AVENUES TO THE ARTS

A General Arts Textbook

by

LEON C. KAREL, Ph.D.

Northeast Missouri State College
Kirksville, Missouri

AVENUES TO THE ARTS

SECOND EDITION, 1969

Library of Congress Catalog Card Number 68-8836

This book was set in Linotype twelve-point Bodoni Book. Section headings are set in type foundry Bodoni Extended Italics and Capitals. Illustrations are by the author.

TO MY WIFE, NAN

FOREWORD

TO THE TEACHER

The field of related arts is still new to the schools of our nation. Its rapid growth has come in response to a search for some way in which to upgrade the quality of education in the arts. This search was occasioned by the close scrutiny of the entire curriculum which occurred in the post-Sputnik era. Rising to the challenge, sciences and mathematics, languages and social studies pioneered new, advanced programs. The arts' turn has now come.

Why a course in the related arts? The logic of such an offering is more readily seen if we compare school arts programs with those in other areas. The sciences, for instance, offer three features to every student. First, they base their work on a "scientific method" which is, in effect, a way of thinking that enables the student to deal with phenomena in the manner demanded by the discipline of science. Second, the sciences offer a general science course to all students in which this method of thinking is taught, and through which a broad view of the entire field may be seen. Third, the several areas of science are then offered as alternative paths for the interested students. Other areas of knowledge have similar structures in our schools. We see general courses in history, government, physical education and other areas, all of them teaching a general method of dealing with the material of that area, and all offering a broad view of the whole field.

Not so in the arts! Here there has been no general course, no method of thinking, no opportunity for the student to explore the whole field. Art, music, drama, and literature go their separate ways. The student who gets into one of these is often scheduled out of participation in the others, and the student who cannot or will not perform finds no place in any of them. Instructors in the several arts know little about the others, having been trained in a rigidly specialized curriculum through college. Hence, any cooperation among them which might help unify and strengthen the arts in the curriculum is missing.

The related arts course enters the picture as the general course for the aesthetic area. It seeks to educate all of the students in understanding all of the arts, so that as adults they will choose wisely what they see, hear, and purchase. This education takes the form of instruction in basic art principles, together with practice in making value judgments. It is the author's firm conviction that a course in the arts

iv

must result in raising the student's standards. The arts, unlike the sciences or social studies, are intimately bound up with the student's personal opinions, his likes and dislikes, and his values. A general arts course should seek to direct and educate these opinions, supply an objective basis for the likes and dislikes, and to lay firm foundations upon which the student can be encouraged to build his own value standards.

The total field of the related arts is so widespread, so pervasive in our everyday lives, and so fascinating, that the instructor will have little difficulty in keeping his classes interested. As the course is repeated, the teacher will find himself developing new, outreaching interests, new insights into fields outside his own major area, and indeed, fresh viewpoints on materials which he had thought understood. The related arts area is fascinating and infinitely varied, and it should continue to grow in interest with each succeeding year of teaching.

TO THE STUDENT

If you enjoy popular music, are puzzled by modern art, thrill to a good movie, or suspect that contemporary poetry is nonsense, this book is for you! It seeks to explain all of these things and more, in a way that the average, non-artistic student will be able to grasp. Furthermore, it explains the arts from the viewpoint of the "consumer." When you have played in a band, acted in a play, written a story or painted a picture, you were learning these arts from their performance side. In a few years, however, you will in all likelihood put aside performance in the arts and, like the vast majority of people, deal with the arts only from the standpoint of the consumer.

Being a consumer, however, has its obligations. Just as a spectator of football needs to know the rudiments of the game in order to enjoy it more, so the art viewer or the music listener needs to know about the inside workings of these forms of entertainment. All of us are constantly being besieged by the arts in one form or another. We get them constantly via TV and radio, in magazines, on billboards, in the market when we shop, in church while we worship. Most of us miss a great deal because we don't know enough about the arts either to fully enjoy what we are exposed to, or to be critical about the manner in which the arts are being used on us. Even more important is the area of masterworks of the arts, the great paintings, compositions, works of architecture and sculpture. If we miss much in the everyday world of the arts, think what treasures are going undiscovered as we pass up chances to delve into these supreme works!

This book will give you some of the necessary understandings and insights which you need in order to live intelligently and fully in the modern world of the arts. The author wishes you a most interesting journey through its pages, and hopes that you will emerge at the end into a world that you didn't realize existed!

ACKNOWLEDGEMENTS

The author wishes to thank the following people:

Dr. Max Kaplan, for ideas concerning the broad areas of knowledge.

H. Douglas Cotton, President of Barton-Cotton, Inc., for permission to use the color plates in this book.

Kathleen Mann, of Charles Scribner's Sons, for permission to use the seven steps in creative thinking from the book *Applied Imagination* by Alex Osborn.

Regina Lindhorst, Nadia Chilkowsky, Gertrude Lippincott, Lucy Venable, and the late Katrine Amory Hooper for assistance and encouragement with the chapter on dance, and with the dance notation examples.

Jim Soderstrom for ideas and diagrams of speech sounds.

Sandra Crawford, for work on the typescript.

H. Greene Simpson and his staff for invaluable advice on matters of typography, illustration, and composition.

My wife, Nan, for encouraging me to attempt this book, for standing by during its writing, and for proofreading the results.

TABLE OF CONTENTS

TABLE OF ILLUSTRATIONS

TABLE OF COLOR PLATES

INTRODUCTION

LEARNING TO LEARN

AREAS OF KNOWLEDGE

The sum total of human knowledge is so vast that the very thought of trying to acquire a broad education seems fantastically impossible. Fortunately, we are able to divide this huge body of knowledge into several distinct areas, and then devise courses of study which enable the younger generations to cope with it.

One of these areas is that of "analytic" knowledge. It consists of knowledge gained by experiment, testing, laboratory observation, analysis, and the like. The various branches of science belong to this area, and they all share a particular way of thinking which is known as the "scientific method."

A second area is that of "assumptive" knowledge. Here we are dealing with knowledge handed down from the past. We cannot test its truth in a laboratory, but must use different means, such as checking sources, verifying written records, comparing contemporary accounts, and so on. The various branches of history are examples of assumptive areas. When a student writes a good term paper, complete with footnotes and bibliography, he is working with assumptive methods.

Yet another area is that of "skills," and deals largely in the perfection of physical processes. Playing an instrument, learning to type, driving a car, participating in sports, learning shop and home economics techniques — all of these share in the skills area in varying degrees.

The area of "moral" knowledge, while not customarily included in our schools, is an important one. Here we are concerned with right and wrong, with questions of good and evil. The home and the church share the heaviest burden of teaching in this area, although clubs and societies share in it, too. Movies, television and magazines are powerful sources of instruction in this morals area, and not always for the better.

The one area in which we are most interested, however, is that of "aesthetic" knowledge. Here one studies the sensory world of man with its colors, lines, shapes, tones, rhythms, odors and tastes. In contrast to history and science, both of which attempt to rule out the personal feelings of the observer in order to be objectively accurate, the arts thrive on such personal feelings! One's opinions, likes and dislikes, preferences and emotions are trained by providing facts and experiences on which they may be based. The ultimate goal of this area of study is twofold; first, the training of the creator and interpreter of art works; and second, the training of the consumer of those works. It is this latter phase with which we are concerned.

To illustrate the four areas of knowledge found in the school curriculum (we are omitting the moral area) let us take a single incident or phenomenon, an automobile accident. This one occurrence can be seen from all four points of view, depending upon which method of thinking is used. For instance, the scientist sees the crash as a problem in physics, calculating the momentum, speed, angle of impact, and so on. The historian, on the other hand, sees it as one of a series of accidents on that same intersection, dating back several years. His viewpoint is that this incident has a "past" which might help us to understand it. The skills-oriented observer may regard the accident as a failure of reflexes, lack of proper training, neglect of precautionary measures, and other factors in which the driver should have been competent. Note that each of these views leaves out the emotions, using the senses of the observer only to record and explain what has happened.

The artist, in strong contrast to these others, sees the event *with* his senses, using his emotions to feel and understand. He may, if visually oriented, respond to the lines of the crumpled metals, the colors of scarred paint and torn upholstery, the texture of metal against foliage, or of the human body against hard steel. The artist who deals in sound may think in terms of the crash of impact, the cries of the injured, the screech of rubber on pavement, or the grating of chrome on glass. The artist who deals in words will try to select those which sound like what they mean, and may seek symbols for the event which could turn it into a lesson for all of us, rather than just another statistic. The artist will always try to imagine what it feels like to be in an accident, and may attempt to recreate the thoughts and emotions of those involved.

The above explanation does not suggest that the scientist and the historian are incapable of feeling. After all, they are human beings. However, when acting in their professional capacities, they try to exclude their personal emotions and biases in favor of objective reporting and study. Perhaps this is a strong reason for surgeons not to operate on members of their immediate family. In such a situation, it would be very difficult for a surgeon father or husband not to become emotionally involved, and this might result in a loss of professional competence for the moment. This might also suggest why some of the best history books about wars are written by people who were not personally involved, and even removed by several generations.

Perhaps it will now be seen that the different areas of knowledge are, in reality, ways of looking at the world about us. Almost anything can be dealt with in several of these ways, and the well-educated person must know which method to use, and when. A historical problem cannot be solved scientifically, nor should a scientific problem be dealt with historically. When Einstein's famous theory was first announced, Adolf Hitler got a large number of eminent German scientists to publicly refute the proposition. Their statement was published in several of the leading newspapers of the day. When shown this, Einstein is reported to have said, "If I am really wrong, it would take only *one* to prove it." Hitler was applying historical techniques to a problem which needed scientific methods.

The ability to make use of one method does not necessarily confer upon its user the ability to use the others. A great historian might be a very poor judge of things of science, and a great scientist might not be able to judge truth from lies in a statement of propaganda. Neither might have good taste in the field of the arts! Each type of approach must be learned and practiced. There is no other way.

WAYS OF LEARNING

Five basic questions serve to introduce this topic:

1. *What is learning?* There are various levels of learning ranging from the type which a child undergoes when he touches a hot stove, to the highly creative thinking which results in the production of new ideas in advanced fields. The sort of learning we are seeking in this course is shown by *changed behavior* on the part of the learner. If the child keeps on touching the stove, we strongly suspect that he has not learned from his experience. If the student does nothing differently and better after he completes a course, we might strongly suspect that here, too, learning has not taken place, no matter what grades were given or what examinations were passed.

2. *How does learning take place?* As we saw in the case of the burned child, some learning is a result of trial and error. Man has improved greatly on this method by condensing his previous experiences into book form. When you read a book which explains how something is to be done, you are really getting the benefit of another's previous experimentation. All of the trials have been made by the author, and you can now start with his experience to guide you!

Most school learning is a combination of study from books and some type of practical experience on the part of the student. Theoretically you might learn to be an architect by beginning with small buildings, erecting larger ones, and learning as you went along, but this would be an extremely costly and lengthy way of going about it. Instead, the modern way is to study the basic knowledge from books, aided by the lectures of instructors, and follow this by an apprentice period with older architects who can oversee your work and catch mistakes. In this particular related arts course, you will get much of your knowledge from books, too, coupled with many trials at thinking about and judging the arts. In this way, you will be able to perfect your evaluation skills and deepen your understanding of the arts much more rapidly than you might if you were to attempt it unaided.

3. *Where do we learn?* The idea that we learn only in school is far from true. As a matter of fact, most people learn more before they get to school than they ever do in their years of formal education, and many learn more outside of school during their school years than they do in classes. We constantly learn during play, at home, from papers and magazines, radio and TV. We will discover that these outside-of-school sources are rich in the arts, and can become effective means of continuing our education long after school is over.

4. *Who learns, and who teaches?* Everyone learns; students, teachers, parents, everybody! Some people learn at a great rate all of their lives, and others slow down after their formal education is finished. Some jobs encourage learning, others stifle it. Being "in a rut" simply means that the circumstances do not promote learning, hence the feeling of routine dullness.

Students are often surprised that teachers continue to study and to learn. It has often been said that one really begins to learn when he starts to teach someone else what he knows. Students who review for exams in groups often find that explaining something to one another is an excellent means of making sure that thing is fully understood.

As for the question of who teaches, the answer is the same; everybody. Although your classroom instructor is the paid professional teacher, each member of the class teaches to some degree. You will find yourself explaining something about the arts to others, perhaps to parents or friends. You may not say a word at times, yet be teaching by your example. Any time that two humans meet, each teaches and each learns something.

The most effective means of learning is to *teach yourself* to understand. Forget for the moment that there is a paid professional teacher in the class. If there were no such person, and if you wanted to learn about the arts, could you set out to master the subject? Of course you could! You would have to spend a lot of time in the library, and you would have to make up your mind to follow a schedule of work, but it could be done. You will find, after graduation, that anything you want or need to learn will be acquired in much this same fashion. Starting at the bottom of your chosen field, your progress will depend in large measure upon your ability to prepare yourself to move ahead. This is usually a matter of additional study and learning. The better you become at self-teaching now, the greater advantage you will have later on.

5. *Why learn?* Basic though this question may be, some students have not yet answered it. We learn because we are faced with problems. From the moment we enter this world, problems are there. To begin with, our parents solve many of them for us, but later on we learn to cope with our own problems. Some of the problems that you are beginning to meet today are quite serious. These may involve your choice of a profession, planning for your future, your marriage, and establishment of a home. Some people meet these problems by not doing anything to prepare, and very often this results in disaster. Others plan and work to solve these problems, and these people have a better chance of success. Part of your school work, your reason for learning, is to give you the practice and preparation for meeting the larger problems that will soon be crowding in upon you.

We have just considered five questions about learning. Have we, then, *learned* anything? Perhaps, but the best test must be based upon whether this new knowledge has resulted in any changed behavior. Usually just reading something in a book, even memorizing it, has little effect on one's behavior. To change behavior requires conscious effort, trial, experience, and repeated attempts to put the "book learning" into practice. Suppose we take an example of a book statement about the arts, and see what kind of application is necessary in order to turn that printed statement into a "changed response" on the reader's part.

"The arts are one of man's most important activities." Now this statement seems simple enough. Anyone can read it and quickly commit it to memory. If the question were put on an examination, "How do the arts rank among man's activities?" we could all answer "Most important," with no trouble at all. Does this mean that we understand the statement? No, it does not, unfortunately. In order to really learn what the statement means, we would have to take active initiative and begin asking some questions on our own. A good set of questions would begin with the same words as the five questions on the previous pages — *what, how, where, who,* and *why.*

1. *What is meant by "the arts"?* We find that the arts include visual areas of painting, sculpture, and architecture as well as auditory areas of music and literature. There are combined areas of both sound and sight, as in cinema, opera, ballet, and drama. Some would include applied arts, fields of fashion, ceramics, metalwork, furniture, and even cooking and flower arranging. All of these areas share something artistic.

2. *How have the arts come to be so important?* Is it possible that they rank with the great business activities, scientific discoveries, political movements and technological inventions of man? Research into this question will quickly show that the arts ranked *far higher* in most civilizations of the past than did business, science, or politics! We treasure the great arts of the Greeks, not their commerce. We stand in awe before the medieval cathedral, not the political system under which its builders lived. Today vast sums are spent on beauty, from eye-catching designs for products to the combined arts of music, drama, and painting which sell these products. We spend more money for beautifying ourselves than we do for most other things. The pursuit of aesthetic goals, trivial or lofty, occupies much of contemporary man's time. Small wonder then that "the arts" rank high among man's activities.

3. *Where do the arts come from?* The urge to produce and be surrounded by beauty is apparently a deep-seated human need. The housewife "sets" the table rather than simply scattering dishes and utensils at random. On special occasions the food is prepared for visual beauty as well as for good taste. None of this improves the nutritional value of what is eaten, but its aesthetic value is improved greatly! The husband, without realizing the source of his artistic impulse, will pay a considerable sum of money for a two-tone paint job on his new car, for extra chrome and white sidewall tires. None of this changes the car's efficiency, mileage or speed. But its appearance is helped, and the man is willing to pay for this.

The professional artist shares this desire for better-looking things, but his artistic impulses have been trained and channeled into more technically difficult activities. He can design a skyscraper or write a play, while we can only arrange flowers or write letters. Yet at bottom we share a desire to see beauty and to create it. Our relationship to the professional artist should be the same as to the "pro" in sports. When a great natural talent is combined with years of training and practice, our nation honors the combination, provided it is the area of sports. Less frequently do we pay tribute to the skilled and talented artist. Perhaps when the average American knows as much about arts as he does sports, our artists will get the same generous treatment here as they get in other nations.

4. *Who says the arts are that important?* This question would not occur to most students. To question a printed statement seems somehow improper! Yet the wise man never wholly believes all that he reads, and insists on checking first. A quick look at the writings of famous men will show that the arts are indeed regarded highly. Listen!

Art precedes philosophy and even science. People must have noticed things and interested themselves in them before they begin to debate upon their causes or influence.

---Robert Louis Stevenson

A man who has a taste in music, painting, or sculpture is like one that has another sense when compared with such as have no relish of those arts.

---Addison

Obviously no animal would be capable of admiring such scenes as the heavens at night, a beautiful landscape, or refined music; but such high tastes are acquired through culture;---they are not enjoyed by barbarians or by uneducated persons.

---Charles Darwin

The man that hath no music in himself,
Nor is not moved with concord of sweet sounds
Is fit for treasons, stratagems, and spoils;
The motions of his spirit are dull as night
And his affections dark as Erebus:
Let no such man be trusted.

---Shakespeare, "Merchant of Venice"

---a property of all good arts is to draw the mind of man away from the vices and direct it to better things---

---Copernicus

Harmony is meant to correct any discord which may have arisen in the courses of the soul, and to be our ally in bringing her into harmony and agreement with herself.

---Plato

Art is not an end in itself; but a means of addressing humanity.

> ---Mussorgsky

The list is endless, and includes names from virtually every field and historical era.

5. *Why aren't other areas more highly ranked than the arts?* We read daily of the wonderful accomplishments of science and technology. As man moves out into space we see visible proof of science's progress. Is not all of this far superior to a lot of paintings and poetry? This depends on what we are searching for. Of course science has done tremendous things, especially in our lifetime, but it cannot reveal the most important area of all, that of man himself! Science delves into the molecular and atomic structures of things, and into the forces which move them, but science cannot deal with the problems of love and hatred, of fear, hope, courage, patriotism and liberty. The scientist can analyze sounds to the smallest vibration but only the artist can mold these sounds into a great symphony which will inspire man. The science of color has been investigated thoroughly by researchers, so that today we have instant color photography, color television, and full color printing, but only the artist can show us how to make use of these inventions to satisfy our need for beauty. The scientist is creating the tools for us to use---the artist often shows us how to use them in the best way. The scientist has created more and more leisure time for the average American---the artist will have to show him how to utilize it, lest he become bored, apathetic, and misuse the time given to him.

The arts, then, remain one of man's foremost activities. The fact that our nation at the moment does not give the arts a foremost place in the scheme of things is of only momentary concern. Up to the present generation, we have been too busy with settling and developing our nation, too busy with material things. Now we are turning our attention to the arts, and they will again attain their accustomed place in the lives of men.

"The arts are one of man's most important activities." Here is the original statement, but see how much more we understand after having questioned its meaning. We could ask many more questions, and each one would lead us into some new avenue of knowledge. As children we constantly asked questions, but somehow most of us have lost our inquisitiveness. The time to regain it is right now, and the subject to ask questions about is the area of the related arts.

THE ROLE OF THE STUDENT

Man loves to create patterns of all kinds. His life is full of them, ranging from church rituals to almost meaningless gestures such as handshaking and tipping the hat. His games are patterns within which exciting contests may be waged. Were it not for these man-made patterns, life would be pure chaos, violent and meaningless, much like a football contest with no rules, no referees, no time limits, no field, and no holds barred!

It often helps to visualize your school experience as a man-made pattern. Long before you were born, the pattern was set, the rules made, the conditions established. Occasionally parts of the pattern will be changed, just as game rules are altered from time to time, but by-and-large, school life remains the same because this type of activity has served the requirements of our society well for quite some time.

You may think of yourself as one of the "players" in this game of going to school. If so, do you know what the object of the game is, and what the rules are? You should! First of all, the game has several objects, or purposes. One which is sometimes obvious is to keep you off the streets, or put more elegantly, watch over your development until such time as you are deemed fit to enter society. This varies a great deal from one society to another. In primitive places, children begin very early to help the family earn a livelihood. Our higher level of culture and greater wealth allow us to keep many more of our young people in school much longer than in any other society in history. With increased automation and higher standards of training required of the laboring force, the teen-ager is simply not needed or wanted for the purpose of work. The school, therefore, is given the job of keeping him occupied somehow until he becomes older and presumably wiser.

A second object of the school is to train that teen-ager to fit into the working class. For this, he must be given a surprisingly sophisticated education nowadays, ranging over basic sciences, communications, foreign languages, arts, and many skills. The fate of the student who drops out is by now well known-----it is only the person who fits himself through education who can find the type of work that will allow him to join the ranks of the self-supporting.

A third goal of your school has to do with preserving the past. America has a fantastic history, and as one of the oldest nations in the world with a continuous form of government, that history is well worth studying. Some of the new nations of the world have no history, hence have few guidelines by which they can steer their future course. Luckily, we have learned from our past, and from the mistakes we have made. Our schools want each one of us to fully understand that past, in the hopes that our nation will continue to prosper and grow, led by a knowledge of what we have done and where we came from. With this in mind, it is easy to see that a course in related arts should present some of America's great achievements in this important area. Each American ought to know, for instance, that his nation has produced world leaders in at least two of the art areas, cinema and architecture. Such men as Sullivan and Wright in architecture, and Griffith and Welles in movie-making are as famed in their fields as Da Vinci and Beethoven in painting and music. The arts, then, can contribute much to every American's understanding of his past.

A fourth objective of your school is to prepare you as a functioning citizen of the United States. There are many ways in which your school does this. One is through your classes in government and civics. Another is through academic activities in which you learn to work together on committees, to elect officers and run a meeting, to vote and abide by majority rule. As a matter of fact, as you consider the courses you take in school, you discover that a great many of them are not useful in preparing you for a job, but instead are for the purpose of preparing you for active citizenship. Here again the arts come into play. Writers have often spoken to us about democracy, and dramatists have taught us many valuable things about the society in which we live. Painters have shown us the American scene, and poets have stirred us to think about the real values of life. The arts do carry a heavy load of ideas, along with their intrinsic structures. We shall study both in this course.

There you have some of the goals of your school, and you can perhaps see a little more clearly how you fit into these goals. Now that you know what the "game" is all about, here are some of the "rules" under which you are expected to operate.

Rule No. 1:   The student should try his best to learn all he can in school. Just as we despise an athlete who won't do his best, we should look down on the student who gets by with less than his top performance. We all want to strive as hard as we can in sports, so as to bring credit to ourselves and to the school. An even better way is to learn to our fullest capacity so that later on the school can be proud of what we have become. Your own school would certainly be proud if Red Grange or Stan Musial had gone to school there. It would be just as proud to have a great thinker in its student body, an Edison or an Emerson. Few of us will ever rise to such heights as these men in their respective fields, but we can all try our best. Let us honor the student who tries hard in any area.

Rule No. 2: The student should think of himself as being on the same path as his teacher. The instructor is, of course, farther' ahead by virtue of his longer years of study and experience. He can and will help you to start out on that same path, and is glad when you begin to move ahead under your own power. The class room should never become a contest arena between teacher and student. Friendly cooperation gives you, the student, the best conditions in which to learn.

Rule No. 3: The student must actively enter into the learning process. Unless there is constant thinking, self-questioning, and mental effort, nothing much will happen. The acts of note-taking, outlining, or underlining the textbook, while they may have value, are not nearly as important as deep thought! A competent stenographer could take down the teacher's presentation in shorthand, and type it perfectly, yet unless she *thought* about the material actively, she would learn relatively little. Work with what you hear and see and read. Put this information to use, analyze it, improve on it, question it, create with it, but never merely copy it down.

Rule No. 4: Make books your principal learning tools. If by some miracle Socrates, Columbus, Raphael, Jefferson, and Edison were brought back to the world of the living for just one day, people would want to ask them questions, and seek their advice. Yet in our school libraries we have their writings, which are in a way even better than a personal visit, for in their books these men took care to say the important things they were thinking, in logical order, not interrupted by any casual or trivial remarks. Search your library for its treasures---you will find a great many. Knowledge is power, and books contain that power, all stored up and ready for you to switch on. The mechanism which contains that switch is your brain. Use it.

Rule No. 5: Constantly test your capacities. School is that portion of your life which society has set aside to allow you to develop your mind and find out what you can do. It is in this part of your life that you will discover your talents and potentialities. If you operate at less than your full potential, you will wonder all the rest of your life whether you could have really "been something." The athlete enters a sport or activity with the intention of seeing how far he can go in improving his performance. The student must do the same. Remember, the responsibility for learning is very largely yours. Your instructors will help, but the main burden falls on your shoulders.

PROBLEMS:

The following are suggested as mental exercises for the student. There are no "right answers" to these problems, no set amount of work that must be done to answer them. The runner does not ask, "How fast do you want me to run in this race?" The student does not ask, "How much should I do on this assignment?" Go as far into the problem as you have the resources to go. The farther you penetrate, the better will be your grasp of the material.

Problem One: After a study of the Table of Contents of this book, tell why you think the author begins with "learning to learn" rather than with a study of the arts themselves.

Problem Two: Find examples in your own experience which illustrate your need for "learning to see" and "learning to hear."

Problem Three: In the introductory section "To the Teacher," the author speaks of the student's need to gain skill in "making value judgments." Explain this phrase, and show your own need in this area.

Problem Four: Make a list of the ways in which you are a "consumer" of the arts during just one 24-hour period. Analyze these experiences to see how well you understood what was going on, how you were being motivated and stimulated by the arts.

Problem Five: Think over the subjects you have studied in school thus far, and divide them into areas of knowledge. Then write a short critical analysis of what you find.

Problem Six: Show that you understand the several areas of knowledge by interpreting in four different ways several of the following incidents or objects:
a. A boxing match. b. A wedding cake. c. A singing canary. d. A man jumping from a tall building. e. An astronaut circling the earth.

Problem Seven: The book suggests that there are several levels of learning, and cites two extremes. Make up a list including these at the upper and lower limits, and insert between them other levels of learning that you may have experienced or observed.

Problem Eight: Using the combination of book-plus-experience as a means of learning, show how you could learn the following:
a. To build a brick wall. b. To sell cosmetics door-to-door. c. To recognize edible mushrooms. d. To paint in oils. e. To design an electric automobile.

Problem Nine: Make a list of things you learned before you began your formal schooling. Select the three most difficult items, and try to explain how you learned them.

Problem Ten: Put yourself in the instructor's place, and list the problems that arise in connection with this class. Rate these in importance. Which do you think would cause you the most trouble if you were the instructor?

Problem Eleven: Apply the "what, how, where, who, and why" question technique to the following statements. Write out each of your five questions for each of the statements below:

a. Democracy is better than Communism. b. Modern art is no good. c. We ought to be stricter with teen-agers. d. Life in the city is getting worse every year. e. Columbus discovered America in 1492.

Problem Twelve: Think about the five rules for students, and add others that you would like to see included.

Part One

LEARNING ABOUT THE ARTS

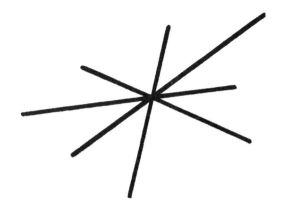

CHAPTER 1

THE EXTENT OF THE ARTS

Geographic Extent

When one investigates the extent of the arts throughout the world, the astonishing discovery is made that there is no nation, no tribe, no area which is without them. In certain places such as Europe we find all of the arts flourishing side-by-side. Most of the world's capitals feature painting, theatre, sculpture, architecture, and opera. Even in provincial towns both here and abroad, the arts will be found. In this country, no matter where one goes, the local schools will be teaching literature, with music, drama, and painting often included in the curriculum.

One might expect to see fewer arts in primitive societies, and this is probably true. On the other hand, people living in such societies often have a rich artistic experience in areas directly connected with their daily lives. While we are more likely to be spectators of the arts, the native is a more active participant, spending much time beautifying his weapons with carving and painting, weaving cloth, making articles for his home, and so on. Even in the barren north, the Eskimo carvers produce statues of bone or stone which are prized by collectors all over the world. The color plate "Bison Lying Down" (Color Pl. 1) is a work of art dating some 30,000 years before Christ!

Geographically, the arts vary according to wealth and resources. Obviously a primitive tribe or a backward nation cannot produce an opera company. This can only be the product of a highly developed society, one in which young people can study music for many years, in preparation. The youth in a primitive society must learn to hunt and find food, to subsist in an often hostile environment. There is no time to devote to long-range artistic pursuits, no years of schooling in which to train the talents and skills necessary for a career in the arts. Our own early years as a nation were much the same. We were always engaged in taming the land and wresting a living from it, and so were unable to afford the luxury of the arts, except in a small way.

Today, a nation's level of civilization is gauged by the type and quality of its art productions. For instance, few Americans know anything about the Canary Islands. They might be desolate and primitive, or occupied by savages for all we know. However, let it be mentioned that on these islands there is a symphony orchestra and a repertory theatre, an art gallery and an opera company, and immediately we know that here is a "civilized" place to visit. Our fears of danger or primitive conditions are gone. We have measured the culture by the arts it has produced.

The arts not only have geographic variations, but they can travel across the face of the earth from one area to another. Obviously there were few highly developed arts here in America before the white settlers arrived. Indian crafts, songs, dances and architecture had reached a certain level, but the Indian lived a nomadic life which prevented him from developing these beginnings into full-blown arts. With the arrival of the Europeans, a westward flow of the arts began which has lasted into our lifetime, and which has only recently begun to reverse itself. For 300 years we imported our music, painting, building styles, fashions, books and statuary. Our native artists largely followed European leadership, and our art patrons demanded and got European art and artists. A few traces of this directional flow linger on. Our fashions are still set in Paris, and we still have opera sung in foreign languages, a practice not followed in other countries.

Since the mid-1900s, however, American architects, painters, dancers, movie-makers, and other artists have become widely accepted throughout the world, and today America has become a pace-setter in many of these fields.

Geographical influences have made themselves felt in other ways, too. During the early 1900s, there was a strong wave of Egyptian influence in art and fashion following archaeological explorations into the tombs of the Pharaohs. Buildings showed Egyptian motifs, and literature and the movies took up Egyptian themes and settings. Much later a Japanese influence spread across the United States and Europe, brought about by studies of Japanese print-making, architecture, and poetry. Primitive sculpture has had a similar vogue, leaving traces behind it of aboriginal styles and subjects in the works of modern dance composers, sculptors, and painters.

The arts, then, do show regional, national, and geographical variations, but above all they prove that all peoples in all parts of our world contribute to the arts, and find them necessary to their well-being.

The Historic Extent of the Arts

We not only find the arts spread the length and breadth of our world, we find them spread backward through time, too. Take painting, for instance. Beginning with our contemporary painters, we can go back a generation or two to Renoir and Van Gogh, back farther to Watteau and Fragonard, beyond that to Rembrandt and Da Vinci, and even earlier to the Christian painters of the eighth and ninth centuries. Painters, we find, were honored in Roman times, as can be seen from the beautiful frescoes that have been unearthed as the buried cities of Pompeii and Herculaneum have come to light. The Romans were greatly indebted, however, to the Greeks, from whom they took many of their artistic styles and techniques. Greek painters, early though they were, had been preceded by the Egyptians, who painted many likenesses of their gods and rulers. (Color Plate 2) We have traced painting back to several thousands of years before Christ, but there are evidences of even earlier painters. In caves of Spain and France, one can see wall and ceiling paintings of life-size bison, drawn by pre-historic man at least 25,000 years ago! (Color Plate 1) The art of painting seems to have been with man from the dawn of time.

Not all of the arts are as old as painting. Music, while undoubtedly present in crude forms from prehistoric times, had to wait until about the year 1000 A.D. to start its development as an independent art form. Up till that time, it had been the accompaniment for dance and song, and had to be passed on from one generation to the next by rote learning. This prevented any development of complexities, and hindered any sort of steady growth in the art. When each generation had to memorize all of its music, the task of holding it all in the memory pretty much kept further advances from taking place. The same sort of thing was a factor in the early development of literature. In the days before writing was common, primitive societies had "bards" whose job it was to memorize all of the old ballads, the epic poems, the stories and tales, and repeat them to the younger generations. The bard was a living history book, honored for the precious store of past learning he carried in his head. Later on, troubadours and minstrels served somewhat the same functions, carrying from one place to another the stories, gossip, adventure, and news of the day. These people were welcomed in every court and country. They travelled a great deal, and served a definite function in their society. Although the music and the literature they performed was interesting and valuable, a means of writing it down had to be perfected before it could start the long developmental process that would result in a Mozart or a Shakespeare.

The different ages of the arts, then, stem from their basic natures. Some of the arts are "direct" while others are "indirect."

The Direct Arts

If a painter, sitting with paints and brushes before his canvas, has an idea for a painting, he proceeds to execute that idea directly into visual form. His mental concept is translated into a visible medium, and there it stands for all to see. He finishes the work, and barring unforeseen damage, it will remain precisely as he left it, a record of his artistic achievement.

The sculptor is in much the same position as the painter, except that he will entrust the casting of a metal statue to trained craftsmen working from a model which he has prepared. The artist closely supervises the casting process and puts the finishing touches on the final version of his statue.

The architect is in a somewhat different position in that he does not actually build the building himself. It is always constructed by a crew of men working under a contractor. The latter follows the plans drawn up by the architect. However, these plans are so detailed and accurate that the contractor has very little choice of what he does. He is merely following orders, so that it may truthfully be asserted that the building is really the architect's creation.

The Indirect Arts

The composer who has the idea for an orchestral work cannot turn this idea directly into music, in the same way that a painter can transform his idea into lines and colors. Instead, the composer must first write an elaborate set of directions called a "musical score" and from this make a separate set of playing parts for each musician in the orchestra. Then these players must rehearse their parts under the direction of a conductor, and finally the music is heard at a concert. Now it might be thought that this differs very little from an architect's plans being carried out by a crew of workmen under a contractor. The fact is that the composer's musical directions are not nearly so precise as those of the architect, and herein lies the trouble. The conductor and his players have considerable leeway in just how they choose to perform the piece of music. One conductor may play it faster than another; one may prefer certain places louder, or softer. Some players may feature a harsher tone, while others prefer a sweeter one. The work may sound brilliant when performed by a professional group, and horrible in the hands of young amateurs. Of course, this uncertainty and variability can also add to the interest --- it would be quite dull if every performance were exactly like every other. In contrast, in the world of architecture, a second building built to the same plans would turn out exactly like the first, or so nearly like it that there would be little interest in comparing the two.

Works of literature, especially poetry and drama, are presented under the same conditions as music. There is always the actor who must interpret the author's intentions to the audience. It often comes about that the actor gets all the attention, and the original creator of the play or movie is almost forgotten. Have we not frequently gone to a movie just because our favorite actor is in it, and do we not listen to the music because of the singer or player, regardless of what he is performing?

Now what does all this have to do with the relative ages of the arts? Simply this; the art of painting could come earliest because no form of "writing" or "notation" was necessary. Sculpture was also a very early art to develop, for the same reason. Architecture was to come a little later, as ways of drawing plans were slowly developed. The earliest builder was a kind of architect-contractor-laborer who probably drew plans as he went along, supervised the work, hired helpers, and stayed on the job from start to finish.

Literature had to wait until written language was developed so that it could assume a permanent form. In early times there were the legends, epics, stories and tales, and some of these survived long enough so that eventually they were written down and saved. It is thought that the *Odyssey* and the *Iliad* were of such origins, as was *Beowulf,* and the tales of King Arthur and his Knights of the Round Table. Possibly a great body of such literature could have come from the American Indian, but he had no written language complex enough to preserve it. Most of the Indian legends are preserved only in fragmentary form today.

The cinema depended on many technological advances for its growth, and is a good example of how an art may be born from new means of recording information. Present-day experiments are being conducted into the possibilities of an art based on light-waves, and another avenue is being explored leading toward an art based upon the sense of smell. The comparatively recent invention of the tape recorder and other electronic devices have made possible a new kind of musical composition. Formerly the composer had to depend upon a kind of "middleman" to perform what he wrote (Example No. 1-1). The composer (A)

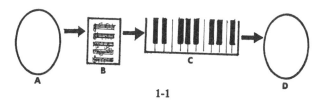

1-1

writes his music in the form of "directions" (B) which are then played by a performer on his instrument (C) so the music may finally be heard by the listener (D). Now, however, some composers are writing by creating magnetic patterns directly on the tape, thus bypassing the performer. (Example 1-2) Such a method, whatever else its difficulties, does give the composer the same final authority as the painter.

1-2   1-3

Recently a means of developing dance notations has been discovered. In earlier times dances were taught by rote, or sometimes notated by comparatively simple means, as in Example 1-3. Now a much more thorough type of notation has made it possible to write

directions for any kind of body movement used in dance. An example of it is shown in 1-4, and more will be shown in a later chapter. With this notation system rendering personal contact between teacher and student less necessary than formerly, the art of dance may become as widespread as music, painting, or poetry.

The arts, then, appeared and started their development at various times in history, depending on their ability to be captured in permanent form. The direct arts (painting and sculpture) began with this problem already solved. Architecture came along somewhat later. Early development in writing brought literature in as one of the arts (Color Plate 2) as shown in the Egyptian picture. Music, though known in ancient times, waited until almost 1,000 A.D. before a system

1-4

of writing it on paper enabled the art to develop into an independent one. Dance is just now being freed of its dependence on rote learning, and other newer arts will doubtless be coming along in the future.

PROBLEMS:

Problem One: Look at the houses in your town, or in a nearby larger city. Notice how the size, style, and materials of houses vary from one part of town to another. Explain this "geographic" difference.

Problem Two: The primitive tribesman finds an artistic outlet in decorating his tools, his weapons, and himself. Find as many parallels to this as you can in our present-day society.

Problem Three: List at least ten items of artistic evidence that America is in an advanced cultural stage.

Problem Four: Find out what you can about the growth of the arts in earlier days in your school, community, county or state. Was there ever a local town band, a community chorus, a theatre, or opera house? What about early painters and sculptors, earlier buildings not now standing, and former schools or academies?

Problem Five: Can you find in your own experience any occasions when artistic influence was exerted from a foreign country? Don't overlook the world of fashion, auto design, popular music, cinema, and the like.

Problem Six: List the advantages that a teen-ager living in Europe would have over one in this country when it came to understanding the historical significance of the arts.

Problem Seven: The text lists a number of famous painters dating from ancient times to modern. We in America can claim the invention of the movies as an art form. Find out who some of our great directors and innovators were, and list their contributions to the art.

Problem Eight: Analyze the phenomenon known as the "paint-by-number" kit and compare it with musical notation, architect's plans, and a play script.

Problem Nine: "The so-called *indirect arts* must rely upon notation or writing for their preservation." Comment on the accuracy of this statement, and indicate some advantages and disadvantages of such notes and words.

Problem Ten: List the hazards of preserving the direct arts over the centuries, contrasting these with the preservation of the indirect arts.

CHAPTER 2

THE MEANING OF THE ARTS: GREAT IDEAS OF MAN

Every work of art possesses a dual nature. First of all, it stands alone as a single object or event to be analyzed for its construction, its materials, its use of the artistic elements, and so forth. Second, it stands as a product of a man and an age, a historical record of the time in which it was produced. In order to understand a work of art fully, both of these natures have to be comprehended.

For example, a poem may be analyzed for its rhyme scheme, meter, line length, use of vowel and consonant sounds, imagery, figures of speech, and other constructional features. But it must also be seen as an utterance by the poet who, in turn, represents a particular historical era, a national sentiment, and so on. We need to know why the poet said what he did, as well as how he said it.

In the visual arts, we might select a bank building from the American mid-west, built in the early 1900s. The building's features include the Greek columns and porch, post-and-lintel construction with interior iron frame. Details of the lighting, heating, and sanitary facilities would increase our knowledge of the bank building. But we must also find out why the banks of that era were designed to look like Greek temples! What caused bankers in every part of the nation to choose this particular style, and why is it not now used? What influence led architects to imitate an ancient form of

2-1

architecture in a new, vigorous, and expanding country? A total grasp of this kind of structure will include both the technical and historic aspects. This places a definite obligation on the "consumer" as shown in the accompanying illustration, Example 2-2. The artist (A) is a collector of impressions, a kind of super-sensitive person who has been trained to see and hear things in the world about him that most of us overlook. As he collects and works with these impressions, he comes upon an idea for combining them

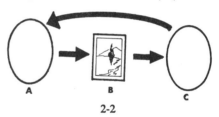

2-2

in a new and interesting way, and in order to let others share his ideas, he puts them down in the form of a work of art (B). This may be a painting or a statue, or it may be a musical performance or a dramatic production, in which case he has written a "set of directions" allowing someone else to reproduce the work. In either case, the work finally reaches the consumer (C), you or me. The artist has done his work --- now we must do ours.

We must try to understand what the artist did to produce his creation --- how he used his lines, textures, colors, or his rhythms, tones, and harmonies. When we can analyze the work for its constructional contents, we must try to grasp its meaning as a "message" from the artist and from the period and society in which he lived. We can truly say we understand the work of art when we can put ourselves in the artist's shoes, think as he thought, feel as he felt, plan as he planned. This responsibility is indicated by the arrow leading from the consumer back to the artist. If an artist is really great, we will seldom if ever be able to accomplish this completely. If the artist is a beginner, or a child, we may understand the work rather thoroughly. On reflection, it seems likely that the attraction of many great works is that we do not understand them thoroughly, and there always remains something unexplained for a further viewing or hearing.

If artists deal in ideas, what ideas are commonly found in their works? Three idea-areas seem uppermost, forming a kind of triangle which encompasses many artistic expressions. The three points of the triangle are GOD, MAN, and NATURE. Ever since the arts made their appearance, the artists have dwelt on these three basic points. For instance, the ancient cave paintings of bison show that prehistoric man thought a good deal about his relationships with the world of nature. Perhaps he felt that by painting pictures of these huge brutes he would be better able to bring them under his control. His attempts were almost certainly in the area of religion or magic. Perhaps he looked on the bison as a kind of god, to be made into an image and revered, or as a figure of fear, to be conquered.

If we are in doubt as to prehistoric image-making, there can be no doubt that Egyptian artists several thousands of years before Christ were actively engaged in picturing and writing about man's relationship to his gods, and to nature, as seen in Color Plate Number 2.

The Greeks took up the age-old theme not only in their poetry and drama, but in magnificent statues and temples which showed their love of order, simplicity, proportion, and balance. Far from fearing their gods, the Greeks gave them human qualities and weaknesses. The GOD-MAN-NATURE triangle was a most prominent theme for Greek works.

If one looks at Medieval arts, he sees the triangle balanced in quite a different way. The artists of the 1100s were mystical in their approach, concentrating upon the after-life rather than the present world, and thinking of the Deity as spiritual rather than in man's image. Music first makes its appearance as a written art about this time, and the early works are exclusively religious in nature. Looking at the total arts of this era, we see a strong focus upon the spiritual world and man's relationship to it, with little consideration of nature, except as a sort of necessary evil to be endured.

By the Renaissance period, some three to five centuries later, man's interest had shifted to another corner of the triangle, to himself. Pictures of the Holy Family looked like the artist's countrymen in local costume and setting, robust and anatomically accurate, rather than spiritually elongated in the earlier fashion. More interest was shown in nature, too, with popular songs of the day stressing "delightful pleasant groves," "the silver swan," and "between the acres of the rye." Shakespeare showed this preoccupation with man and nature by writing penetrating studies of treachery, ambition, weakness and love. His comedy, "A Midsummer Night's Dream," combines social and natural settings with a romantic touch of supernatural, yet one could scarcely say that it dealt with man's relationship to his Creator.

As we approach modern times, we find artists more and more concerned with man alone. Science had begun to unlock many of nature's secrets in the 1700s, and has continued to do so at an ever-accelerating pace. Artists have followed the growing importance of science with alarm, sensing that as man puts more and more faith in discovering the secrets of nature, and in his own ability to guide himself, he is losing contact with the third side of the triangle. Thus we find poets in the 1800s crying out against the blight of the landscape by coal mines and factories, of the enslavement of men by machines, and even against the child labor practices of the day. We find painters showing us the sordid side of city life, its senseless rush and unfeeling attitude. Architects of the 1930s devised a type of "modern" architecture that was so functionally lacking in ornamentation that it shocked us into demanding some redeeming features of beauty, some relief from the purely machine-oriented building. Composers depicted the noises of steel mills and power dams, while others created dissonances to match the social conflicts of the world man has made for himself.

Finally we have emerged into the chaotic, unplanned world of the present-day arts, in which the concept of randomness held by some scientists is echoed by formless approaches to art in many areas. Musical compositions no longer require performers to read notes steadily from start to finish, but encourage the players to follow their own inclinations. Some of these works have no set beginning or end, but may start and stop anywhere. This certainly tells us something about the contemporary idea of man's place in the scheme of things, and what he feels to be his reason for existing. Paintings may also reflect this. A not-uncommon technique consists of dribbling, splashing, throwing or squirting paint on the canvas in haphazard patterns which are not fully controlled by the artist.

Thus we may begin to sense, in this necessarily brief sketch, that artists mirror the thoughts of their times, and that their works can be valuable guides to the ideas and feelings of many different ages of the past. Whatever the prevailing ideas of an era may be, one or more of the arts is sure to sense and record them.

The section just completed has to do with "learning about the arts" and has dealt with both their geographic and historic extent. If the reader has begun to follow the author's advice in constantly asking questions, he may now be asking himself, "What method of instruction will be followed in this course and this textbook?"

The material studied thus far has been introductory. The arts have been discussed in a general way, and the student's role has been mentioned. All of this is intended to stimulate and awaken the curiosity, to sharpen the interest preparatory to really getting into the main subject. The next three parts of the book are devoted to the fundamentals of hearing and seeing. You will be shown what to look for and what to listen for in the arts. Next, in Part Five, we will look for the meaning behind the things you see and hear. In Part Six you will begin to apply your skill in observation, and your new-found understanding, to unfamiliar areas of the arts. In Part Seven, you will study the observing and understanding processes themselves, and in the final section of the book, help is offered in judging the arts.

You will notice that, aside from the early reference to the historical and great ideas approaches to the arts, there is little of this material found in the rest of the book. This is deliberate, the intention of this text and course being to train the student's observation and to lay foundations for critical judgment. The ultimate goal of the course is the preparation of an intelligent consumer. If the student can study the arts from the historical and great ideas approaches in other courses, he should by all means do so. This will give him a total perspective that neither aspect alone can furnish. But for the present, this course will confine itself to the principles of the arts, and an investigation into the manner in which works of art are created.

PROBLEMS:

Problem One: Show briefly how the following works could be seen from two points of view, the constructional and the historic:

a. Our national anthem. b. The White House. c. The poem, "Old Ironsides." d. The Statue of Liberty. e. Your county courthouse. f. The latest hit record. g. Your own home. h. Coins of different dates and nations. i. Tombstones.

Problem Two: In the diagram of "Artist-Work of Art-Consumer," tell where an actor would fit in, and what his responsibility would be.

Problem Three: The book says that an artist is a kind of super-sensitive person who collects impressions. Try to become such a person, yourself, for a period of 30 minutes. Record what you see that you feel is either beautiful or interesting. Do the same for another 30 minutes, recording what you hear.

Problem Four: A work of art may be thought of as some kind of "message" telling us something about the artist and his world. Discuss how this fact might be put to use in the raising and educating of small children.

Problem Five: Find one or more aspects of the GOD-MAN-NATURE theme in:

a. Popular Songs. b. Movies. c. Advertising. d. Short Stories. e. Poetry.

Problem Six: Find in a history book what the people of some particular era thought and believed. Then find a work of art from that same era which carried out such thoughts and beliefs.

Problem Seven: With the arts today inclined to become somewhat unplanned and chaotic, architects continue to build well-planned and efficient structures. Comment on this apparent departure from the general trend.

Problem Eight: Discuss the artists' growing concern in the 1800s with man's relationship to nature, in light of today's developments in nuclear energy.

Problem Nine: The artist who deals in an area other than literature may find himself unable to speak directly to people about the complex world situation in which we live. What suggestions have you for such an artist?

Problem Ten: Artists have often been accused of drawing so far away from the ordinary consumer that no communication can take place between them. Offer your ideas on this subject.

Part Two

LEARNING TO SEE

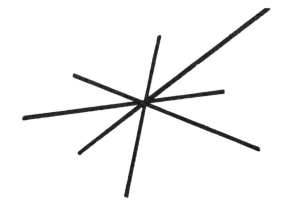

CHAPTER 3

LINES—TYPES AND FORMS

A line is often a record of some action which has taken place. Every so often we will see black tire marks on the pavement, perhaps curving off onto the shoulder. We know a car has skidded, trying to stop at a high rate of speed. We see lines left by skyrockets, by water cutting a path through dirt, or by a falling star. Lines are fascinating, and catch our eye readily. The lines of a car or a dress help sell that particular product. We often use lines to help us estimate one another, as when we judge a person's age by the wrinkled lines of his skin, or his character through handwriting.

Types of Lines

We often classify lines by their general character, and by the way they are made. In the first category, we have simple straight lines; horizontals, verticals, and diagonals. The horizontal line is a line of rest, of peace and relaxation. It is also a line of weariness, death, and monotony. This line is often seen in landscapes, (Ex. 3-1) dividing the picture into horizontal sections sometimes slightly curving to avoid too much sameness. Even the general horizontal shape of the painting tends to lend that air of quiet peacefulness. The vertical straight line has an air of quietness about it, too, but it is a more poised, ready-for-action line than the horizontal. The example of tree-forms (Ex. 3-2) shows the use of this line. The third kind of line, diagonal, contains

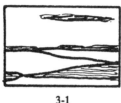
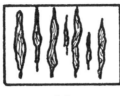

3-1 3-2 3-3

the greatest feeling of action, force and movement. Without even showing any subject, the lines suggest (Ex. 3-3) strife, commotion, and disorder. Why do lines have this connection? Fundamentally, the lines you see are simply ink printed on paper; one kind cannot move any more than the others. How, then, do they create these illusions?

We find that the artist closely follows the forces of nature, and he uses lines the way nature uses them. Suppose you noticed a large telephone pole (Ex. No. 3-4) lying on the sidewalk in front of your house one day. This pole has assumed a horizontal position, and contains no energy at the moment. Just before noon, six husky men arrive and stand the pole up, balancing it on one end. You watched these men work hard

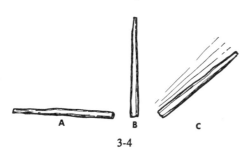

3-4

to lift that pole. Where did all their energy go? A minor part, of course, went into the grunting and sweating of the men, but by far the greatest portion was stored up in that pole! Suppose the men were to walk off leaving it unguarded, just balanced. This would be a criminal act because the pole could so easily be toppled over onto someone. The person who was hit by it, would in effect be hit by six strong men! So long as the vertical position is held, the pole retains its energy, but as it begins to fall, it assumes a diagonal position, the line of action! This then, is the reasoning behind our feelings for different kinds of straight lines.

Curved lines, too, take their feelings from natural forces. The graceful "slow" curve takes more time to change direction. The busy "fast" curve changes direction many times in a short space. Thus in Ex. No. 3-5 we have slow curves reminding us of the slow circles of a swan on the lake, while the fast curves of Ex. No. 3-6 are more like the water bugs that dart about on its surface. The hawk glides in slow curves, the sparrow dips and darts in fast ones. One often sees a skater

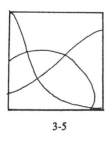

3-5

3-6

begin a figure-skating exhibition with slow curves around the arena, but invariably the climax is a series of the fastest curves possible, a "spin" in the center of the ice.

Since straight and curved lines may be found in almost any visual art work, let us glance at some of the color plates to see how lines are used. In "Bison Lying Down" (Color Pl. 1) we see nothing but curved lines except for a few diagonals in the animal's legs. All these looping, swirling lines help give the painting a look of action, fierceness, and life. The plate which follows it, the "Stela of Dedu" (Color Pl. 2) makes much more use of vertical and horizontal straight lines. This accounts for the static, unmoving quality of the two people and of the whole scene. Look now at the Rembrandt etching "The Sacrifice of Abraham" (Color Pl. 7) which contains such a lot of quick curves showing action, struggle, anguish and impending death. Contrast this with the "Madonna and Child" (Col. Pl. 6) and note the slower curves, the arched picture frame, and the general vertical poise of all the figures. Everything leads upward in this picture.

Forms of Lines

There are numerous line forms in the visual arts, and in order to narrow down the field somewhat it is necessary to select some of these and omit others. Among those most often seen in art works are the following:

Skeletal Lines -- these are made by following the main directions of the eye-movements one might have in looking at the object or by visualizing its internal structure, shown in Example 3-7.

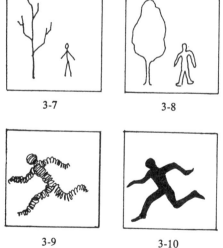

3-7   3-8

3-9   3-10

Outline Lines -- made by following the outer edges of the object, as shown in Example 3-8, and omitting the interior structure.

Contour Lines -- made by following the three-dimensional shape of the object, as seen in Example 3-9.

Edge Lines -- made by the edges of a solid object. In the case of Example 3-10, we imagine a line encircling the figure of the man but of course there really is no line there, only the edge of the black against the white.

Some artists make use of freely drawn lines in their work. Note the excellent lines of Picasso's "Mother and Child" (Color Pl. 13). Here the figures are drawn over a neutral background with a bare suggestion of solidity of color or material. Only the line is used to create a feeling of reality, and it is sufficient. In contrast, the "Madonna and Child" of Milano (Color Pl. 6) has pure line less in evidence, though one sees it readily enough. In "Young Woman with Water Jug" (Color Pl. 8) the lines are created by edges of things, the map, window, cape, and so on. Line in its pure form is seen in the slanting rain of the "Storm on the Great Bridge" (Color Pl. 3). One never sees the air filled with black lines during a storm, but we accept this convention readily.

3-11

Contour lines may be seen in the Rembrandt etching (Color Pl. 7) as the shading lines follow the general surface contours of the rocks. They may also be seen in the photograph of the Lever House (Color Pl. 4) following the floor levels around the corner of the building. As in Example 3-11, depth may be suggested merely by following the three-dimensional shape of the subject being drawn.

PROBLEMS:

Problem One: Imagine that a gigantic spaceship has been voyaging for 500 years to a distant star with several thousand people aboard. Write a short essay on the changes that might take place in the visual arts of these people after several generations, in so far as "line" is concerned.

Problem Two: Select two large magazine ads which appeal to you. Make a line analysis of each to see whether this particular element is used effectively.

Problem Three: Check some recently built homes and some built in the 1920s or earlier. Compare the "lines" found in each.

Problem Four: Make the same kind of comparisons in fashions of these two eras, or in automobiles. Give reasons for the changes in line over the years.

Problem Five: Draw skeleton-, outline-, and contour-line pictures of your hand, all on one sheet of paper.

Problem Six: Practice making line analyses of the other color plates in this text.

Problem Seven: Practice drawing the contours of a basketball, a water tower, a banana, and a balloon.

CHAPTER 4

COLORS

A second great visual art element is color. We see it almost everywhere we look, but few of us know just what it is. Color is caused by different vibration speeds of light waves. These waves in turn are a part of a larger series of "electromagnetic waves" which include such familiar uses as radio, radar, TV, X-ray and so on, shown in Example 4-1. Light waves must be the exact length for our eyes to receive. If they are a bit too long (slower-vibrating) they will be infra-red light, and invisible. If a bit too short, they are ultra-violet light, also invisible, and harmful.

Nearly everything we see is visible to us because light is reflecting off it into our eyes. Some things, like the sun or a light bulb, make their own light. Every other object is seen by reflected light. Most light is made up of many frequencies mixed up together, producing the effect of "white" light. If such white light is sent through a triangular shaped section of glass it will be split up into its separated wavelengths and come out the colors of the rainbow, as shown in Example 4-2.

If the fact is understood that white light has the colors already in it, then it is easy to see what will happen when the artist uses paint colors. Paints are in reality "light blotters," and will soak up all wave lengths but one. Red paint for example absorbs orange, yellow, green, blue, indigo, and violet wave lengths, reflecting only the red light. Something in the size of the molecules in red paint or dye will reflect that particular wave

gov't channels
AM radio
TV, FM radio
radar
heat, infra-red
visible light
ultra-violet
X-rays
gamma, cosmic rays

4-1

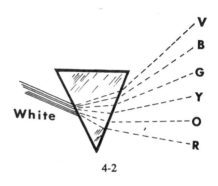

4-2

length, and that only. Other colors work in the same fashion.

Color, then, depends upon what portion of the light is being reflected. This is why, if you mix all the various paint colors together, the result will be a dark, dingy gray. Since each paint color absorbs all but its own light frequency, the more colors that are added, the darker the mixture becomes. Color may be discussed under three headings.

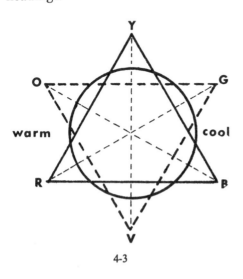

4-3

1. *Hue* -- this is the correct term for what we commonly call "color." In paint-mixing, three basic hues will produce all the other hues. These three, called primary hues, are Yellow, Red, and Blue. (See Example 4-3) They are mixed to produce the three secondary hues, Orange (R plus Y), Violet (R plus B), and Green (B plus Y). There are sub-mixtures possible -- a lot of red mixed with less yellow would be a "red, red-orange," and so on.

The color wheel is an interesting device to help keep the relationships among these hues clear in our minds. First we see the primary hues linked by a solid triangle, and the secondaries by a dotted one. The vertical dotted line divides the wheel into a "warm" left side and a "cool" right side. The association of green and blue with ice, cool water, and so on, is common. Red and orange on the other hand are thought of in connection with sun, desert, fire, and other hot subjects. The left side of the wheel is also known as the "advancing" side and the right as "receding" or "retreating." Warning signs are in red or orange while inconspicuous objects are found in blues and greens. The hues yellow and violet are capable of being on either side, depending upon the other hues used with them. Yellow and violet in a desert scene look hot, and in an arctic scene cool.

Let's look over the color plates again for some of the hues we have been discussing. In Mondrian's "Broadway Boogie-Woogie" (Color Pl. 10) the hues are all primaries. The gray areas are not colors but something called "neutrals," to be discussed later. The lively look of this painting stems from its use of primaries. The picture "I and My Village" (Color Pl. 14) uses red, blue, green and some yellow. "Young Woman With Water Jug" (Color Pl. 8) has the same three primary hues, though much darker. So does "The Wise Men" (Color Pl. 5) in stained glass. Artists the world over use these primaries widely. However, there are still other things to be learned about the wheel.

When a painter makes use of hues which lie next to each other on the wheel, he is using an "analogous" scheme. Such a picture as the "Bison" (Color Pl. 1) is all of one basic hue. The Egyptian "Stela" (Color Pl. 2) has similar unity of hue, in this case yellow-orange. The Picasso "Mother and Child" (Color Pl. 13) is painted with analogous hues. Very frequently women wear outfits of analogous hues, a blue skirt with green jacket and accessories. Blue-violet and orange-yellow have been favorite analogous color schemes.

A final consideration on the wheel is the idea of "complementary" hues. Very frequently women wear outfits of analogous hues, a blue Red and green, blue and orange, and yellow and violet are complementaries. They tend to clash when placed side by side in equal amounts. When mixed as paints, complementaries neutralize one another, making a dull gray. The addition of just a little green paint in a large amount of red will give the red a duskier, not-so-vivid color. This is called "toning down" the red. The brightness of any hue can be toned down by adding a little of its complementary. One notices complementary color schemes in fashions, where a red dress may have a very slight touch of green in a bracelet or pin, and in interior decoration when a blue room has a bit of orange added for accent in the cushions or draperies. So much for hue.

2. *Value.* The color wheel gives us only the mixtures available from the primaries and secondaries. No matter how these are mixed, they will not produce certain other colors. For example, there is no brown on the wheel nor any possibility of such a color, for brown is orange with black added. This brings us to the second color factor, "value." In its simplest consideration, value is any gradation between pure black and pure white. The accompanying value scale (Example 4-4) approximates 10 steps between the two extremes. The difficulty comes in applying the value scale to colors. The hue "orange" at the extreme top of this scale would be a very pale tan, in the middle a rich orange and at the bottom a deep, dark brown. Red would vary from a delicate pink at the top to a black rose at the bottom, and so on. Most colors of this type have trade names like "coral" or "electric blue" or even "desert flamingo," meaning very little so far as telling how they are made up. It is more accurate to call such a color "Red-8" or simply "R-8" to indicate a blackish-red.

4-4

Notice in "Young Woman With Water Jug" (Color Plate 8) the different values of blue. There is a very light, almost white-blue in the walls, a darker blue in the headpiece and collar toward the window, still darker on the left side of the girl's head, darker yet in the cloak on the chair, and darkest of all in her skirt -- five values of blue! Almost as great a range of blue values is seen in "The Wise Men" (Color Pl. 5). In contrast, Mondrian (Color Pl. 10) does not vary the values of his hues at all.

3. *Intensity.* When a hue is mixed with its complementary, the intensity is reduced and the hue dulled. Some dulled, slaty blues may be seen in "Storm on the Great Bridge" (Color Pl. 3) and in "Singer Building" (Color Pl. 11). All of the hues appear to have been dulled in this work, from the orange in the lower right to the blues elsewhere. Neither of these has the Mondrian's pure blues. Having added a third factor, it is now possible to designate any color by a hue-value-intensity figure. The deeper blue at the lower right-hand corner of "Storm on the Great Bridge" would be something like B-7-5 for instance. One note of caution; many times it is virtually impossible to tell how a certain color is arrived at. All paints are not alike chemically, and will not produce identical color mixtures even if a formula is carefully followed. Paint stores for interior paints now usually have mixing machines with formula books to allow the buyer to match his sample to a predetermined mixture. Even then, the paints will be slightly different when they dry.

PROBLEMS:

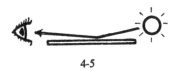

4-5

Problem One: If you hold an LP record so that it is on your eye-level, and then let a light shine off it into your eyes, (as in Example 4-5) you will see the colors of the rainbow on the surface of the record. Explain this.

Problem Two: Set up an experiment in which you view various colors under colored lights. Explain the results.

Problem Three: Find out the basic difference between sonar and radar, and explain in general terms how they work.

Problem Four: Explain why pure black and pure white are not obtainable in paints.

Problem Five: Compare and explain "subtractive" and "additive" color mixing.

Problem Six: Using water colors or "tempera" (show card color) make a color wheel. Then experiment with the different hues which it is possible to attain. Try complementary and analogous color schemes.

Problem Seven: Try making a few value scales of the main hues. Note in which ones it is easiest to obtain gradations of value, and explain.

Problem Eight: Find examples of several color schemes in advertisements, homes, fashion, and the like. Discuss each one.

Problem Nine: Collect samples of one hue at varying intensities. Arrange them from whitest to blackest.

Problem Ten: Analyze the variations of the red hues in Klee's "Revolution of the Viaducts" (Color Pl. 16).

Problem Eleven: Discuss the artist's use of red and green hues in "Manchester Valley" (Color Pl. 15).

CHAPTER 5

TEXTURE AND VALUE

Texture may be defined as the surface appearance of objects, or the way they feel to the touch. Hence, textures can be both seen and felt. We get some idea of the latter when we stroke a kitten's fur, or touch sandpaper. Most of the textures used in the arts, however, are not touched but only looked at.

We learned in the section on color that reflected light is the common means of perceiving colors. This is also true of textures. When we look at a shiny chrome surface, such as an auto hubcap, we know it is smooth without ever touching it because of the mirror-like light reflections from its surface. A rough board casts minute surface shadows, giving it the typical look of roughness. It is these surface shadows that painters try to imitate in their works, arranging the paint colors in such a way as to duplicate the light and shadow interplay on the surface of the object they're painting. At certain times, painters have concentrated on such texture imitation, going to great pains to reproduce the texture of sparkling glass, fur, fresh-cut oranges, metal and human skin. At other times, painters have been more interested in another kind of texture, the actual surface of the painting itself.

When the painter sets out to create a real texture, he must, of course, use a painting medium which is capable of taking varying textures. The medium which is most often used for this purpose is oil because the painter can vary it from a quite thin and runny liquid to a thick, heavy one. None of the other mediums of painting can be manipulated in this way. Watercolor dries the same thickness on the paper and cannot be built up in rough ridges. Note the Van Gogh painting, "Starry Night" (Color Plate 9) with its heavy streaks of oil swirling through the sky. Contrast this with the very thin oil as seen in Picasso's "Mother and Child." Now look at Vermeer's "Young Woman With Jug" to see the beautifully *imitated* textures of linen, metal, cloth and glass. By his imitations of light and shadow, the artist gives us simulated textures in this painting, while Van Gogh shows us *real* texture in his rough surfaces. In order to add textural interest to their works, painters in recent decades have embedded materials of various kinds in the paint surface. Pieces of newspaper, cloth, screen wire, string, ashes and other materials may be seen as part of the painting surface.

One interesting surface texture variant may be seen by closely examining the "Madonna and Child" (Color Pl. 6). It will be seen that the borders of this painting are embossed with a design. Halos of similar nature are found over the heads of the mother and child, and slanting lines stream outward from them in all directions. This effect is achieved by stamping the gold surface of this painting, much as a leather purse or belt may be embossed. Beneath this very thin gold leaf surface there is a layer of soft red clay to take the impression of the stamp or die which the artist uses. Such "tempera" paintings were created as religious offerings in the medieval era, and were made as costly as possible. At times jewels were powdered to make the colors for the paint!

The textures used by painters are sometimes real, sometimes imitative. In sculpture and architecture they are nearly always real. Once in awhile we see a wood surface painted to resemble marble, or metal finished to look like wood, but this is generally regarded as cheap, and not often done. Sculptors and architects know that every medium has its own beauty, and need not pretend to be something else. If we must build with wood, let us admit it honestly. If our statue is clay, then we should make the most of that medium's qualities.

Real surface textures may be arranged in approximately five degrees; rough (jagged rocks, rubble), coarse (gravel, sandpaper), matte (egg shell, leather grain), smooth (finished wood) and shiny (polished metal, glass). Each texture reflects a different amount of light, and in a different way. Rough textures scatter and absorb light in a haphazard, nonuniform way. Shiny surfaces reflect light so exactly that images can be seen in them.

Sculptors choose surface textures to match the subject they will portray. Thus, a statue of a beautiful woman would be done in marble, which may be polished to a lustre and which has a creamy, soft look about it. A rugged athlete might be cast in bronze, and the statue left unpolished.

Architects consider textures carefully in choosing their materials. They know that wood has a warm, inviting look and can be finished or rough, painted, stained or varnished. An office suite with wood panelling, and one lined with brick will have quite different feelings about them. Often exteriors of buildings will exhibit a variety of textures ranging from stone and brick to metal and glass. Note in the picture of Lever House (Color Pl. 4) the varying textures one sees. The shiny, cool, glass surface contrasts strongly with the red brick buildings around it, and with the concrete slab tower in the distance.

Value

We have already seen how a scale may set up varying degrees of value from pure black to pure white, and how these can be carried out in colors. Paintings have, in addition to their color-values, an overall value (not to be confused with their monetary value). A painting such as "Broadway Boogie Woogie" (Color Pl. 10) is considered "high" in value, that is, bright and light. Picasso's "Mother and Child" (Color Pl. 13) is a little less bright, but still high on the value scale. Vermeer's "Woman With Water Jug" (Color Pl. 8) is still darker, perhaps in the middle of the scale. "Storm on the Great Bridge" (Color Pl. 3) is gloomier still. At the dark end of the scale is Van Gogh's "The Starry Night" (Color Pl. 9). A picture such as Chagall's "I and My Village" (Color Pl. 14) mixes lights and darks together to form a "contrasty" picture. See how lively it looks compared with the Japanese print, for instance, or the Van Gogh.

Value in sculpture is concerned with the way light falls on the statue, and the shadows it casts. Look at your own hand, noticing that the underside is usually shaded while the upper surface is reflecting a lot of light. The face also catches light falling from above, usually, to form highlights on the forehead, cheek bones, and nose bridge. Shaded areas will be seen in the eye sockets, on the lower edges of the lips, and under the chin. A common trick used by directors of horror movies is to reverse the light-and-shadow patterns of the face by having the light come from below. Even the most kindly face looks sinister when illuminated in this way. Sculptors know this, and take care to have their statues properly lighted and placed.

Architects pay great attention to the way their buildings look in different kinds of light. If a structure is absolutely plain, it will cast only one large shadow, and will look just about the same from sunrise to sunset. If, however, there are projecting details, such as window frames, cornices, ledges, screens and so on, these will catch and reflect light in shadow patterns which change constantly with different kinds of weather. Such a building will not look as monotonous as the bare one. Many buildings add water pools and reflecting basins to give additional light sources. Night lighting by means of spotlights and interior lights can add a great deal to the visual interest of the structure.

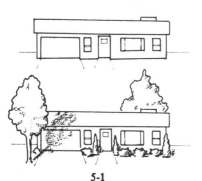

5-1

We often consider value in our

own homes when we plant trees and shrubbery. The small plants have no real function except to break the monotony of the ground line and to cast shadows. The larger trees will throw off water vapor and help cool the air. Many people plant vines as yet another way to add shadows to a house. In Example 5-1, we see two houses of identical type, the upper being without shrubbery or trees. Note how much more pleasant and interesting the landscaping makes the lower house.

PROBLEMS:

Problem One: Count the number of different textures used on the interior of your automobile. Range them from "rough" to "shiny," and tell why each was used.

Problem Two: Find out from a paint dealer or interior decorator what "texture paint" is and how it is used.

Problem Three: In what ways may the texture of wood be changed? Collect samples of woods with different surface textures.

Problem Four: Find examples of some great painters of the past who specialized in imitating textures. Examine their work closely to see what they did, and how it was accomplished.

Problem Five: Explain why one cannot see his reflection in a sheet of sandpaper but can in polished metal or glass.

Problem Six: Find examples of sculpture in which you feel that the texture matches the subject well.

Problem Seven: Note several old houses in your neighborhood or town. How do they compare in exterior textures with recently built ones?

Problem Eight: Find examples in magazines of photographs which are high, medium, low and contrasty in value. What does this value level have to do with the subject in each case?

Problem Nine: Explain "back-lighting" in photography.

Problem Ten: Examine local buildings for night lighting. How does the shadow pattern change from daylight to night lighting?

Problem Eleven: Examine Color Plates 2, 3, 8, 9, 10, 13, and 15. Arrange them as to value, from lightest to darkest. Also select the ones with least contrast and most contrast.

CHAPTER 6

DEPTH; VOLUME AND PERSPECTIVE

A. *The Illusion of Depth in Painting*

In this chapter we are dealing with the three-dimensional aspects of the visual arts. This takes two forms, the imitation of depth in a flat painting, and the real three-dimensional qualities of sculpture and architecture. Let us consider ways by which the painter can achieve the illusion of the third dimension.

1. *By Use of Color.* Earlier, in our study of the color wheel, it was mentioned that the left side of the wheel represented advancing colors, and the right side receding ones. Artists sometimes make use of this fact to bring a sense of depth to the flat surface. Something of the kind (though not intended) can be seen in the Japanese print (Color Pl. 3) in which the two orange panels in upper right and lower left stand out from the gray surroundings as if they were closer to the eye. The red squares and rectangles in the Mondrian work (Color Pl. 10) also seem to stand out.

An even more common use of color is in creating the illusion of the blue haze common to our atmosphere. We see distant objects only because of the light reflected from them to our eyes. If these objects are far off, this light must travel through many yards of air, which contains billions of gas molecules, moisture droplets, dust specks and so on. Naturally all of this tends to filter out some of the light rays, so that only the shortest wave lengths get through, and these are the ones causing the color "blue." The distant objects, then, look a hazy blue to us. In higher altitudes and dryer climates, the air is much thinner, that is, it contains fewer molecules. Distant objects retain more of their original colors, so that the newcomer to those parts at first will badly misjudge distance. Notice how the painter generally colors his distant backgrounds with this same bluish hue.

2. Depth in painting can also be obtained *by use of forms*. The artist can manipulate these and produce in his work the illusion of depth. Forms may be used as follows:

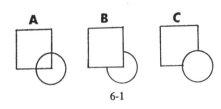

A   **B**   **C**

6-1

a. Overlapping forms -- here the artist uses, let us say, a square and a circle, (Example 6-1). He can make it seem that one is in front of the other by overlapping. At A, the two are drawn out fully, with the result that it is impossible to tell which is the nearer. In B and C, one form is made to blot out the other, with the result that the square seems nearer in B, and farther in C.

b. Foreshortened forms -- here the artist causes the "near" edge of the object to be larger, shortening its length until one is persuaded that the object is protruding from the flat surface. (Example 6-2).

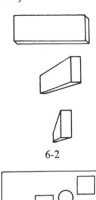

6-2

c. Positions of forms -- as we look around us, we notice that the nearest objects are generally below our eye level, and farther ones tend to be higher up. Painters use this fact to bring another depth illusion to their works. In Example 6-3, we see squares and circles rising from the lower edge of the picture to the top. Although none of them is nearer to the eye than any other, we feel that the higher ones are farther away.

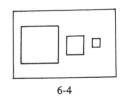

6-3

6-4

d. Size of forms -- if the size of objects in the painting is made to vary, our mind will persuade us that the smaller object is farther away than the larger. This is seen in Example 6-4, where the squares seem to recede into the distance. Judging distance by size is learned early in childhood. The baby will reach out for anything which attracts its attention, such as a bright light or even the moon. The story is told of a man, blind from birth, who had his sight restored through an operation. The first day he could see, he looked out the hospital window and tried to touch the cars in the street ten floors below!

3. *Line* may also add the illusion of depth.

a. Converging lines are often used to show distance and depth on a flat surface. In Example 6-5, we see two lines which converge to cre-

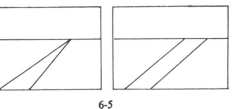

6-5

ate the idea of a highway stretching across a vast plain. If these lines are parallel, the illusion vanishes, the picture remains flat. Converging lines are frequently seen in pictures of houses and buildings. In the photograph of the Lever House, (Color Pl. 4), the use of converging lines is clearly seen. Lay a straightedge along the lines of this building, or the others in the picture, and you will find that each line is directed to an invisible "vanishing point" somewhere off to the left of the picture as seen in Example 6-6. You will notice another one off to the right, where the lines of the narrow edge of the building meet. Two vanishing points are created when we view a building from a corner position.

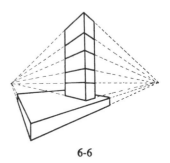

6-6

Creating the illusion of depth by the use of converging lines is easy once the basic principles are grasped. First we begin by looking at the building head-on. Our vanishing point is wherever *we* are; as we move to one side or the other, up or down, the vanishing

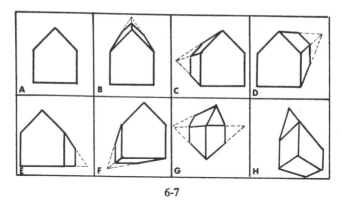

6-7

point moves with us. In Example 6-7, we can see only the front of the house at A, because we are directly in front of it. At B, we are above it, and can see the roof. At C, we have moved off to the left, but are still above it. We can now see roof and side. At D, we are above and to the right. At E, we have taken a position below the level of the house, so that it looks as if it is set on a hill, and at F we move to the left, staying low. Finally, at G and H we leave our position generally in front of the house and move to sharply angled positions, whereupon we get two vanishing points.

Painters at one time were captivated by the discovery of the laws of perspective, and they made their paintings as geometrically accurate as possible. Now, however, the painter may use his knowledge to distort perspective, and thus give his painting a brooding, sinister look, or perhaps an air of unreality. Note the tiny group of buildings in the Chagall painting (Color Pl. 14). Perspective lines are thoroughly mixed up, giving an even more dream-like quality to an already fanciful scene.

b. Clarity of line may also add to the depth illusion. We know that the more distant an object is, the less we are able to make out its details. The painter may internationally paint certain objects with clarity of detail and others with less detail so as to promote the illusion of depth. Note in the color plate of the Lever House that the closest building on the right shows a great deal of detail, down to the individual bricks. More distant structures show only larger features, and the farthest ones, such as the tower at the extreme right are only outlined.

B. *Depth and Space in Sculpture*

The painter must work to achieve the illusion of depth on a two dimensional surface, but the sculptor already has the third dimension as an integral part of his art. He needs, however, to choose how he will exploit this third dimension, and generally his choices fall into the following categories:

1. Relief Sculpture -- this kind of sculpture is found on coins, plaques, tombstones, and many other places. The figures do not stand free, but are a part of the background, projecting out from it but still attached. This has a number of advantages, among them the fact that a background scene may be shown behind the figures, such as landscape, clouds, trees and so on. Free standing sculpture cannot show such objects. A further advantage is found in the positions which the sculptured objects may assume. If the relief is in stone, the figures may be standing on tiptoes, while a free standing stone figure in that position would break of its own weight.

2. Free standing sculpture uses space completely, allowing the observer to see the statue from all sides. Such statues usually have a limited subject matter range; either showing the human form or else a restricted number of animal forms such as horse, dog, tiger, etc. Sculptors do not make free standing statues of buildings, mountains, trees, insects or the ocean, though painters frequently use these for subjects. The sculptor of a full-round statue must take into consideration the fact that his work may be viewed from all sides, hence must make it good looking from many angles.

Another consideration is that of weight. A life-size statue in stone will weigh several hundred pounds, and that weight must have adequate support. It is for this reason that many stone figures will have an animal placed by the legs, or a flowing garment which acts as a base, or perhaps a tree stump which will help support the statue's weight. Sculptors who use wood or metal have mediums with higher "tensile strength," that is, with ability to bend without breaking. Metal statues frequently are hollow, adding to their lightness. This allows poses which would be impossible in the statue carved from stone.

3. A third use of depth and space occurs in the "interior spaces" of a statue. In "Child With Cat" (Color Pl. 12) we have a statue which allows us to see only its exterior surface. Some sculptors would like us to see some of the interior, and have in recent years made

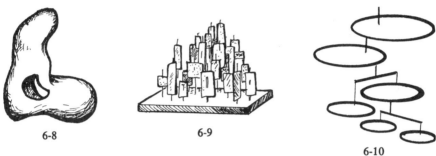

6-8   6-9   6-10

statues such as Example 6-8, with holes in them, statues of wire and metal which can be seen through, as Example 6-9, and even moving sculptures such as Example 6-10, which whirl and sail through space. One sculptor even designs large and complex works to fit against the floor, ceiling and four walls of a small room so that when you step in, you are *inside* the sculpture. If this seems strange, just remember that any room, with its furniture, light fixtures, rugs, etc. is a kind of sculpture which we live in. Some of the earlier, elaborate styles of interior decoration with their mouldings, chandeliers and ornamentation everywhere were in effect room-sculpture to be viewed from within.

C. *Enclosed Space in Architecture.*

Whereas sculpture only occasionally makes use of interior space, architecture uses both exterior and interior space all the time. Buildings have an outer and inner volume, and the two are not necessarily closely

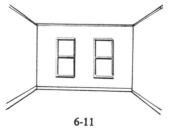

6-11

related. Sometimes we approach a small home and are surprised upon entering to see how spacious it seems. At other times the larger house may seem cramped inside.

Interior spaciousness is as much a result of eye-movement as any other factor. In Example 6-11, we are looking into a room which is empty. There is nothing to stop

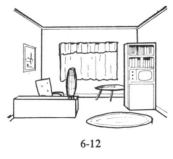

6-12

our eye movement as it travels from the near edge to the far wall. In Example 6-12, however, the room space has been broken up into areas so that the eye no longer has a clean sweep to the far wall. Instead, it is stopped by the sofa, bookshelf, pictures and chairs. Thus, oddly enough, a room looks larger when it is filled with furniture than when it is empty. Of course, a room can be too cluttered up, and look crowded and small.

The dimensions of the interior volume are quite important to the "atmosphere" generated by the room. In the accompanying illustrations, Examples 6-13 and 6-14, the cubic volume of the two rooms remains the same, but their effect is totally different. Room 6-13 is low-ceilinged, suitable as the setting for a convivial gathering of people. It could be a

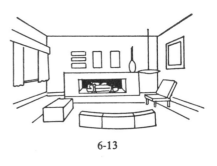

6-13

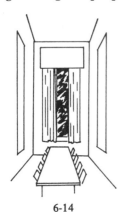

6-14

large office where many desks and typewriters added to the noise, or it could make a good night club or game room. Example 6-14, however, is lofty, cold, reserved. It would be good as a Church or a room for the meeting of the Board of Directors. There would be no gay music or loud laughter here, but hushed tones and serious discussion. Yet both rooms are the same, except that one has been tilted on its side!

Interior space, eye-movement, and dimensions are all factors in architecture. Their successful achievement is a matter for much study and planning.

PROBLEMS:

Problem One: Find some examples of paintings showing depth illusion, and others where the painter presents only two dimensions. Explain why the artist wanted depth in the one case but not in the other.

Problem Two: What problems in depth perception will be encountered by men on the surface of the moon, and why?

Problem Three: Find a painting, if you can, in which *all* of the means of depth illusion are used. Identify each one on a freehand sketch of the work.

Problem Four: Cut out a cardboard frame about 6" wide and 4" high. Then hold it close to your face so that the scene in front of you looks like a picture within that frame. Now sketch the relative position of near and distant objects, showing where they fall in that frame.

Problem Five: Make a drawing of several buildings set in an open field. Mark one vanishing point on your paper, and use this same point for all the buildings. Now repeat the drawing, but this time use a different vanishing point for each building. Compare the two drawings for stability, interest, physical accuracy and sense of reality.

Problem Six: Find examples of relief sculpture, other than coins, in your town. List only sculpture with a subject, not non-objective work such as window-trim or mouldings. Identify and locate each example so a field trip may be taken by the class to visit the sculptures you have found.

Problem Seven: Do the same as problem six, only for free-standing sculpture with a subject.

Problem Eight: Visit the site of a house to be built and note the space which has been marked off on the ground, or laid in the foundation. If possible, look at empty rooms of new, unfinished houses. Take their measurements, comparing them with furnished rooms in your own home. Write up what you find.

Problem Nine: Visit various churches, supermarkets, bowling alleys, and college or high school meeting rooms. What variations are found in the ceiling heights?

Problem Ten: List as many suggestions as you can find for making a small room look larger. Consult home-makers' magazines for such hints.

Problem Eleven: Explain illusions of depth in Color Plates 1, 2, 15, and 16.

Part Three

LEARNING TO HEAR; MUSIC

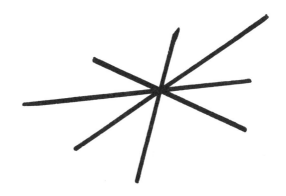

CHAPTER 7

PITCH—TONAL PATTERNS

In Part One, we learned some general things about the arts. For one thing, some of them are based on the sense of sight, which we have just studied, while others deal in sounds. The visual arts are also known as "space arts," and the audible arts as "time arts." One of the time-sound arts which all of us know from other classes, is literature. The other, music, is not so well understood. Many people cannot read its notation and fewer still can explain its structures and meanings.

Music has a unique advantage, its ability to affect the subconscious mind. No other art can penetrate so deeply into that area of the brain which controls our basic bodily functions. A person under anaesthetic will show increased heartbeat, blood pressure, skin sensitivity and muscular tension if a march is played. Play a soothing lullaby and these unconscious responses change in the opposite direction. No other art has this power. Poetry read into his ear, or a painting put before his opened eyes will have no effect. This direct road to the subconscious explains why music can stir us so deeply, and also why advertisers use music to accompany their appeals on radio and television. They know that no matter what we are doing, their music is causing a response in us, and properly managed, this response can be linked to the sale of the product.

Music, then, can stir the emotions but this serves as a handicap as well as an asset. People are likely to listen with their emotions and not their minds. The music becomes a kind of background for daydreaming and fantasy. Such listeners could not tell you how the music was constructed, whether there were two themes or three, what style was represented, what instrumentation was used, or any one of dozens of objective features. They had reacted to it, but without understanding. To listen to music in this way may be thoroughly enjoyable, but the listener must not deceive himself into thinking that he understands it when he does not!

Musical understanding --- the kind which penetrates into the construction of the music --- is difficult but eminently worthy of study. Music composition has been called man's greatest achievement, and when we perceive it for what it really is, that claim does not seem excessive. A work of music is a pattern made up of vibrations in the air, spread out over a span of time! Our ears can pick up and translate into sound, air pressure waves between 16 vibrations per second and approximately 20,000 vibrations per second. If the rate of vibration goes either above or below these limits, we cannot "hear" the pressure waves. The area of study which is concerned with sound waves is called "acoustics," and offers many fascinating insights into such problems as echoes, sound-proofing, sonar, and so on. Our present study must be confined to music as an art, rather than as a science, however. A later chapter of this book explores the hearing mechanism.

A musical composition consists of literally thousands upon thousands of different vibrations coming to our ears with only split seconds between them, some long, some short, some single, some multiple, combined into complex groupings, and all of this lasting as long as a half-hour or more. Out of this chaos of sound, the trained listener is able to pick out the main musical ideas or themes, list them in order of appearance, tell when they may have been repeated, how they were changed, what instruments played them, and top off his performance by identifying the composer and approximate date of composition, all of this with a piece of music never heard before! A similarly difficult task would be hard to imagine in the visual arts. Suppose, for instance, you were taken on a tour of a great castle, shown a hundred different rooms, moving swiftly through each one without once looking back, sometimes being led through rooms you'd seen earlier, and never having a chance to see the whole castle from a distance. At the end of your tour, could you draw a fairly accurate floor plan of the building, placing each room in its proper area? Most students cannot draw a floor plan of the school they have attended all year. To do such a thing would require a good memory, which could be greatly assisted by taking notes and making sketches as you toured. These aids are the same for the good music listener. He must know how to hold music in his memory, and be able to take notes on interesting features quickly.

Music's Four Elements

The art of music depends on four broad factors for its identity and effectiveness. These are: *Pitch, Duration, Volume and Timbre.* They can be illustrated quite simply. Play a tone on the piano. This single note may be measured for the four elements just named. If the tone "A" (Ex. 7-1) is located just right of the keyboard center, that

7-1

tone will be vibrating at the rate of 440 times per second. That is its *Pitch*. This tone can be heard for 15 seconds before it dies out. This is its *Duration*. It can be measured as having a certain level of loudness. This is its *Volume*. And finally it can be determined by the ear that the tone is coming from the piano, not from a trumpet or human voice. This aspect of the tone is its *Timbre*.

In exploring these four elements of music, we discover that there are important subdivisions within each. For instance, pitches may be strung out one after the other in the form of "motives," or "melodies." Sometimes they are played all at once, forming "chords" or "harmony." Duration, the length of time a tone is heard, may involve "rhythm," a series of different tone lengths coming one after another. It may also deal with "meter," the pulse or beat of the music, and "tempo," the music's speed!

The other two factors, volume and timbre, are not so complicated, although in the latter we become involved with the various families of instruments, kinds of orchestras and bands, and so on.

Musical Notation -- (Pitches Only)

In order to get into the business of learning how to listen to music, we will have to tackle the tough problem of learning how to write it down. Unless we can do this, at least on a limited scale, we will not really understand much of what we hear. Actually, the writing of music need not be the bogey-man most of us have dreamed up. We have all seen a simple but effective kind of music-writing on popular sheet music. The familiar grid-and-dot notation tells us (Example 7-2) where to place our fingers on the fretted finger-

7-2

board of a guitar, banjo or ukulele. Anyone can learn it.

The conventional system of notation is a cumbersome, difficult system to learn. A much easier one will be used here, which will enable the student to write and play simple music within a fairly short time. Later on, if he wishes to pursue his musical study, the student should learn the conventional staff, clefs, key signatures, and so on.

First, a section of the piano keyboard is shown in Example 7-3, with the letter-names of the tones on it. The black keys will remain unnamed for the moment. Below the keyboard we have the piano-staff, so named

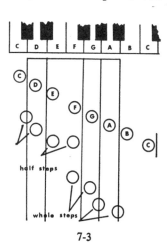

7-3

because the lines represent the black keys of the piano. In using this staff, play the notes from the top of the page to the bottom. Any tones which are on a horizontal line are played together.

The next thing to learn is that the distance between any two adjacent tones on the keyboard is called a "half-step." Notice that sometimes the white keys have a black one between them, and sometimes they do not. Whenever two tones are separated by a tone between, the distance between the outer ones is called a "whole-step," as seen in the lower part of Example 7-3.

Musical Scales

Between the lowest and the highest tones of music there are several thousand distinct pitches, too many for the composer to use, and for the listener to keep straight. No painter ever attempts to use all available tones, tints, hues, and shades. Similarly, no composer tries to use all of the available pitches. In selecting a few for use, he creates a "scale", usually of eight tones, the last of which is just twice the vibration rate of the first, this distance being called an "octave." One of the easiest

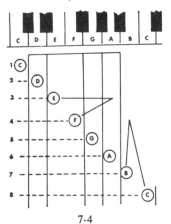

7-4

scales to play begins on "C" and moves to the right on the keyboard to the next "C", an octave higher, notated in Example 7-4.

Notice that this scale has a pattern of whole-steps and half-steps, so that there is a whole-step between each pair of tones except for numbers three and four, and seven and eight, where there are only half-steps. This pattern of scale is called a "major" scale. Once we have the pattern, we may build a major scale starting anywhere we like. For instance, let us begin on E, building another major scale. This time we will reduce the size of the piano staff somewhat. After all, its purpose is to make writing more compact, rather like shorthand. If one has to draw a piano-keyboard-size staff there would be no advantage over using a picture of the keyboard. With this smaller staff, as shown in Example 7-5, we have room for additional lines to take care of higher notes. Compare the scale pattern here with the one starting on C, and it will be found to be identical. The major scale will, if properly written, come out the same each time.

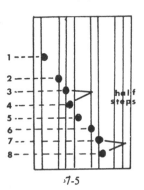

7-5

Notice that the eighth tone is always in the same relative place on the staff as the first tone, and that the half-steps always fall between scale steps 3 and 4, and 7 and 8. If all of these check, you have written the scale properly. One more matter; these new tones which are on black keys are called "sharps." Our new scale now reads as follows:

"E—F sharp—G sharp—A—B—C sharp—D sharp—E"

The regular alphabet letter still applies but if the tone has been moved to the right onto a black key, the word "sharp" is used to designate the fact. In some scales the tone has to be moved to the left in order to make the whole-steps and half-steps fall into their proper pattern. This scale on F (Example 7-6) is an illustration. The fourth tone of the F scale cannot be a "B" because this would make a whole-step where there should only be a half-step. Therefore the tone is moved to the left, the half-step is created, and the scale proceeds. The new tone is called "B flat." It could not be called "A sharp" because we already have an A in the scale.

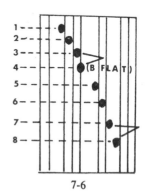

7-6

PROBLEMS:

Problem One: Music is used as a part of many ceremonies in our societies. Because of its power to reach the emotions music is excluded from one formal situation where we don't want it, the court-room. List the things that could be done with music if it were so used.

Problem Two: Find examples in history, the Bible, and my-thology where music's power to affect the emotions is shown.

Problem Three: Find five different types of music used to sell products, comparing the styles or kinds of music with the products being sold.

Problem Four: List the reasons why music with a story or plot might be more popular with the average listener than music without.

Problem Five: Look up the subject of "acoustics" in an encyclo-pedia, and be able to explain what is meant by "reflection", "refrac-tion", "diffraction", and "absorption."

Problem Six: Explain the physical reason why one tone on the piano sounds higher or lower than another.

Problem Seven: Look up the step and half-step pattern of other types of scales, such as melodic minor and harmonic minor scales. Practice writing these.

Problem Eight: Write a scale with all half-steps, and another with all whole steps.

Problem Nine: Find several other ways of indicating musical pitches in addition to those mentioned in this chapter.

Problem Ten: Explain why the piano keyboard has its peculiar arrangement of black and white keys.

Problem Eleven: Prove that you understand the principle of major scale construction by building all twelve possible scales.

Problem Twelve: Invent other scale patterns of your own and experiment with these.

CHAPTER 8

PITCH—HARMONIC PATTERNS

With only a little practice the student should be able to play all major scales slowly on a piano. From there it is only a short step to playing harmony, for many of our common harmonies are based on the scale tones. If, for example, we choose the first, third, and fifth tones of the F major scale, we have what is known as "tonic" harmony, often indicated simply

8-1

with the Roman numeral "I," shown in Example 8-1. The notes, being on a horizontal line, are to be played simultaneously. This tonic chord is the most important of the scale, and may be played in any combination of the three tones. Notice that the scale tones 1, 3, and 5 are arranged in several ways in the example.

As the different chords are added, the same system of forming them is followed. Another useful chord is that built on the fourth tone of the scale, called the "subdominant" and indicated by the Roman numeral "IV." Here the 4th, 6th, and 8th tones are used together, again in any order. A third chord of great usefulness is the "V" or "dominant" harmony, built by using the 5th, 7th, and 9th (same as 2nd) tones of the scale.

In Example 8-2 we see the C, F, and E major scales, each with its I, IV, and V chords. Students should try to find these tones on the piano, and learn to hear and play them. These three chords may be used to accompany music such as hymns, popular songs, folk music, and much else. The different scales are useful for shifting the

C
SCALE
I
IV
V

F
SCALE
I
IV
V

E
SCALE
I
IV
V

8-2

music up or down so as to fit it to different types of singing voice. In addition, the same melody repeated in several different scales will not seem as monotonous as if played in the same scale, so we find that scales are useful to avoid monotony.

You will find that twelve different major scales may be built on the various white and black keys before the octave is reached, and duplication begins. Each of these twelve has its I, IV, and V chords, which you know how to find. In addition, the II, III, and VI chords are quite useful. These are formed in exactly the same way, by skipping every other tone in the scale. The VI chord, for instance, would contain the 6th, 8th, and 10th (or 3rd) tones of the scale.

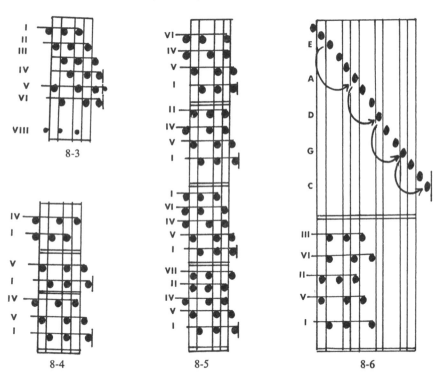

8-3

8-4

8-5

8-6

Chord Progressions

All the useful chords (you will notice that VII is seldom used) have been written out in Example 8-3. Now that we have them, how are they to be used? We find that music tends to use chords in "chains" or "rows" one after another, in some kind of logical pattern. At the end of the chain, we invariably find the I chord. Next to the last, we usually find the V chord unless the piece of music is a hymn, where we find a IV chord used instead. Thus most ordinary pieces end with the chords V-I, and hymns end on IV-I. Quite a few pieces will combine these for a IV-V-I ending. It has a most familiar sound when played on a piano. In Example 8-4, we have all three kinds of chord progression.

If we wish to add chords to these to make our chains longer, we may add some of the other chords in front of these. A fairly common practice is to add on a chord which has two tones of the scale in common with the one which will follow it. If the previous progression began IV-V-I, we will want to add a chord to the beginning of it which has two tones in common with IV. There are two in our collection, the II and the VI. Either of these will be suitable, as shown in Example 8-5. To carry the progression back even further, we might use the I chord at its beginning, and even the VII which we usually don't use would not sound bad here. Try playing the chords in the lower section of Example 8-5 to hear their effect.

One other common way of building chord progressions is by preceding each chord with one which is four notes to the left on the scale, shown in Example 8-6.

Remember that any of these chords may be used in any of the twelve major scales. For instance, in the scale which begins on the first line at the left edge of the staff, the chords are as shown in Example 8-7. This scale and set of chords, which are no harder to figure out than any other we have tried, may be compared with conventional notation as seen in Example 8-8. Note that one must add signs to the conventional staff, including the treble clef which indicates what particular pitches the five lines will stand for (they may change from one piece to another), the flat-signs, and so on. Note also that steps and half-steps cannot be distinguished from one another in this type of writing. Finally, the lines of the

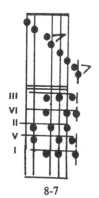

8-7

8-8

staff bear no logical relationship to any keyboard or fingerboard of an instrument, so that the learner has a difficult time of it to grasp the sense of what he is trying to play.

PROBLEMS:

Problem One: Write out the I, IV, and V chords for any scale. Then arrange the notes in these chords in such a way as will "fit the hand" and make playing them easier. Note where each note of the chord must move to get to the next chord. Now practice this movement on the piano until it becomes automatic.

Problem Two: The twelve different keys or scales have other uses besides accommodating the voice range. Make a list of such uses.

Problem Three: Select a familiar hymn in a hymnal, and figure out what chords are used in it. If you cannot read the notation, get a musical friend to tell you the name of the chord tones and the scale they are built on. From these, you will be able to identify the chords.

Problem Four: Sit at a piano and experiment with chords of your own making. These need not be of the types we have studied. When you accidentally discover one you like, write it down. Then try to analyze it, to determine how it is made up.

Problem Five: The chords studied so far have been built by selecting every other note of the scale. Try this method with other types of scales than the major. Note all the interesting variations that happen when the scale pattern differs.

Problem Six: Try making up chords by using notes which are next to each other on the scale. Try using every fourth note, and also use the regular chords, but add another tone at the top. These last are usually quite interesting.

Problem Seven: Chords may be "broken" by playing their tones one after another rather than simultaneously. Try this, using a measure with three beats in it. Let the lowest note of the chord come on the first beat, the middle note of the chord on the second beat, and the top note on the last beat. A few measures of such broken chords are shown in Example 8-9.

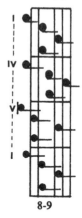

8-9

CHAPTER 9

DURATION—METER AND TEMPO

The music we have written thus far may sound well enough if we are interested in chords and tones but there is more to music than this. One wants to hear a "beat" and be carried along by a steady tempo. In order to achieve this, we will need to add definite durations to our pitches. We shall begin by counting slowly, "One-two-three-four, One-two-three-four" over and over, timing the counts against a second-hand of a watch until we are counting exactly one per second. Now

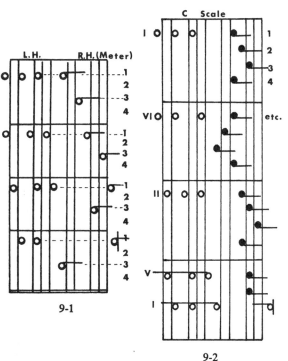

9-1

9-2

we begin to play the chords with the left hand and the melody with the right, as shown in Example 9-1. If this proves difficult, two students may cooperate, one playing the chords and the other the melody. Meanwhile, a third person might carry on the steady counting.

Note that the chord and the melody tone which are directly a-ligned with the meter count are played together just as the voice says that number. If this practice is carefully observed the music should sound as intended.

The horizontal "bar lines" which divide each four beats from the next four are placed there merely to help the player keep his place.

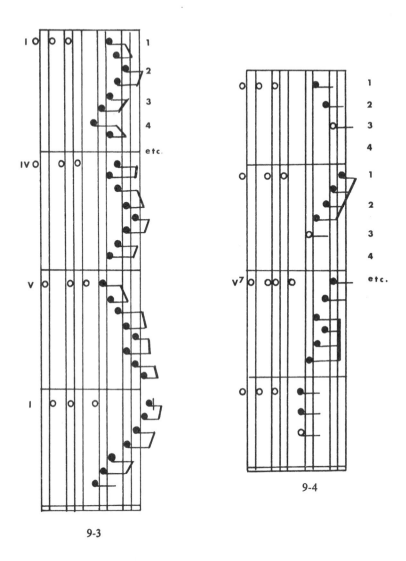

9-3

9-4

The space between these bar lines is called a "measure." This piece is four measures in length.

The basic 1-2-3-4 beat with which we began is a useful kind of meter. Many interesting things can be done with it. In the next example, 9-2, we see four melody notes per chord, one on each of the four counts. Only at the very end do we depart from this pattern. It is possible, as in Example 9-3 to have more than one note on a beat or count, in which case the music would be written as indicated.

Most music, unlike the examples just given, is a mixture of different lengths of notes. A more typical phrase would run something like that in Example 9-4. This might easily be reversed so that the left hand and the right hand are made to exchange parts. This makes a simple eight-measure composition when played together with the previous example, the second half being shown in Example 9-5. Notice that in the V chord there are four notes, giving it a fuller sound. This added note is two tones up the scale from the top note of the chord or seven tones from its lowest note. It is indicated as a V7 chord for that reason.

By this time, the student will have figured out that the different types of notes used in the melody indicate different time values. This may be more easily seen in the chart of note values, Example 9-6. The pitch aspect of the tones is easily seen on the piano-staff, but unfortunately, the duration of the notes is not. A hollow-headed note does not really *look* any longer in time than a solid-headed one, and why should it? In the accompanying chart, we have made the long

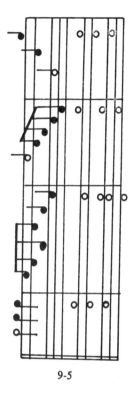

9-5

notes actually look longer proportionately than the short ones. In Example 9-6, alongside the graphic representation there is the conventional note-head. Study these until you have made the connection between the appearance of the note-head and its time length. Notice that this kind of visualization represents the old-time player-piano roll, where a long-held tone was actually a long slit cut in the paper, as seen in Example 9-7.

In the following example, 9-8, the player-piano graphic notation is compared with conventional notes. The latter are much more useful, inasmuch as they require a good deal less space and need

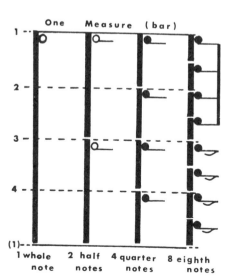

9-6

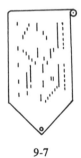

9-7

not be measured out and drawn so carefully. Thus, as long as we keep counting the meter (1-2-3-4) steadily, we can write a whole note in a fraction of the space it would take to write eight 8th notes, for instance. Under the graphic notation as seen in Example 9-9, a four-count whole note would have to be as long as the eight 8th notes because it lasts as long.

In Example 9-10, we see another means of indicating tone length, the "tie." The note on the left-hand side of the example is normally a two-count note, but it has been "tied" to a one-count note, this making a

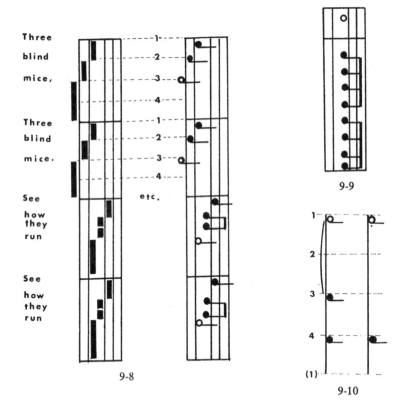

9-9

9-8

9-10

total three counts. This same length may be written by placing a dot just beneath the note, which automatically adds half its length to it. Again we get a total of three counts.

The same thing may be done with the one-count quarter note. Tie it to an 8th note and give it a total length of one-and-a-half counts, or put a dot beneath it for the same value. In Example 9-11 both ways are used. The ties make the quarter notes longer, and so do the dots. In each case, the quarter-note gets one-and-a-half counts.

Rests

It is not sufficient to indicate pitch and duration. There must be a way to indicate silence, too! Just as the empty spaces between objects in a painting are important to its design, so the silent places in a piece of music may be of interest.

In order to indicate places of silence, signs called "rests" are used. There is a rest which corresponds to each type of note, as shown in the following chart, Example 9-12. In Example 9-13, we see a melody with rests in it. In playing this piece, remember not to play during those counts where rests are found.

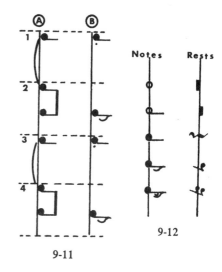

9-11

9-12

Tempo

A minor, but necessary sub-element of music is "tempo." The first music which we worked on was counted at a tempo of one beat per second, which might be indicated as "quarter note equals sixty." If it were taken twice as fast, at 120 beats per minute, the basic harmony, pitch, and rhythm would not change, but the total effect of the piece certainly would! From a rather mournful, plodding composition, it would turn into a vigorous march.

We have two choices in indicating a tempo for music. It can be done with a number, as above, or it can be indicated with a word or two. "Very slow" and "Moderately fast" are seen on music as tempo directions. More commonly used are Italian terms, among them the following:

Largo..... very slow and drawn out
Adagio.... quite broad and slow
Andante...moderately slow, walking tempo
Allegretto.. moderately fast
Allegro.... briskly, fast
Vivace.....extremely fast

9-13

84

These tempos are not set exactly by counting beats with a watch or metronome, but are left to the performer's discretion. This tends to make the musical interpretation more flexible, less rigid. The Italian terms are used in most of the serious music we hear, frequently as titles. The educated listener should become familiar with their meaning.

PROBLEMS:

Problem One: Figure out the number of counts or beats in a march written in "1-2-3-4" meter if the tempo is 120 beats to the minute and the piece is three minutes long. How many beats would it have if it were 128 measures long, and what would be its length in minutes in that case?

Problem Two: Count the number of measures in a popular tune. Count those in a march. What can be said about the lengths of the two kinds of music, and their internal structure? Note: a measure bar in conventional music is a vertical line rather than a horizontal one.

Problem Three: Work out a new (to you) major scale and then write a chord progression to a 4-beat meter. Fit a melody to these chords, using mixtures of whole, half, quarter, and eighth-notes. The piece should be at least eight measures long.

Problem Four: Write a part for two percussion "instruments" which may be anything from handclapping to regulation drums. Use notes and rests in your parts. Let the players' parts be on adjacent vertical lines, with separate rhythm parts at least some of the time. See Example 9-14 for correct format.

Problem Five: Look up tempo indications in printed music, and see how many you find that are not in the textbook. Look up their meanings, and insert them in their proper place in the list of those you have already studied.

9-14

CHAPTER 10

DURATION—RHYTHM PATTERNS

As seen in the previous chapter, the basic musical element of "duration" has three aspects, meter (the steady beat or pulsation of the music), "tempo" (the speed of the music), and "rhythm" which is yet to be explained. In an earlier chapter, it was stated that the term "color" was often misused. We talk about colors when we really mean "hues." In the same way, "rhythm" is often misused for the term "meter." Many people say that they like the strong rhythm of a march, when what they really like is the hypnotically compelling beat or meter, which makes them want to tap their feet. Much currently popular music has rather simple rhythms, but the heavy, steady meter carries it along. What, then, is rhythm?

Rhythm consists of a series of durations which follow one another. Under this definition, almost anything that produces sounds produces rhythms. Glass chimes tinkling in the wind create rhythms, a two-year old child banging on a piano creates rhythms, and the footfalls of a group of people walking down the street form rhythms. Your accents as you read this sentence aloud form rhythms. Thus we see that practically everything that creates sound creates rhythms. Only those things which create steady sounds lack rhythm. The hum of the electric fan, the wail of a police siren, the buzzing of a fly --- these have no rhythm because they do not have a series of durations, only one tone.

By far the greatest proportion of our music not only has rhythm but that rhythmic component is arranged into patterns. It is extremely rare to hear music whose rhythms are not grouped into patterns of some kind. Perhaps the closest thing to patternless rhythms in music is heard in the chants sung in the Roman Catholic Church. These are really *not* without pattern, but the pattern is less evident than in most of our music. The reason for this is that these chants follow the rhythms of the words which are being sung, and word rhythms, unless taken from metric verse, are not likely to incorporate strong rhythm patterns within themselves. Let us take a few ordinary sentences as an illustration:

> *"May I please have a drink of water?"*
> *"My name is Betty Harrison --- what's yours?"*
> *"Isn't this a wonderful day?"*

86

These sentences all possess rhythms, but the rhythms are not grouped into patterns so that our attention is called to them. If we were to set up such patterns deliberately, we would begin to get the sort of rhythm patterns that are found in poems and pieces of music.

"May I please have a drink of water?
May I please have a drink of tea?
May I please visit with your daughter?
May I hope she will visit me?"

Music Rhythm Patterns

Let us imagine a very long tone being held by an organist. As long as he holds the key down, the tone will sound. Such a tone, as noted earlier, possesses the four elements of music, pitch, volume, timbre, and duration. But the latter element is only present in its simplest form, one long tone. In order to make it musically interesting, the player must vary the lengths of that tone, break it up into shorter and longer time segments. Let us imagine him idly tapping the organ key while thinking of something else, producing a series of durations which are random, chance rhythms, as shown in graphic form in Example 10-1 (A). Now these same rhythms may be regrouped to form patterns, just as words may be repeated in accent patterns. Such a patterned grouping is shown in 10-1 (B). Now the ear and eye can pick out groups of rhythms which seem to fit together. The eighteen durations fall into three groups of six to make a recognizable pattern. In Example 10-2 we see the same pattern written in conventional rhythmic notation. Notice how much less space is taken up by the latter, as compared with the graphic notation of the former. Imagine how large a piece of popular music would have to be if it were printed in graphic notation instead of the conventional notes we use! It would be as long as a player piano roll instead of the few pages we customarily see.

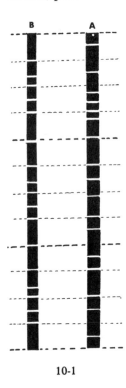

10-1

Musical rhythms are rarely as simple and repetitious as the ones just studied. Many of them are extremely complex, with patterns of repetition that are not immediately apparent to the listener. Let us examine some of the ways in which a composer works with the rhythmic aspect of music. A simple tune which we all know is "My Bonnie Lies

·Over the Ocean." In Example 10-3, we see the first phrase written out in rhythmic notation. The phrase begins with the word "My" and ends with "ocean." The second phrase has exactly the same rhythmic pattern

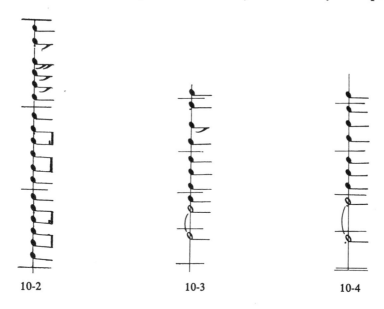

10-2   10-3   10-4

except for the very last word, "sea." Now we have a repetition of the words " My bonnie lies over the ocean," together with the same rhythm pattern for the third phrase, and we end with the words, "O, bring back my bonnie to me," which introduce a new rhythmic pattern, consisting of seven equal durations followed by a long tone, shown in Example 10-4. The chorus which follows repeats both words and rhythmic pattern, again except for the very last word. If we were to write out a "formula" for this type of pattern structure, it would be designated as AAABCC. Within the overall form, there are some interesting repetitions. Note that the new pattern of Example 10-4 is repeated in the last half of the tune, with the words echoing this repetition. Such internal structure makes this short piece what it is. Without it, the music would probably have been long forgotten.

An even more complex rhythmic structure is to be found in another well-known piece, the hymn "Joy to the World." In order to make its rhythmic patterns clear, we will print it as indicated by these patterns:

(A) "Joy to the world, the Lord is come
(B) Let earth
(B) Receive

(B)   Her king.
(C)   Let every heart
(C)   Prepare Him room
(D)   And heaven and nature sing
(D)   And heaven and nature sing
(E)   And heaven, and heaven
(F)   And nature sing." (last part of A)

It is revealing to see how Handel, the great composer, set the poem to his own rhythmic patterns, and to note how vastly different these patterns are from the rather trite ones of the poem in its original form.

"Joy to the world, the Lord is come.
Let earth receive her king.
Let every heart prepare him room,
And heaven and nature sing."

The poet, Isaac Watts, used a far more repetitious rhythm pattern than did Handel. The two are compared in Example 10-5. Handel's musical rhythm patterns force us to give great emphasis to the words, "Lord is come" drawing them out much more than we would if reading them in Watts' poem. Listen to how the song emphasizes the word "every", and how it turns the last, dangling line of the verse into a sort of imitation of heaven and nature singing, echoing the news. Only by means of musical rhythms can such effects be assured. A reader of poetry may, to be sure, get these same effects as he reads, but another reader of the same verse may not. The more precise rhythmic notation of music assures that the desired effects are gained each time.

JOY
TO
THE
WORLD,
THE
LORD
IS
COME.
LET
EARTH
RE-
CEIVE
HER
KING.

10-5

Rhythm and Meter

Much of the interest in music is gained from the interplay of rhythmic and metrical forces. Usually we find the meter going along smoothly and steadily, either in triple or duple accents, while against this steady background, the rhythmic patterns change from time to time. Music in which meter and rhythm are identical is rare. Perhaps the best known example of such a piece is the chant sung in many churches, known as the "Doxology." This tune has a note on every beat. There are no places in it where the tones come faster than the beats, or slower. As a result, the music sounds quite stately and impressive. However, if this were to go on much longer, we would tire of it. The tune is sung once and only consists of 32 notes in its entirety, so we have no chance to become bored with it.

Other well-known tunes are found to have a regular relationship of two notes to the beat, or three, or four. "Yankee Doodle" will be found to carry two notes to the beat, while much of "Oh, Dear! What Can the Matter Be?" is set in three notes to the beat. "Old MacDonald" has long stretches in which a four-note pattern is heard on each beat. Of course, there are many more tunes which mix up the meter-rhythm relationships constantly. "Comin' Through the Rye" contains a good many variations on the basic meter, just in the first phrase.

10-6

One large area of music depends for much of its interest upon subtle and persistent tensions between meter and rhythm, the area of jazz and blues. A few years ago, a popular band recorded a version of the old tune "Little Brown Jug." In the original music, the meter-rhythm relationship is a very close one, as seen in column A of Example 10-6. The popular version, however, made use of many more durations in the pitches of the tune, and was written something like column B. The differing relationships are quite evident.

Students of jazz and popular music styles will recognize that each particular era in the development of American popular music had its own particular rhythmic patterns. A single common pattern of durations has varied significantly from one generation to another resulting in the well-known styles of our American jazz past. Anyone who has listened to the records of such jazz greats as King Oliver, Louis Armstrong, Benny Goodman, Glenn Miller, Stan Kenton, and Gerry Mulligan, will find a different type of rhythmic figuration in each. Undoubtedly future generations of popular music writers and players will develop new kinds of rhythms to set their styles of music apart from those of the past. Style in music, depending heavily on rhythm for its distinctiveness, is no mysterious thing. Elements of different styles are taken up in a later chapter.

PROBLEMS:

Problem One: Find a piece of music which you can use to explain meter, rhythm, and tempo. Use it in a short demonstration before the class.

Problem Two: Play a record at varying speeds, noting what happens to rhythm, meter, and tempo. Report the effect of this music when played at 33, 45, and 78 RPM.

Problem Three: Analyze the rhythmic patterns in a piece of currently popular music. Compare these with patterns found in a "classical" work. Write your report on the differences noted.

Problem Four: Spend an hour or so around the house or outdoors listening for rhythms not in music. Does nature or man produce the more? Do they hold your interest long? Why? What was the most interesting rhythm pattern heard? Try to write it out in notation.

Problem Five: Analyze the rhythm patterns of two of the following hymns:

      a. O Little Town of Bethlehem b. It Came Upon A Midnight Clear c. Silent Night d. Deck the Halls e. God Rest You Merry Gentlemen f. O Come, All Ye Faithful

Problem Six: Compare the word rhythms with the music rhythms in a hymn or old favorite song. If they vary significantly, try to explain why, and tell which you prefer, the word or music rhythms.

Problem Seven: Comment on any visual rhythms found in the Klee painting (Color Pl. 16) or Pickett's picture (Color Pl. 15).

CHAPTER 11

MOTIVE AND MELODY

In Chapter Seven, we learned how to read and write one aspect of music, pitch. We found out about steps and half-steps, and the pattern of the major scale. In Chapter Eight, we learned how pitches could be combined into harmonies, and a little about the formation of these harmonies into chord progressions. We then left pitch for a time, taking up the element of duration. Then in Chapter Nine, we explored meter and tempo, and in Chapter Ten, rhythm. Although it was excellent to treat these aspects of music separately for the purpose of learning about them, they are never found separated in actual music. Pitches and rhythms are always heard together, accompanied by meter and tempo, often underlined by harmonies. When pitches and rhythms are so combined, we call them "motives" or perhaps "melodies."

Motives. A motive is a small musical fragment combining pitches and rhythms, which can be readily identified as a complete musical idea. Motives have been compared to bricks in a building. They are often small, inconspicuous units which are repeated and varied to make up a large structure. Just as individual bricks in a wall may be laid in such a way as to form larger patterns, so individual motives may be used in music to create larger sections, themes, and so on. In Example 11-1, we have a number of motives which are well-known to all of us. The first (A) is the clock chime motive which has been often used in tunes, and the second (B) is the same motive reversed. The motive at (C) is a famous one which is immediately repeated in that hymn. At (D) we see a motive which has a striking rhythmic pattern, and is again repeated with a somewhat different pitch series but the same rhythm. At (E) the motive is also repeated, but with one note left off. Slight variations in motive rhythms or pitches are not considered as creating a different motive. So long as the listener can identify the central idea of the motive, it remains the same one being repeated. Note that it is usually the rhythm that identifies the motive, rather than its pitch. In Example 11-2, we see a familiar motive at (A) followed by a quite different one at (B). In both cases, the pitches are identical! When the rhythmic aspect changes greatly, we no longer

92

recognize the motive as the same. Notice on this example that the meter is written in a different way. The two fours seen at the top of section "A" signify, first that there are to be four beats or counts in each bar, and second, that a quarter-note is the basic unit, receiving one of those beats. The three-four meter signature of part "B" indicates

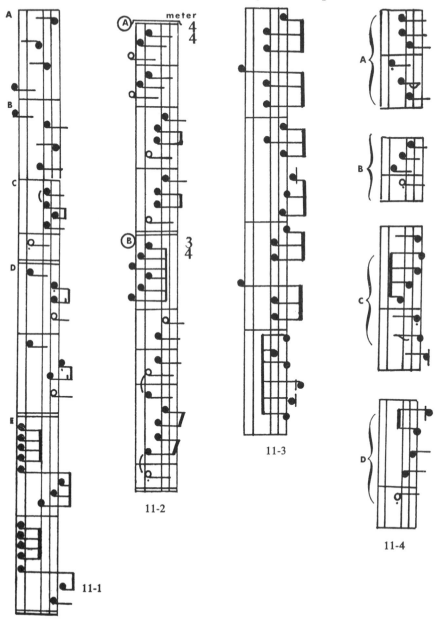

11-1

11-2

11-3

11-4

that there will be three beats in each bar, and that a quarter note is the basic beat. If the signature were six-eight, there would be six counts in a measure, and the eighth-note would be the basic beat unit, and so on.

Music is found to be filled with pieces having identical pitches in their themes, but rhythms so different that we do not recognize the pitch similarity. The first four notes of "Silent Night" are the same as those of the *"Toreador's Song"* from *Carmen,* yet nobody catches the similarity. Popular songs have been made by taking pitches from themes found in serious music. The tune *"I'm Always Chasing Rainbows"* comes from a melody by Chopin, more or less intact. The first six pitches of both melodies are, however, those of the hymn *"More Love to Thee."* A famous court trial arose from the similarity of the popular song *"Avalon"* to an aria from Puccini's opera *Tosca.*

Many pieces are made up of motives being repeated over and over. The famous opening prelude of Bach's *Well-Tempered Clavichord* is such a piece. Another is the old-time dance tune *The Irish Washerwoman,* which begins with a three-note motive and continues with it in the same vein for a long time, repeating the one rhythmic motive endlessly, as shown in Example 11-3. The repeated "triplet" figures constitute the entire piece. (A triplet is a type of rhythmic notation in which three notes are played on one beat.) Another well-known tune built on a rhythmic motive is *"Yankee Doodle."* Many other tunes constructed in the same way will be identified by the listener now that he knows what to look for.

Melodies. Oftentimes several motives are used to make up a melody. The four motives shown in Example 11-4 make up the tune *"America,"* with several repetitions, of course. The completed tune, with repetitions marked, is shown in Example 11-5.

Many melodies are made up of motives repeated over and over. This type of construction has its counterpart in several areas of the visual arts. In architecture the motive has been likened to a brick. Carrying this analogy farther, the melody might be compared to a beam which spans longer distances, unites larger areas of the structure. The motive may be repeated many times, and so may a melody. In Example 11-6 we see a melody repeated in this way, against a few changing chords to relieve the monotony.

The beginner in music writing need not fear being repetitious. Repetition of motives and melodies is the lifeblood of music. The composer must give his listeners a chance to hear these smaller "building blocks" more than once as a memory aid. Note how Example 11-6 keeps repeating the same phrase, only changing it a little at the very end to provide a conclusion.

11-7

11-8

11-5

11-6

Writing Melodies.

Having seen something of how melodies are made up, we can now try to fashion a few of our own. One of the easiest ways to begin writing a melody is to set up a chord progression first, and then simply use the same tones in your melody as you have in the chords. In Example 11-7 this is done. The music written by such a "formula" will probably sound simple and plain, but so are the first sentences we write. As we keep on writing both music and English, we learn to be more complex and original.

A melody which follows the chord tones is apt to sound a bit like a bugle call. If we add other tones to it, it will sound somewhat smoother, more singable, as in Example 11-8. Note that the non-chord tones used here are still tones found in the scale from which the chords are built. For the present it would be well to use no tones in the melody which are not in the scale. In this particular example, the tones which belong to the chord are "hollow" while the non-chord tones are "solid" black. Do not worry about playing these in time, with a steady beat. We are only interested in the pitches at the moment.

Notice that the non-chord tones are usually sandwiched in between the chord tones, which makes them sound smoother. However, smoothness is not as important as interest. If a melody is interesting, we will overlook a rough, dissonant sound here and there. As in any creative work, no matter how elementary, the artist must strive for his own individual statement. At first, the beginning composer has little technic with which to say anything profound, but as he writes more and hears more his musical statements will improve. All of us have improved in our written English; there is no reason why our music writing cannot improve as readily.

One improvement we can strive for almost as soon as we have written a few short melodic phrases, is that of length. The chief obstacle for the composer, at least the beginner, is the problem of what to say once the first short melodic phrase has been written. We will find that the seasoned writer is able to take that short phrase and somehow work with it for a much greater length of time than the beginner. Works of young composers abound with thematic material, while the works of older composers generally use fewer themes, and exploit them more fully. We have noticed this same tendency in people's speech. The four-year-old rambles from one topic to another as he tells us something; the mature speaker can stay on one theme, developing it more fully.

In Example 11-9 we have one means of gaining length in a piece of music. Instead of basing the work on a short motive, or even a four measure theme, we have set up a longer melodic line of eight measures, then repeated this. Many pieces of music begin their repetition only after eight bars have been played, especially popular music. The common pattern here is eight bars (A) repeated, then eight bars of contrasting music (B) followed by the first eight again. The form of such music is commonly designated as AABA.

PROBLEMS:

Problem One: Write a one-measure motive, then repeat it using different pitches with the same rhythm. Make at least an eight-bar piece out of it.

Problem Two: Set up a chord progression of four or more harmonies, then fit a motive to the various chords and construct an eight-bar piece by repeating the progression.

Problem Three: Find a recording of popular music in which a motive is used repeatedly. Analyze the work, and report to the class.

Problem Four: Using the same chord progression as in Problem Two, write a melody which spans the first two bars, then repeat this for two more.

Problem Five: Experiment with a melody which uses some notes that are not in the scale on which the accompanying harmonies are based. That is, if you are basing your chords on the "C Scale", use a few black key tones in the melodic line.

Problem Six: Search through popular music, hymns, marches, and so on for two pieces of music having the same opening pitches in their melodies.

Problem Seven: Listen to serious musical works for their use of repeated motives and themes. Choose one composition and write a thematic analysis of what you hear.

Problem Eight: Write as long a melody as you can, using a simple repetition structure such as AABA, ABBA, etc. If you can add harmony here and there, so much the better. Use rhythmic variation and repetition to hold it together.

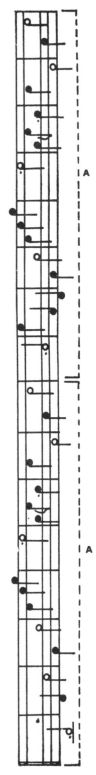

CHAPTER 12

VOLUME AND TIMBRE

Having dealt with the various aspects of two musical elements in Chapters Seven through Eleven, we turn our attention to the remaining two elements, Volume and Timbre.

VOLUME. In addition to pitch and duration, music also has "loudness" as an element. We have seen how pitch and duration may be written in musical sign-language. Volume, too, is notated, but rather imprecisely. Traditionally, music is printed with volume directions as follows:

ppp . . . . *(very soft)*
pp . . . . *(quite soft)*
p . . . . *(soft)*
mp . . . . *(moderately soft)*
mf . . . . *(moderately loud)*
f . . . . *(loud)*
ff . . . . *(quite loud)*
fff . . . . *(very loud)*

The letters are really abbreviations for Italian terms, which are often used by musicians when talking about degrees of loudness in music. The letter "p" stands for "piano", "pp" for "pianissimo", and "ppp" for "pianississimo." We have heard this same kind of word ending in the army terms, "general" and "generalissimo." The letter "m" stands for "mezzo" (pronounced "met-so") and means "middle" or "medium." We come across the same term in hotels, where the "mezzanine" is midway between the lobby and the first floor. The remaining letter, "f", stands for the Italian term "forte," (pronounced "for-tay"). One recalls that the original name for our common piano was "pianoforte" which indicated that it was able to produce both soft and loud tones. The other degrees of loudness on the list stand for "fortissimo" and "fortississimo" of course.

Sometimes composers will use other languages to give volume directions to the performer. One occasionally finds pieces with the directions "Loud" or "Very Soft" printed at the beginning. By far the greatest percentage of composers, however, use the Italian terms.

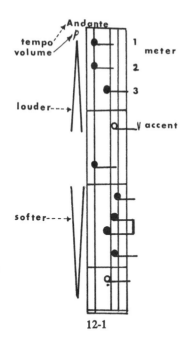

12-1

In addition to these, one finds several other volume indications in music. In Example 12-1, we see three such signs. The inverted "V" which is labeled "louder" indicates a gradual swelling of the dynamic level. This is also sometimes written into the music as a word, "crescendo." Its opposite, the "decrescendo" is shown just below it. The third sign for a loudness change is the small "v" labeled "accent." This indicates to the player that he must make that one tone slightly louder than its fellows. For a louder accent, the composer might use the letters "sfz" meaning "sforzando," adjacent to the note he wishes emphasized.

Uses of Volume. Students of music sometimes overlook the usefulness of volume changes when writing compositions. The problems of pitch and rhythm writing are so great that one forgets that the volume element may be used to great advantage. As an illustration, review the Example 11-5, *"America."* If this were played or sung at a single level of loudness, it would be dull, indeed. Every time we hear it performed, however, we hear volume changes in it. The first phrases are usually produced at a rather low volume level; then the next two are given a crescendo. The volume climax comes at the end of the phrase "From every mountainside" and the last phrase sinks back to the first dynamic level. Contributing to the effort of the volume increase at the climax is the fact that the pitch level reaches its highest point at the same time. The two together create an effective climax. Something similar occurs in our national anthem, where the pitch and the volume rise together near the end, on the words "O'er the land of the free."

Many composers combine volume levels with sections and repetitions in their music. Thus, if a piece has a repeated first section, this section may be repeated at a softer or louder level the second time. Marches usually consist of sections repeated at contrasting levels of loudness. The great bulk of dance music written in the 1600s and early 1700s was based on the AABB form, each section being quite long (as compared with modern dance music), and each section being repeated at a contrasting dynamic level.

Sometimes composers will build a lengthy section of music by repeating the same theme or motive louder and louder. Ravel's *"Bolero"* is such a piece, starting very softly, and gradually building the same repeated phrase into a tremendous climax of thundering sound. Aside from changes in instrumentation and loudness, this piece is one long repetition of a short melody.

Accents are also used to effect changes in music. If a melodic motive or theme is accented one way, and then repeated with other, different accents, the effect will be different. One might well compare such treatment with accents in speech. If we read aloud the words, "I like modern art" with several different accent patterns, we will discover that the sentence can mean several quite different things:

I like modern *art* (but not modern music).
I like *modern* art (but not earlier art).
I *like* modern art (I don't hate it).
I like modern art (I don't care what you think).

Try this shift of accent on Example 11-9, first accenting the initial note in each bar, then shifting the accent to the second note, or the third, where possible. The effect will be something like creating a new meaning for the music, just as in the English sentence.

Sometimes this device of stressing certain tones in a melodic line is used to point out the presence of a hidden melody within the larger melodic line. One often finds this in "variations" where the original tune can be picked out of its context by emphasizing it with accents. In Example 12-2, we see that the accented notes are those of the tune *"Drink To Me Only With Thine Eyes."* Such a variation style was common in the early 1800s but is not seen as much today. Examples 20-8 and 20-9 are also concerned with this use of accent.

TIMBRE. The last element of music to be considered is that having to do with the kind of sound heard. Broadly speaking, music uses two types of sounds, vocal and instrumental.

The human voice has been divided into four broad classifications; soprano, alto, tenor, and bass. Each has its characteristic tonal quality created by the interior physical properties of the mouth and throat, vocal cords,

12-2

lungs, sinuses, and so on. Within the four categories, there are numerous subdivisions such as coloratura, lyric, and dramatic soprano; contralto; lyric and heroic tenor; baritone, bass-baritone, and basso profundo. These classifications not only refer to the pitches which are within the range of the singer, but to the type of vocal quality possessed. Thus a bass may actually be able to sing as high as a baritone, but his voice has that dark, heavy quality which distinguishes it from the somewhat lighter, mellower baritone sound. The student will be able to catch these differences by listening to trained voices, either on record or in person.

Instrumental timbres are, of course, created by mechanical means. One might think of the various musical instruments as machines built to produce desired pitches and timbres. Such machines may be divided into broad classifications, depending upon the method used to produce the pitch, in most cases.

String Instruments are those which use stretched strings to produce tones. The tone is sometimes produced by bowing on the string, sometimes by plucking it, and sometimes by hitting it with a mallet or hammer of some sort. Among the first classification are the violin, viola, cello, and bass viol. The harp, guitar, banjo and ukulele fall into the plucked-string group, and in the last category are the piano, zither, balalaika, and others.

String instruments range in size from small ones (violin) to large ones (bass viol). The smaller an instrument is, the higher it is capable of sounding, and the larger, the lower. Actually, the violin, viola and cello are all versions of the same instrument, built in varying sizes. Some string instruments, like the harp and piano, are built to get both high and low pitches. This is possible because these instruments use many strings, one for each pitch, where the others use only four strings and shorten them with the fingers to produce many pitches.

String instruments blend well with one another, produce beautiful tones, can play more than one tone at a time (especially the piano and harp) and are accounted among the finest instruments man has invented.

Woodwind Instruments are essentially tubes of wood or metal with holes in them. These holes are covered by the fingers to lengthen or shorten the tube, giving different pitches as desired. The tone itself is produced by a vibrating object at one end of the tube. In the flute, this "object" is simply the fluttering air caused by the flutist blowing across the opening through a carefully controlled hole between the lips. In a clarinet and saxophone, the vibrator is a bamboo "reed" which is set in motion by the air from the player's lungs. In the oboe and bassoon, there is a "double reed" to produce the initial vibrations which are greatly magnified by the enclosed air in the tube. One can illustrate each type of reed simply. Producing a tone by blowing across your thumb knuckles into your cupped hands is something like the flute method of creating a tone. Adding a sharp blade of grass between the thumbs is like the action of a single reed on a clarinet or saxophone. Blowing air between the edges of two thin sheets of paper is like the action of the double reed.

Like the string family, the woodwinds come in different sizes. Starting with the piccolo and flute, we find also about a half-dozen different sizes of clarinets (sopranino in E flat, soprano in B flat, E flat alto, B flat bass, E flat contrabass) in the band, and a clarinet in A in the orchestra. In the saxophone family there are four common ones, soprano, alto, tenor, and baritone, and several others not so commonly seen. The double reeds come in two sizes each, the oboe and English horn; and the bassoon and contrabassoon.

Brass Instruments are always made of metal, though not usually true brass, and are like the woodwinds in that their tone is produced at one end of a long tube which amplifies it and gives it a characteristic timbre. In each case, the tone is generated by the player's lips which are "buzzed" against the mouthpiece. Unlike the woodwinds, the brass instruments do not get their pitch changes by opening and closing holes with the fingers. Instead, they add or subtract lengths of tubing, thus producing higher or lower tones as desired. In addition, there is another means of getting pitch changes on a brass instrument, that of blowing "harmonics."

A "harmonic" is possible on a stretched string, on the enclosed air column in a woodwind instrument, and on the air column of a brass instrument. Harmonics are used much more in brass playing than in the other two families. In order to understand this musical phenomenon, let us imagine a long rope with one end tied to a tree, and the other held in the hand. We now begin to swing the rope as if we were about to have someone start skipping rope with it, as seen in Example 12-3A. The rope is now swinging on its "first harmonic," sometimes called the "funda-mental." Now let us twirl our end faster, and we see that the rope will begin to swing in two equal loops, its second harmonic, as seen in 12-3B. If we had a sufficiently long rope and strong hand we might even get it to subdivide into three, and four loops. If so, the segments in the four loops would each be rotating two times as fast as those in the two loops, and four times as fast as the one loop.

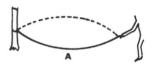

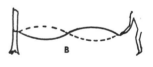

12-3

While a rope is difficult to swing in anything more than three loops, a stretched string on a violin or guitar can easily be induced to subdivide into quite a few more. Have a musician friend bow a string bass, and while he is doing so, run one finger slowly down the string. At certain places your finger will suddenly divide the string at exactly the right place to allow it to produce a harmonic tone, and you will be surprised to hear a clear, light note pop out. As you continue on down the string, other harmonic tones will appear and disappear. When you have gone past the mid-point of the string, you will be repeating the harmonic tones in reverse order. The same thing is possible with a guitar if you will bridge the strings lightly with a finger while strumming with the other hand. As you come to the dividing points on the string, the harmonics will be heard as light, ethereal chords.

Harmonics on woodwind instruments are used mostly to shift from one "register" to the other. You will note that a woodwind instrument can play only so many notes by lifting the fingers and opening holes. After all the holes are opened, the player must shift to a higher harmonic and cover all the holes again, starting over on a higher pitch level. It is possible to produce a harmonic by blowing gently into a bottle, then blowing very hard. The second tone will (if done properly) be higher than the first. Normally only the second harmonic may be produced in this way. The human lungs cannot produce enough air pressure to make the air in a bottle subdivide into three or four parts, though it is possible on musical instruments. The author once had a musical demonstration performed by an auto mechanic armed with a soft drink bottle and an air hose at a service station. Third and fourth harmonic shrieks were audible all over town!

Brass instruments rely constantly upon harmonics. A bugle is nothing more than a single metal tube upon which the bugler can, by changing his lip vibration speeds, produce a number of harmonic tones. The familiar *"Taps"* is a tune made up of the 3d, 4th, 5th, and 6th harmonics, as are virtually all bugle calls. Any brass player can demonstrate harmonics merely by holding the instrument to his lips and playing various tones without touching valves or slide. When additional notes are wanted, the player can get them by lengthening or shortening the tube as he either presses down valves (which add more tubing) or moves the slide (which on the trombone also adds length).

Percussion Instruments get their tones by being hit in some fashion. Commonest of the percussion are the various drums. The bass and snare drums seen in marching bands can only play rhythmic parts, but the kettledrums, or tympani, are able to produce pitches also, by varying the tension of their drumheads. Other common percussion instruments include the cymbals, the triangle, castanets, gongs, rattles, and so on. The xylophone and marimba are classed in the percussion family, being made of varying-sized bars of wood or metal which give out a series of pitches when struck. Occasionally, one finds the piano classed among the percussion family because of its method of producing the pitch from hammers striking the keys.

Miscellaneous Instruments not previously assigned to any family include such common ones as the accordion, which gets its tone from metal reeds within the instrument, and the harmonica, similar but smaller. There is also the pipe organ, which is technically a wind instrument but of such vast dimensions as to almost rate a category of its own. Sometimes the pipe organ, the accordion, the piano, and the celeste (a small instrument which produces its sound from metal bars struck by keyboard hammers) are grouped into a category called simply, "keyboard instruments." Various older instruments such as the spinet, the clavichord, and the harpsichord would also be found in this group.

Electronic Instruments constitute the final group, and create their tones from electronically generated sources. Occasionally one hears a radio develop a high pitched squeal, a result of a malfunctioning tube. The electronic organs which are so common get their tones from a controlled squeal of this type, carefully treated and modulated to produce a pleasant sound. In recent years, a new source of musical tones has been discovered and exploited, magnetic tape patterns. Composers in this area need large amounts of equipment with which to generate tones and record them, add other tones, re-record, blend, and otherwise manipulate the results so that a musical effect may be obtained. Examples of this type of music may be heard on records. In some works one hears pitches far higher than anything possible on ordinary musical instruments, and rapid-fire rhythms which no human technique could possibly execute. Through the electronic medium, the composer can take a few recorded sounds, transpose them to any pitch, make them faster, slower, combine them with other sounds for harmony or counterpoint, and eventually work them into a composition. As was pointed out earlier, the new electronic instruments make it possible for the composer to bypass the performer, if he wishes to do so.

PROBLEMS:

Problem One: Find a piece of printed music, and in it identify all of the dynamic indications, explaining what each means.

Problem Two: Find an example of recorded music in which dynamic changes play an important part. Explain what they do to enhance the work.

Problem Three: Find an example of the old-style variations, and look for places where accents outline the melodic content of a variation. Play this for the class.

Problem Four: Find examples of various vocal timbres in the field of opera, and see if there is a certain kind of character assigned to a certain type of voice. For instance, are heroes likely to be basses or tenors?

Problem Five: What other ways are there for producing tones on a violin in addition to simple bowing and plucking? Find examples.

Problem Six: Explain harmonics as you would to a 10-year-old child. Illustrate with simple examples.

Problem Seven: Why is the instrument called a "bass viol" and not a "bass violin"?

Problem Eight: What was the earliest instrument invented which we still use commonly (aside from the drums)?

Problem Nine: How would one classify the "musical saw," the "steam calliope," the "ocarina" and the "Jew's-harp"?

Problem Ten: Make a musical instrument of the percussion type by one of the following methods:

a. Fill bottles to various levels with water, suspend them by strings from a rod, and strike gently.

b. Cut lengths of hardwood so that they produce a scale when suspended from strings and struck.

c. Drive spikes into a board for varying distances, striking them to produce a scale.

Problem Eleven: Try producing tones on the instruments in Problem Ten by blowing on the bottles rather than striking them. Is the result different? Try bowing the nails with a well-rosined violin bow. Can a tone be produced? Why is it different from the first tone obtained?

Problem Twelve: Try making a "brass" instrument out of a length of rubber hose, a pipe, or a mailing tube. Fashion a mouthpiece out of a wooden spool by reaming out one end to form a shallow cup.

Try buzzing your lips in the cup with the mouthpiece fitted into the tube. Can you produce harmonics? Why is the tone so "crude"?

Problem Thirteen: Demonstrate harmonics on a real brass instrument, first with only the mouthpiece, then with the instrument attached. Why is the latter so much easier?

Problem Fourteen: Check on a local pipe organ, if your town has one, to find out about the number of pipes, their type and material, possible combinations, and type of wind supply. Talk with the organist about the manner in which this instrument operates, and explore its mechanisms, tone qualities, and other possibilities. Report to the class.

Problem Fifteen: If you have the necessary time, obtain two tape-recorders and experiment with making an electronic composition. Try playing a tape you have just made on one recorder, and add something to it, recording the combination on the other. You can play tapes backwards, at varying speeds, make "tape loops" which will repeat something over and over on one recorder while you add something else "live" and record the result on the other. Play the resulting music to the class, describing how it was created. Be sure to allow plenty of time for this assignment.

Part Four

LEARNING TO HEAR; SPEECH AND LITERATURE

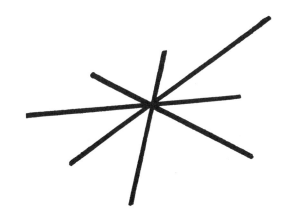

CHAPTER 13

SOUNDS OF SPEECH

We have just completed Part Three, in which we learned to hear music. Now we take up the problem of hearing in the art of Literature. The reason for dividing the two areas is that although our language contains the same basic elements as are found in music, it has in addition others not found there. Music is concerned with sound only, while literature deals in *sounds that have added meaning*. When we hear a tone sung by a human voice, it is just a musical sound, but when we hear a spoken word there is a sound and also a meaning or idea that goes with it. Thus, literature may be studied on two levels, and good literature usually combines both sounds and meanings to reinforce the total effect. For an example, consider the following words written by Alexander Pope (1688-1744), as an illustration of the very thing we are talking of:

"When Ajax strives some rock's vast weight to throw,
The line, too, labors and the words move slow."

We could get the same meaning by saying, "When Ajax tries to throw a big rock" but the very difficulty of pronouncing Pope's words adds to the sense of what he is describing. His writing makes better use of words because he uses both their sounds and their sense.

Speech Sounds

Most people pay little attention to the way in which their own speech is produced. Aside from the fact that it consists of vowels and consonants, little else is known by the average person about the fascinating world of speech sounds. Let's start with the vowels.

Vowels

These are the "singing" parts of our speech, usually spelled by the letters a-e-i-o-u, but there are more than twice that many vowel sounds which we use every day. In order to classify them, a diagram has been drawn to represent the inside of the mouth, in Example

110

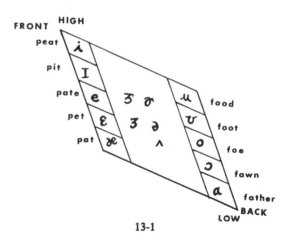

13-1

13-1. The section labeled "High-Front" will be just behind the upper teeth, while the "Low-Back" area is deep in the throat. You will notice that there is a letter of the "phonetic alphabet" included for each of these vowel sounds. If we used these phonetic kinds of letters, a given sound would always be written the same way in every word. As it is, the letters "ea" have one sound in "peat" but a different one in "sweat" and still another in "great"! One of these phonetic signs is called the "Schwa" and can be spelled with a-e-i-o-u in five different words! Its basic sound is "uh," and here are the five words; *a*lone, spok*e*n, penc*i*l, comm*o*n, citr*u*s! When five different letters represent the same sound, it's no wonder Americans can't spell! As a matter of fact, in many other languages, spelling is never studied beyond primary grades because words are spelled as they sound. Educators are now beginning to see that many students' difficulties start with the illogical pronunciation and spelling of our language. Several plans for phonetic alphabets are now making their way into our elementary schools.

In order to feel the basic changes taking place in the mouth as different vowel sounds are called for, repeat the words "peat, pit, pate, pet, pat" rapidly, then just the vowels from those words. You will find yourself saying "yeah." Try the same exercise with the "back vowels." The middle vowels, being less definite as to position, are harder to place accurately. The "Schwa" is one of these.

When the vowel sounds are called the singing parts of our speech, that is exactly what is meant. If any part of a word is to be sung (or hung onto) it will usually be the vowel sounds. Thus it is easy to sing "Keeeeeeeeep" but impossible to stretch out either of the two consonant sounds, "K" or "p."

Consonants

If we could see an X-ray moving picture of our mouth and throat in action as we talked, we would be amazed at the intricate things that go on inside just to produce a few simple sounding words. A rather more complicated chart (Example 13-2) for the consonants shows them to be divided into two classes, the "non-continuents" (those which start and stop abruptly) and the "continuents" (those that can be drawn out somewhat like vowels).

SPEECH MECHANISM USED

CONSONANT CHART	Bi-labial	Velar	Alvelar	Inter-dental	Labio-dental	Vocal Cords
A. Non-continuents	b	g	d			voiced
1. Plosives	p	k	t			unvoiced
2. Aspirate		h (glottal)				u
B. Continuents		3 (zh)	z	ð (this)	v	v
1. Fricatives		ʃ (sh)	s	Θ (thick)	f	u
2. Nasals	m	ŋ (ng)	n			v
3. Affricatives		dʒ (j)				v
		tʃ (ch)				u
4. Glides (w, j [yuh] hw)			l			v
5. Retroflex (r)						

Some Useful Definitions:

"bi-labial"	two lips
"velum"	soft palate
"alvelum"	ridge behind upper teeth at roof of mouth
"inter-dental"	between the teeth (tongue)
"labio-dental"	lips and teeth
"glottis"	opening between vocal cords
"aspirate"	breath sound
"fricative"	sound made by air forced through small opening
"nasal"	sound forced through nose passages
"glide"	a consonant made by gliding from one vowel to another (y equals eeuh; w equals oouh)

palate

velum

tongue

glottis

Simplified Diagram of Speech Apparatus

13-2

Within these two broad classes, there are the "voiced" and the "unvoiced" sounds, which can be easily distinguished. Put your fingers on your Adam's apple and slowly say "downtown." Notice that the movements of the tongue for "d" and "t" are exactly the same, but on the first of the two there is a vibration of the vocal cords, while on the second there is none. Sixteen of the consonant sounds are matched up in this way, a voiced and voiceless pair using the same formation of the speaking mechanism. In most cases the two sounds in the pair have different spellings but some do not. "Saw" and "was" use exactly the same letters, but in one, the "s" is voiceless and in the other it is voiced. The letters "th" are sometimes voiced (as in "*th*is,") and at other times unvoiced (as in "*th*ick").

The columns across the top of Chart 13-2 indicate the type of speech mechanism used, while the categories on the left-hand side indicate the kind of sound made. The more one studies the sounds of speech, the closer he will be to understanding many ordinary features of our speaking habits. For instance, many of us jumble our speech into what must sound like a totally different language to a foreigner who has learned "correct" English. We say "Chagonnadoo" for "What are you going to do?," and "Jopenem" for "Did you open them?" This drives home the point that spoken and written English are quite different from one another. On occasion, someone will speak the written language, and when he does, we accuse him of either trying to show off, or of being very formal. The reverse usually doesn't work well, either. A student's theme should be in good *written* English, not the way he would speak.

A few final remarks concerning the charts; they do not pretend to cover the total range of spoken sounds. Students of foreign languages know that the German "r" and the French "r" are not represented here, nor is the "umlaut" or many other speech sounds which are possible. All in all, linguistics experts catalog some 126 different sounds of speech, of which English uses only 65, and with only 26 letters in our alphabet to spell *these!*

The charts cover only the sounds of our language and how these sounds are transcribed into visual signs, which we call letters and phonetic markings. This does not include the "pitch" of the words, a factor which sometimes makes a great difference in meaning. If the words "I do" are spoken with the pitch dropping at the end, the meaning is one of certainty, but if they are spoken with a rising pitch, then the feeling is one of doubt. In similar fashion, the question "Where?" can be asked with either a rising or falling pitch, and mean two different things. If someone says, "I am going to Europe," and his friend says, "Where?" with a strong pitch rise, the answer will be

"To Europe." But if the "Where?" is asked with a falling pitch, the answer will be "Oh, to Germany and France." In one case the pitch indicated the need to have the statement repeated, and in the other case additional information is wanted. Pitch variation means a lot more in some languages than in others. In Chinese, for instance, one single syllable may mean many widely different things depending upon its pitch pronunciation!

PROBLEMS:

Problem One: Analyze the vowel and consonant sounds of your first, middle and last names.

Problem Two: Write a sentence describing something high using only high vowels, and another using low vowels to describe something deep or low.

Problem Three: Work out a chart of consonants which can be spoken without moving the lips. Then use these to compose a short speech which a ventriloquist could use.

Problem Four: Write a sentence or two describing some noisy action or event, making use of many plosive consonants.

Problem Five: Write a paragraph of ad copy suitable (from the standpoint of word sounds) for one of the following products: nylon hosiery, earth-movers, perfume, chain saws, electric fans, cough syrup, sleeping pills.

Problem Six: Look up the recent work being done with a phonetic alphabet for the early grades. Explain its significance.

Problem Seven: Listen to your friends' speech habits, and write down interesting slurred speech patterns such as "Izzy gunna go?" (for "Is he going to go?")

Problem Eight: Read the front section of a large dictionary, on sounds of the English language. Report on the interesting information you find there.

Problem Nine: Explain why, when we imitate a Frenchman, we write "zis and zat," for "this and that," and when we imitate a German, we write "vass" for "was" and "dere" for "there."

CHAPTER 14

USES OF WORD SOUNDS

We have seen that words have both sound and meaning, and we have looked into the formation of these sounds, to some extent. This is only the prelude to the more important study of how the author or poet uses these sounds in words. Such usage may be grouped under several main headings:

1. *Sounds which imitate.* These include such words as "bang," "whisper," "crash" and "jingle." This word usage is well known by the name "onomatopoeia," and is just one of the ways sounds enter into word meanings.

2. *Sounds which suggest.* If the author is describing a windy day, he may use words which make use of the affricatives and fricatives. These would include the consonants s-z-sh-zh-f-v, th, j and ch. Useful words might include: church, size, sighs, thistle, thrust, thrush, feather, vivid, fervent, feverish, and so on. For a "windy" sounding sentence, he might choose the following:

> *"After father fastened the casement shutters, the strong thrust of the sighing breezes started lashing branches along the sides of the house, scraping and feeling with leafy fingers for some slight fissure to grasp and clutch--a sinister, scratchy sound."*

There is scarcely a word in that sentence which does not have one of the pre-selected sounds in it. This adds to the effect, especially when compared with this paraphrase:

> *"After father closed the windows, the wind began to blow tree-branches against the house, and the noise they made was rather weird."*

Such a use of the consonant sounds for suggesting noises is called "consonance."

3. *Sounds which rhyme.*

a. End rhymes are the familiar kind we associate with rhyming verse, the "moon-June" type. In order to rhyme, two words must match sounds from the last accented syllables to the ends of the words. Thus "brick" and "trick" rhyme, having but one syllable each, and the two sounding alike. Two-syllable rhyming words would be "river" and "shiver," the syllables following the accented one being alike. An example of rhyming words of three syllables would be "article" and "particle," with only the initial syllable changed. "Germination" and "termination" will rhyme for the same reasons. Words of unequal length will rhyme, too, provided they are alike from the last accented syllable on.

"He proved an inspiration
As leader of his nation."

b.   Slant rhymes are used to give poetry a kind of rhyme scheme which is not as exact as that quoted above.

"In the world of fashion
His slighest notion
Was an inspiration."

In this example, the lines do not end on exactly the same sounds, but the pattern is unmistakably there. Such repetition of sounds lends power to the words, giving them a feeling of resonance.

c.   Internal rhyme places rhyming words anywhere in a line rather than only at the ends. This type of sound repetition could be added to the sentence about the storm.

"As father fastened the casement shutter
The flutter of wind from attic to basement
From gable to gutter and over the table
Persuaded the candles to shiver and stutter."

We see here the words "shutter" and "stutter" at ends of lines but "flutter" toward the beginning of one line and "gutter" in the middle. "Casement" and "basement" rhyme, but are not in the same relative position. "Gable" and "table" are found in the same line. This internal rhyme can add a musical kind of sense to the lines in addition to their word meanings.

4.   *Sounds requiring certain speech mechanisms.* Our sound-producing apparatus finds some sounds or sound combinations more difficult to produce than others. We frequently find collections of such sounds in "tongue-twisters," such as the one which begins "Theophilus Thistle, the thistle-sifter . . ." Perhaps even harder is this one: "He snatched the satchel and snitched the schnitzel!"

While authors and poets rarely spend time making up tongue-twisters, they often do search out words which will cause some trouble in pronunciation, so that the smooth flow of words will be halted and the descriptive passage made to sound labored or heavy, for a purpose. Suppose the words were being used to describe a car starting on a cold morning. Not only would appropriate consonants be called for, but they might be employed so as to seem labored and slow.

"It first starts with sluggish shakes, chugs and growls, coughs; frost streams from its pipes, it protests strongly, and finally gives in and runs as smoothly as summer."

The words used are combined in such a way as to cause the reader to pause between them, until the car warms up a bit, and then the words smooth out and flow evenly. Such word usage is found in poetry, especially in modern, short poems. It may also be found in commercial messages designed to sell products.

5. *Sounds repeated for a pattern effect.* We have all known this kind of sound usage. As children we delighted in stories which repeated a phrase over and over. Among such classic phrases are:

"Oh Grandmother, what big eyes you have!"
"The better to see you with, my dear."
"Oh Grandmother, what big ears you have!"
"The better to hear you with, my dear."

The perennial favorite among children, however, is one with even more repetition:

Then Chicken Little met Ducky Lucky and cried, "The sky is falling, the sky is falling!" Then Chicken Little and Ducky Lucky met Turkey Lurkey and cried, "The sky is falling, the sky is falling." Then Chicken Little and Ducky Lucky and Turkey Lurkey met----" and so on.

We can find phrase repetitions such as these in many a fairy tale but they are also to be found in serious literature, as well.

Several excerpts from the Bible illustrate the point:

Behold, my servants shall eat, but you shall be hungry;
Behold, my servants shall drink, but you shall be thirsty;
Behold, my servants shall rejoice, but you shall be ashamed:
Isaiah 65: 13

A time to be born, and a time to die;
A time to plant, and a time to pluck up what is planted;
A time to kill, and a time to heal;
A time to break down, and a time to build up;
A time to weep, and a time to laugh;
A time to mourn, and a time to dance;

A time to cast stones, and a time to gather stones together;
A time to embrace, and a time to refrain from embracing;
A time to seek, and a time to lose;
A time to keep, and a time to cast away;
A time to rend, and a time to sew;
A time to keep silent, and a time to speak;
A time to love, and a time to hate;
A time for war and a time for peace.

Ecclesiastes 3: 1-8

The effect of this kind of repetition is to make the passage more stately, more impressive. Good speakers use the same device when they state:

I say to you this evening that taxes must be reduced.
I say to you this evening that wages must be increased.
I say to you this evening that crime must be controlled.
And I say to you this evening that if I am elected---

Such repetition acts like a hypnotic chant, allows the speaker to take plenty of time to drive home a few simple points, and gives him a great opportunity to build up to a big climax. Without it, he would not be nearly as effective!

6. *Sounds which set a "key" or "pitch level."* Here we are talking largely of vowel sounds, repeated for a sustained effect. This practice, known as "assonance," makes use of the vowel positions seen on the chart (Example 13-1). For instance, if we wish to make our vowels sound light and airy, we will concentrate on the "ee" and "oo" sounds as much as we can:

I've seen fleecy blue skies with a new moon peering through,
keeping an eye on me, too shy to do more than peek-a-boo.

Just the opposite in vowel tone would be this sentence:

Fat clouds awkwardly follow one another as the fall mountains soar aloft, and under foot the path drops into mud and swamp.

In the latter example, the low vowels are repeated with the result that the sentence carries a darker, heavier sound.

In summary, the sounds of speech may be used in a number of ways to add to the effectiveness of the ideas carried by the words. Although this kind of writing may be found anywhere, it is especially apt to be found in modern poetry, which has become a kind of compressed, super-language capable of expressing much with a few carefully chosen words.

PROBLEMS:

Problem One: Make a list of onomatopoetic words which you hear yourself and your friends using in the space of one or two days.

Problem Two: Write a paragraph about a subject which the "nasal" and "liquid" sounds suggest to you, taking care to use many of these in the words.

Problem Three: Write a poem based on rhymes for your three names. Use yourself as the subject for this poem. You may have to use some nicknames for rhyming purposes.

Problem Four: Write several short lines whose ends form slant rhymes. Make the thought coherent in each set of lines.

Problem Five: Write a line or two using words which require the speaker to stop and start between almost every word.

Problem Six: Write several lines which use word endings and beginnings that allow the speaker to deliver the words in a smooth, continuing flow of sound.

Problem Seven: Write a speech of three minutes' duration in which you use repetition of phrases for dramatic effect. Practice delivering the speech.

Problem Eight: Listen to a public speaker (politician, minister, etc.) and write down the use of phrase repetition you hear.

Problem Nine: Find an example of "pitch" level through assonance in modern poetry.

Problem Ten: Write a bit of verse or prose in which vowel sounds are repeated for their tonal effect.

Problem Eleven: Look through the sixteen color plates and select those having much repetition. Find relationships of this repetition to that used in literature.

CHAPTER 15

DURATION ELEMENTS IN LITERATURE

In music, the duration element was subdivided into meter (the beat), rhythm (patterns of durations), and tempo (the speed). Almost the exact features are found in literature!

Meter. Sometimes we find ourselves reading or speaking in a regularly accented pattern of syllables and words. Sentences such as the following make use of regular meter patterns:

The air today is fresh and fine.
Mama, mama, come and see.
Look at the quarterback run with the ball!

As we analyze the meter patterns, we find that they illustrate three common types of meter. The first sentence makes use of the "unstressed-stressed" duple meter known as "iambic."

$$\cup \; - \quad \cup \; - \quad \cup \; - \quad \quad \cup \; -$$
The air | to-day | is fresh | and fine.

In the second sentence, the accent is reversed, for a "trochaic" meter.

$$- \; \cup \quad - \; \cup \quad - \quad \cup \quad -$$
Ma-ma | ma-ma | come and | see.

The third sentence uses a triple meter known as "dactylic."

$$- \; \cup \; \cup \quad - \; \cup \; \cup \quad - \; \cup \; \cup \quad -$$
Look at the | quar-ter-back | run with the | ball!

Another kind of triple meter, accented in the middle of each triplet, is called "amphibrach" meter.

$$\cup \; - \; \cup \quad \cup \; - \; \cup \quad \cup \; - \; \cup \quad \cup \; -$$
To mar-ket | to mar-ket | to buy a | fat pig.

We might even have the last of each three syllables accented, and write a sentence in "anapestic" meter.

$$\cup \; \cup \; - \quad \cup \; \cup \; - \quad \cup \cup \; - \quad \cup \; \cup \; -$$
In the back | of the car | is a gro | cer-y sack.

Generally speaking, meters are coupled with line-lengths to form a compound name by which types of metrical verse are known. Thus, our first sentence would be found to have four accents, or four "feet," and would be known as "tetrameter." Since it has iambic meter, we would call it a line of "iambic tetrameter." A handy table for naming accents and line lengths follows:

(line lengths)		(meter accents)	
Feet Name		∪ —	iambic
1 — monometer		— ∪	trochaic
2 — dimeter		∪∪ —	anapestic
3 — trimeter		∪ — ∪	amphibrach
4 — tetrameter		— ∪∪	dactylic
5 — pentameter		— —	spondaic (spondee)
6 — hexameter			
7 — heptameter			
8 — octameter			

Memorizing all the special names for meters and line lengths is not the most important thing about meter. What *is* important, and moreover useful, is to gain insight into the poet's use of meters for literary effects. The chief interest in poetic meter, like musical meter, lies not in seeing how precisely a metrical beat can be followed, but in seeing how words can stray away from it and return again. Nothing is so deadly as hearing a child read a poem in the exact meter, with every accent given equal weight, and each line read with exactly the same speed as all the others. This is the equivalent to hearing an inexperienced jazz musician play exactly what is written! He, like the reader of poetry, must learn to vary his rhythms so as to avoid that monotony which comes from being always predictable. When the listener senses that basic beat, and hears how the performer strays away from it, a kind of tension is set up which adds greatly to the interest. In poetry, this tension is augmented by the poet himself, as he writes words which break the steady meter of the basic accent patterns. One such device for breaking the metrical swing is the "spondee," a doubly accented foot in the line. We could insert one into our original examples as follows:

∪ — ∪ — — — ∪ —
The air | to-day | smells fresh | and fine.

Note how one has to accent both "smells" and "fresh", which breaks some of the metrical monotony.

— ∪ — ∪ — — —
Ma-ma | ma-ma | quick, come | see!

Here the last three words get equal accents, adding to the emphasis of the sentence.

$$\text{—} \quad \cup \cup \quad \text{—} \quad \text{—} \quad \text{—} \quad \cup \cup \quad \text{—}$$
Look at the | half-back | run with the | ball!

The word "halfback" effectively breaks up the triple meter of the original line, putting more punch into the words at that point.

Note how effectively Shakespeare uses the spondee to break up the iambic pentameter swing of his lines as King Henry urges his men into battle against the French. If the King spoke his words strictly according to the accents of iambic pentameter they would read:

$$\cup \quad \text{—} \quad \cup \text{—} \quad \cup \quad \text{—} \quad \cup \quad \text{—} \quad \cup \quad \text{—}$$
Once more | un-to | the breach | dear friends | once more
$$\cup \quad \text{—} \quad \cup \quad \text{—} \quad \cup \quad \text{—} \quad \cup \quad \text{—} \quad \cup \quad \text{—}$$
Or close | the wall | up with | our Eng | lish dead.

Act. III, Henry the Fifth

But of course no actor would ever deliver the speech in that way; instead, it would be accented more like this:

$$\text{—} \quad \text{—} \quad \cup \cup \cup \quad \text{—} \quad \text{—} \quad \text{—} \quad \text{—} \quad \text{—}$$
Once more | un-to the | breach dear friends | once more
$$\cup \quad \text{—} \quad \cup \quad \text{—} \text{—} \quad \cup \cup \quad \text{—} \cup \quad \text{—}$$
Or close | the wall up | with our | English | dead.

Shakespeare's lines thus gain in effectiveness by being written in iambic pentameter but spoken with varying accents. Notice how the speech opens with two accented words so as to gain the attention of the soldiers, and repeats those words at the end of the first line. Later on in the same speech, the king says:

> "*Now set the teeth and stretch the nostril wide,*
> *Hold hard the breath, and bend up every spirit*
> *To his full height. On, on, you noblest English,*
> *Whose blood is from fathers of war-proof!*"

These lines begin with a perfect example of iambic pentameter, spoken with the same accent as its basic meter carries, but the following line breaks this with "Hold hard" and "bend up." The end of that sentence -- "to his full height," is especially effective inasmuch as it stretches out the words in an imitation of the soldier stretching himself.

The variations which a poet can make on a basic meter are endless. When he wants, the poet can adhere closely to a standard metrical setting, allowing the words to come tumbling along easily and smoothly, as Samuel Taylor Coleridge does in "Kubla Khan."

> *In Xanadu did Kubla Khan*
> *A stately pleasure dome decree;*
> *Where Alph, the sacred river, ran*
> *Through caverns measureless to man*
> *Down to a sunless sea.*

The steady meter of these lines reminds us of the beginning of a tale of adventure, when the narrator begins "Once upon a time there was ---" and the listener gets settled down for a pleasurable experience. The third line, continuing on into the fourth, is a good imitation of the continuous flow of the river until, as it reaches the sea, it slows down and stops. The poem continues:

> *So twice five miles of fertile ground*
> *With walls and towers were girded round;*
> *And there were gardens bright with sinuous rills,*
> *Where blossomed many an incense-bearing tree;*
> *And here were forests ancient as the hills,*
> *Enfolding sunny spots of greenery.*

As the poet changes subject from the flowing river to the spacious land, the meter begins to broaden out. First comes the triple accent of "twice five miles." The next line adds one extra syllable, "were," to the tetrameter, and the following line goes to pentameter. Even that is stretched by the word "sinuous" which, appropriately means "winding" or "coiling." The poet is using meter and line length to broaden out the flow of sound, and to give the reader an auditory image corresponding to the visual one he sets up.

In the next few lines, Coleridge surpasses himself by giving us a sound of tumbling and falling, the words abandoning all pretense of meter and coming any which way:

> *"But oh! that deep romantic chasm which slanted*
> *Down the green hill athwart a cedarn cover!*
> *A savage place! as holy and enchanted*
> *As e'er beneath a waning moon was haunted*
> *By woman wailing for her demon lover!"*

Note the mixture of true rhymes and slant rhymes in "slanted," "enchanted" and "haunted," and the similarity of sound in "wailing" and "waning." The exclamation points help break the word flow, as if the reader were stopping to listen and look about.

Rhythm--In one sense, the element of rhythm has been already dealt with as we spoke of the sound repetitions used by speakers and writers as they repeat phrases. Such repetitions are effective because they set up recurring rhythms, not because they make good sense! Very often they merely repeat what has been said and understood earlier. Let us investigate what might be done by repeating a rhythm pattern in speech. We begin with an ordinary "view-with-alarm" speech, such as might be made by a political candidate.

> *My fellow citizens; I believe we can all agree that our nation is facing a time of trouble. Enemies face us halfway around the world, and our young men are having to leave their homes, schooling and careers to fight and die for their country. But equal dangers confront the nation at home. Crime flourishes, the accident rate on our highways takes an ever-increasing toll, and growing numbers of marriages find their way into the divorce courts. What is the answer?*

This speech has now been revised to take advantage of some of its rhythmic possibilities. See if you can tell the difference:

> *My fellow citizens, I believe we can all agree that our nation is facing a time of trouble. Young men are leaving their schools and homes, facing an enemy far away. Fighting and dying, they are learning a new career instead of the one they had hoped for. Ladies and gentlemen, I think we can also see that our country at home is in equal danger; danger from crimes that increase every day, and rising fatality rates on the highways; smashups of marriages, homes breaking up, and loss of authority. What is the answer?*

If this use of rhythmic phrasing is still not clear, it will become so when the speech is seen as a kind of verse! Note the parallel construction in the two sections, and the metrical flow of the phrases:

> *"My fellow citizens;*
> *I believe we can all agree that our*
> > *Nation is facing a time of trouble*
> > *Young men are leaving their schools and homes*
> > *Facing an enemy far away*
> > *Fighting and dying, they're learning a new*
> > *Career instead of the one they had hoped for."*

> *"Ladies and gentlemen;*
> *I think we can also see that our*
> > *Country at home is in equal danger*
> > *Danger from crimes that increase every year,*
> > *And rising fatality rates on the highways,*
> > *Smash-ups of marriages, homes breaking up, and*
> > *Loss of authority. What is the answer?"*

Tempo. Having studied something of meter and rhythm, only tempo remains of the three aspects of the element of duration. It is perhaps the easiest of the three to grasp, for it is concerned with the general speed at which the literature is read or spoken.

We notice tempo in the voices of our friends -- some speak slowly, some rapidly. We hear changes of tempo as speakers become angry, or tired, or excited. The tempo of spoken words often tells us more about the meaning than the words themselves do, as when someone says very rapidly, "Who's excited? I'm not excited. Of course I'm not excited!" The reverse might also be true, if you said to a friend, "Aren't you excited?" and he drawls, "Oh s-u-u-re, I'm excited."

We speak of the tempo at which a scene is played on stage or in the movies. Some of the most tense, nerve-chilling scenes are played at an extremely slow tempo, as when the unsuspecting victim is about to walk into a trap. The camera slowly glides over the scene, pausing to inspect a dark alley, an open window, a screen door swinging idly. Not a soul stirs in the streets, even the background music has ceased. The victim approaches slowly, and everything is prolonged until the nerves of the audience are stretched to the breaking point.

Just the opposite is the fast-tempo scene in which one thing happens hard on the heels of another. Camera angles switch with bewildering suddenness, we find ourselves looking at one scene, then another in the space of a few seconds. Fight scenes are generally shown at rapid tempos, as are many comedy episodes, including the final "chase", which is still an effective climax for a movie.

Tempo is an important device for each of us to use in his own speech. Nothing can emphasize a point better than suddenly slowing the tempo way down, unless it is the use of loud dynamic accent. The two together are an unbeatable combination! To cite an example, suppose the last sentence before this one were read like this:

Nothing can emphasize a point better than suddenly slo-o-ow-ing the tempo waaaay doooown, unless it is the use of LOUD DYNAMIC ACCENT.

Certainly the addition of the tempo and accent factors would make the meaning of the sentence come across much more clearly and forcefully.

In summary, then, the duration aspects of literature consist of *Meter*, which is the regular pulsation or "beat" of the words; *Rhythm*, the individual sound patterns; and *Tempo*, the pace or speed of presentation. In practice all three are closely interwoven, and are of great usefulness both to the speaker, the reader, and to the writer.

PROBLEMS:

Problem One: Compare the musical meter of a hymn or song with the poetic meter of its words. Write an explanation of what you find.

Problem Two: Listen to conversations, taking notes on any strong metrical passages you hear. Analyze these for meter and length of line.

Problem Three: Analyze several notable speeches and documents for their meter. (Preamble to the Constitution, Gettysburg Address, Pledge of Allegiance, The Lord's Prayer, American's Creed, etc.)

Problem Four: Think of a product which might make use of metrical prose in a commercial. Write such a commercial.

Problem Five: Find lines of poetry containing spondees. Write out and mark at least five such lines.

Problem Six: Write a short simple speech. Then rewrite it to stress repetitions of rhythmic phrases.

Problem Seven: Take notes in the next movie you attend, marking the scenes and the tempos at which they are played. Note where the slowest and fastest tempos are found.

Problem Eight: Illustrate the use of different tempos in speech to enhance or change the meaning of the words.

Problem Nine: Write an original short poem about one of the color plates in this book, making use of patterns in words similar to the visual patterns of the picture.

CHAPTER 16

SENSE ELEMENTS IN LITERATURE

Earlier it was pointed out that words convey understanding on two levels, their sounds and their meanings. Just prior to this chapter, several of the elements of sound have been explored (rhythm, meter, tempo). Now the elements of meaning must be considered.

It is possible to get some kind of reaction from listening to an unknown language being spoken. The recorded speeches of Hitler still carry an effect today even though we may not know what he's talking about. A far deeper effect would result if the *sense* of his words came through to us, as well as their sound. But even here, there may be confusion, for words have two kinds of sense, or meaning.

1. *Dictionary meaning.* Suppose the word "cellar" is looked up in a dictionary. The reader will find something like this definition:

An underground space or room beneath a house.

This is the meaning which the word has for most of us, the meaning which it carries in ordinary usage. We call this its "denotation."

2. *Personal meaning.* Suppose further that when you were small, a cruel person had punished you by forcing you to stay all day and night in a cold, clammy cellar where there was no light, and where spiders and rats and strange noises scared you so terribly that you never forgot the experience. To you, the word "cellar" would probably hold a meaning quite different from the usual one. A certain word, because it is so strongly connected with ideas and memories, may become loaded with an emotional charge, ready to go off when you see or hear that word. Many times each of us has made some innocent remark which triggered an unexpectedly violent response from someone. We may even ask, "What did I say?" after such an outburst.

We quickly learn that certain categories of words are dangerous. Hence, we avoid arguing about politics and religion. The words in these areas too often carry emotional overtones. When one person uses the word "democrat" the word stands for (in his mind) everything good, honest, progressive, patriotic and so on. To another person who hears the term, however, it may mean something reactionary, dangerous, narrow-minded and short-sighted. The two people cannot carry on much of a meaningful discussion if they use the same terms but with different meanings. In recent years, a science of word-meanings has grown up, called "semantics." Its practitioners claim that many of mankind's difficulties have arisen out of the ambiguities of words, and that if we are ever to get anywhere in world-wide understanding and peace we will have to agree on the meanings of the words we use when we talk around the conference tables.

Although word ambiguities are barriers to understanding one another's motives, they offer a rich variety of artistic expression when we turn to literature. The very thing that makes words unsuitable for argument makes them eminently useful in poetry and prose.

FIGURES OF SPEECH

Among the many ways in which our language can be used for artistic purposes, certain "figures of speech" stand out as examples: A figure of speech is a kind of word usage which allows us to convey a meaning which the words do not actually state in and of themselves. Among the commonest figures of speech are these:

1.   Simile and Metaphor.   In the former, a comparison is made between two objects which in themselves show no obvious similarity. A human being does not resemble a rock, yet when we say "The center was like a rock in the middle of the line during the championship football game," the comparison is aptly made. In a metaphor, the word "like" is omitted, and we say the center *was* a rock in the middle of the line. Metaphor is common in such expressions as "He's a good egg," and "She's a jewel."

2.   Use of a part for the whole thing (synecdoche). We often refer to a person as "a brain," that part of him being an outstanding characteristic. For some reason we talk about a hundred "head" of cattle, and bestow the title "fastest gun in the west" on the man who carries that gun.

3.   Use of one word to suggest another (metonymy). The writer may say, "His wife sets a good table" but he is talking about the food, not the table itself. We say of a baseball slugger "He swings a powerful bat" but actually all bats are equally powerful or powerless as the case may be. We are really speaking of ability to hit the ball.

4.   Transposition of word order (hyperbaton).   Our language is so structured that the same words when shifted around may mean something quite different from their literal intent. "This turned out to be a fine day" is an expression of satisfaction but reverse the word

order to "A fine day this turned out to be" and the sense is just the opposite. When someone disappoints us, we say to him, "A good friend *you* are!" which certainly doesn't mean "You are a good friend."

5. Understatement (litotes). "That's no small job you've got" means in effect that it's really a big job. What looks like faint praise in the expression "She's not half bad," is really a strong compliment. Thus the language says one thing but means another.

6. Use of a proper name for a common one (antinomasia). Certain words in our language have been derived from the trade names of the first widely accepted products of their kind. Thus we say "kleenex" when we mean tissue and "coke" for soft drinks in general. Every advertiser hopes his product will become so well known as to enter into the language as a common term. "Hershey bar" is almost synonymous with chocolate candy, and this firm has not found it necessary to advertise its products via the usual channels, yet still keeps up its sales.

7. Personification (prosopopoeia). Words can endow inanimate objects with life, and give them human qualities. "The cruel thorns tore viciously at his tender flesh." This is vivid description, but thorns are not cruel -- only humans and a few animals develop cruelty. "The mountains called it to the seas, which echoed back the name." Obviously mountains do not call anywhere, but the picture is a striking one.

8. Deliberate use of faulty grammar (solecism). The rules of grammar are broken at times in order to say something that cannot be expressed in correct English. The sentence "It won't never get no worse" is not only stronger than "It will never get any worse" but conveys something about the person who says it. A voice was heard coming from a hall full of students asking "Ain't we never going to finish studying them grammar lessons?" The expressive language of this question gives its own answer.

9. Extravagant, exaggerated word usage (hyperbole). To overstate with words may be just as effective as to use understatement. "As Webster spoke, a veritable torrent of words poured forth, shaking the earth to its foundations, blasting the heavens, and shattering the souls of the men who heard him." Of course, Daniel Webster had a voice no louder than most speakers, and certainly shook or shattered nothing when he lectured, but the exaggerated word picture is effective nevertheless. Sometimes hyperbole is used with comic effect "The excruciating pain, the dread consequences, the utter helplessness of mortal man with a hangnail."

10. Use of old forms of speech (archaism). Although now seldom

used, older speech forms are by no means totally forgotten. Their most common use is in prayer, where we say "Wilt thou be with us this day" instead of "Will you be with us today," "The Lord giveth and the Lord taketh away," rather than "The Lord gives and takes away."

11.   Needless repetition or redundance (pleonasm). Our language is full of such phrases as "to repeat again," "stupid idiot" and "free gift." We hear people speak of a "hollow tube," an "audible noise" and a "toxic poison." Even if we recognized each such expression for what it is, we might continue to use them on occasion because of their expressiveness. One advertiser of a bug spray ended his commercial message with a loud, echoing, male voice saying--"and it KILLS THEM DEAD!" The redundance was deliberate and effective.

12.   Contradictory or incongruous words used together (oxymoron).   One of the beauties of our language is that it can place such words as "pretty" and "ugly", "little" and "big" together and still make sense! If someone gave you a large and unattractive vase, you might later remark "It's pretty ugly and a little big" and you would be understood. We hear the phrase "a cruel kindness" and understand the contradiction in terms perfectly well. "We had a lovely quarrel" someone tells you, "and we ended up agreeing to disagree!" A circus employed a short actor once who billed himself as "the world's tallest midget" and attracted crowds of people.

These twelve figures of speech do not exhaust the total list by any means. There are several dozen more, quite rarely used. All of them, however, represent ways in which language may be used to give a new meaning to the words, a non-scientific meaning. Of all languages, English is one of the richest in word possibilities. A few, like Eskimo, do not possess common nouns but give everything a separate name. Thus, we can say "boat" and mean anything from a toy sailboat to the largest ocean liner. The Eskimo has no one word to cover all these examples. Other languages do not have multiple meanings for words, as we do. Consider our word "fast." It can refer to something moving rapidly ("he ran fast") or to something not able to be moved at all ("he stood fast"). It can also mean "to go without food," and "to have an unsavory reputation," and "to operate in advance of the correct rate" (as a watch is "fast"). Think of all the possibilities open to the writer, using words with such flexible denotations! A sentence can mean a great many things. The author once bought a tent which came in a large canvas carrying bag. He took it into the back yard and pulled it from the bag but before he got a chance to try it out, he was called to the phone. He told his son to go out and put up the tent, and came back later to find it back in the bag! The phrase "to put up," in the case of a tent, has two meanings, exactly opposite!

Pronunciation of terms:

Synechdoche — (sin-éck-duh-kee)

Metonymy — (mét-on-a-me)

Hyperbaton — (high-púrr-ba-ton)

Litotes — (lít-oh-tees)

Antinomasia — (anti-no-máze-ia)

Prosopopoeia — (pro-so-po-péa-a)

Solecism — (sóle-uh-sizm)

Hyperbole — (high-pér-bo-ly)

Archaism — (ar-káy-izm)

Pleonasm — (pléa-oh-nazm)

Oxymoron — (oxy-mór-on)

IMAGERY

In addition to the subtle changes in meaning which figures of speech may add to our language, words are also used to create images. When you hear the radio announcer say, "Folks, this delicious, dark-brown, creamy-rich chocolate will melt in your mouth," he is trying hard to create a taste image that will be so strong you will want to buy his product. Almost all advertising is involved with the creating of images, indeed entire corporations work hard at building images of themselves in the public mind. How do words contribute to this process? What kinds of images can be created?

1. *Visual Images.*

Line. As we look back over the visual art elements studied earlier, we remember line, color, value, volume, texture, and perspective. Each of these not only can be seen, but some can be felt (texture, volume) and all are capable of being described in words, with more or less detail. Suppose we wished to create a literary image of the lines in an old woman's face. We might simply say, "The old woman had many lines in her face." This doesn't present a very vivid picture to the reader, however, because all of the visual characteristics of line are missing. A more observant author might write:

1   *The old woman's face was covered with a fine network*
2 *of lines that made her appear to be standing in the shadow*
3 *of a finely woven fish net. As she talked, the lines*
4 *rearranged themselves as if by magic, now appearing for*
5 *a frown, now disappearing in a quick smile only to come*
6 *out on some other part of the face. There were two bold,*
7 *deep, vertical lines in the forehead, leading down to the*
8 *bridge of the nose --- lines giving her face the look of*
9 *poised command and authority. Two diagonals on either*
10 *side of her mouth appeared to add action to the countenance,*
11 *even when in repose. The thin mouth presented a calm,*
12 *horizontal line echoed by similar landscape lines across*
13 *the forehead. Quick curves about the eyes gave her glance*
14 *an unexpectedly gay look. All in all, she presented a*
15 *fascinating study in facial lines, much more interesting*
16 *to look at than the smooth face of a young girl, just as*
17 *a drawing is superior to the blank paper.*

Notice that the paragraph uses many of the things that were studied in the chapters of Part Two. In line 7 the writer has commented on vertical lines, and their effect of poise and authority. In line 9 attention is called to the diagonals, for action. Horizontals are described in lines 12 and 13, and curves in the same sentence. A writer must train his eye to see visual things, so that he may describe them for his readers. His vision should be as acute as the painter's.

Color. One of the more difficult visual images to sustain is that of color, yet the imagery need not be unsuccessful if the writer will only be observant of the many aspects of color. The student of this text will know that there are primary and secondary hues, cool and warm, advancing and retreating. Combinations of colors include variations made by mixing black (shades) and white (tints) with pure hues in various value-scale ranges. And so the writer with a knowledge of color, and an observant eye will be able to record what he sees, while the untrained observer will be able to say very little, even though his skill with words is equally great.

Not only are lines and colors used in visual imagery, but the other elements may also be used. These, however, will appear under other categories.

2. *Motion Images*

The description of motion may follow somewhat the idea of line -- after all a line is the visual record of some movement or other. If lines can be straight and curved, motions can follow the same paths. If curves are slow or fast, motion can have varied tempos as well. Here we cross over from visual to auditory art, since our study of motion is plainly getting into meter, rhythm and tempo. The writer will have to be an observer of the "motions" of music, applying them to his writing to make it more vivid:

The dogs were frisking about in the yard, now covering the lawn in a series of evenly-timed bounces that described a line of Roman arches, from the house across to the trees. Suddenly one would flatten himself to the turf, tail sweeping the ground in a vigorous arc. The others would break the smooth rhythm of their circling runs and enter upon a combination of dashes and pauses that created a visual symphony of doggy notes written in joyous rhythm on the green grass.

3. *Tactile Images*

Texture being not only seen but felt, the writer will need to visualize his description both from the eye and the fingers. Here he will find words useful which imitate the rough or smooth textures with rough or smooth sounds of their own. Words like "scratchy" and "oily" by their very sounds suggest the textures they denote.

A second kind of image closely connected with the sense of touch is the "thermal" image. Here the sensations of heat and cold are described, but it is quickly seen that these have not been as carefully developed as the areas of line and color. We have only a few general levels of temperature, and only a few words to record them. Words like cool, chilly, cold and frigid, or warm, hot, and sweltering are scarcely sufficient to build much of a varied picture. So the writer depends on comparison ("It was hotter than the hinges of Hades") or personification ("The heat licked at his boots, gnawing at the blistered skin inside") or metaphor ("The wind was a gigantic icicle forcing itself down his throat").

4. *Images of taste and smell.*

These are sensory areas which, like the tactile senses, have not been exploited for artistic purposes. Of the two, taste is likely to have been more developed in the average person, but even here most of us are far from expert in identifying subtle tastes, classifying them, and analyzing their components. A few people have brought their sense of taste to a pitch of perfection rivalling the musician's ear or the painter's eye. Such people may be employed as "tea-tasters," who test blends of tea by sipping and sniffing. These men are able to identify the separate ingredients of a brew made of a dozen different varieties of tea leaves! Perhaps even more remarkable are "gourmets" who specialize in fine foods. Such experts can often identify ingredients of many sauces, gravies, and soups after a brief taste, can tell where the grapes grew that the wine was made from, and take an artist's pleasure in the taste of good food. Their sense of taste would rebel at some of the hamburger-joint cooking we eat uncomplainingly, just as a fine musician's ear will not tolerate even a slightly out-of-tune chord that sounds good to the average listener. This doesn't mean that such people never eat hamburgers -- they do, and enjoy them. But they insist on food that is cooked and served properly, and who can blame them? It is said that as a nation, the French appreciate good food most highly and expect to get it in most of their eating places. The English are reputed to care the least for the taste of their food, and will cheerfully tolerate meals which would be considered tasteless almost anywhere else.

Perhaps one day the senses of taste and smell will be brought to the same state as seeing and hearing are now, and whole arts will be built up around them. If that should happen, the writer will then be able to set up word images to describe those senses.

5. *Aural Images*

We know enough about music, after working through the six chapters of Part Three, to use musical images in our writing with some effectiveness. The following passage will illustrate some of these:

> *I was awakened by the repeated motive of a songbird.*
> *It seemed to follow some kind of avian scale for four ascending tones topped off by an accented climax in quite a different key, as if it had all of a sudden discovered a new harmonic progression. Underlining the song was a woodpecker's sixteenth-note percussion, and regularly at every fourth bar, there came fortissimo the bass note of the neighbor's bull.*

In summary, it has been suggested that where imagery is concerned, the writer must always be inferior to the visual artist. Images are more immediate and striking when perceived by the eye than by the "mind's eye." The saying goes, "One picture is worth 10,000 words," but don't underestimate literature. After all, it took words to present *that* picture!

PROBLEMS:

Problem One: Write out a list of words which you think have private meanings (connotations) for you. Write these meanings, and then look up the dictionary meanings (denotations).

Problem Two: Look up the term "semantics" in an encyclopedia and find out something about this new area of learning.

Problem Three: Write a paragraph or a short verse in which you make use of a number of figures of speech. Use examples other than this textbook provides.

Problem Four: Find as many of the twelve figures of speech in poetry or prose as you can. News stories may be useful sources.

Problem Five: Investigate the characteristics of different languages, concentrating on the unique possibilities of each for the creative writer.

Problem Six: Collect a number of ambiguous statements which show how easily a writer can mislead his readers through words which have more than one meaning.

Problem Seven: Write a paragraph in which visual imagery is used on one of the following subjects (or one of your own choice): a stock-car race, a diving contest, a fashion show, a battle, a 3-alarm fire.

Problem Eight: Imagine a time in the far-off future when the sense of smell will be developed to the same degree as sight and hearing are now. Discuss the kinds of art works which would be designed to appeal to that sense, under the following headings:

    a.   What will the works be about? What subjects might they have?

    b.   What will their purpose be? Who will enjoy them?

    c.   What will they be made of? How will the "artist" make them?

    d.   What "elements" will they embody? Line, texture, rhythm?

    e.   What over-all structures or forms might they follow?

Problem Nine: The same ideas as in the previous problem can be applied to the sense of taste.

Problem Ten: Also the sense of touch.

Problem Eleven: Write a paragraph using word images to describe Color Plate 15.

Part Five

SEARCHING FOR MEANING

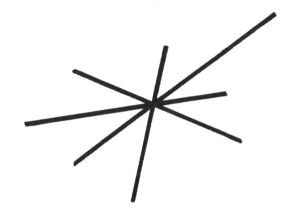

CHAPTER 17

STRUCTURE IN THE ARTS

Having learned "to hear" and "to see," we are now in a position to plunge even deeper beneath the surface of the arts. We have begun to realize that a single work of art may have many layers or levels on which it can be approached. These could be described as follows:

Subject level -- the person sees only the subject of the painting or statue, or grasps only the plot of the story or movie. He criticizes the work of art on its faithfulness to things he sees or hears in the outside world. The younger the person is, the less he will be able to grasp of even this surface-level of the arts. An infant reacts only to the bright colors or loud sounds, and cannot tell what they stand for. In music, a "surface-level" listener usually allows the musical sounds to set off a daydream which he enjoys so long as the music plays.

Medium level -- the viewer becomes interested in the material of the statue, how it is used, what techniques were required, etc. Painting and architecture may be admired from this standpoint, too. Many people derive pleasure from seeing how materials are used in a building or home. In the audible arts, the performer's technique in handling the medium frequently outweighs all other artistic considerations. Thus, many people go to the movies to see the actor, not the play; they also attend concerts and opera because a great singer or player is featured. For this same reason, listeners will sit where they can see the pianist's hands, or watch the instrumentalists in the orchestra.

Background level -- a more practiced student of the arts will know something about the work besides its subject and medium. He may begin to learn some of its background, who created it, and what period of history it came from. Such information can be quite valuable in shedding light on the work in question. It would help, for instance, to know that Beethoven's *Third Symphony* was written at the time Napoleon was rising to power. Beethoven hated hereditary privilege and thought that a man should be respected for his own abilities, not for his family connections. Napoleon, making his way over kings and princes, was his ideal, and Beethoven dedicated the work to him. Before it was published, however, Napoleon had proclaimed himself an emperor, and brought the composer's wrath down upon him. The original dedication was changed quickly, but the work remains a tribute to a hero.

Elements Level -- although a person reads diligently about the background of a work of art, he will never come to grips with that work until he can evaluate its "elements," the basic features of its construction. These we have studied under the various headings of pitch, timbre, volume and duration; or line, color, value, volume, texture and perspective. The trained critic picks out these features of what he sees or hears, notes their usage, and gauges the value of the work, in part, by their presence and their effectiveness. Where the untrained observer will talk about how the painting "looks just like the farm I grew up on" the trained observer will discuss the horizontal lines, the color scheme, the value contrasts, and so on. In music, he will take note of motives, themes, harmonies, timbres, and other elements.

Structural level -- at the center of understanding lies the grasp of the structural design of the work of art. In the visual arts, this is but a short step from the perception of the elements but in the audible arts the problem is greater. Music students often understand the elements of pitch, duration, volume, and timbre but fail to comprehend how these have been woven into a musical form. Likewise, few moviegoers penetrate the structure of a film they may have seen several times.

A truly thorough knowledge of a work of art must include all of these levels, and there is no "right" level on which to approach a work. Even after years of listening practice, many music-lovers prefer to hear a new work on a purely sensual level the first time. Sometimes a too-thoroughly-analytic approach destroys the charm and freshness of a work, but whether this is the case or not, the educated consumer will, if he chooses, be able to penetrate the work at all of these levels.

Structure in General

The whole idea of structure or form in the arts is the creation of plans or patterns. The artist seeks to impose his will on the medium or material with which he works. Take stone, steel, brick, wood and cement, and dump them on a pile and you have the materials of architecture without the plan or form. Let these be organized according to a good plan and the result is an architectural masterpiece. What are we really admiring when we gaze at a great cathedral? Certainly not the stone of which it is built -- we can see that in any rock quarry. We are admiring the plan of organization created for that stone by a human mind! Similarly the structures of music, painting, literature and sculpture are valued for the fact that they are concrete realizations of man's ability to think creatively.

A structure or form, then, represents man's mind; this goes without argument. When we see a painting done by a monkey, we feel angry or cheated somehow (even though it may exhibit interesting colors or lines) because we want the arts to be *human* creations! This urge to order materials into man-made designs is so common that we scarcely notice it. Cutting the lawn and trimming the hedge are, in reality, forcing materials of nature to conform to our ideas of what looks good. We make flowers line up in rows because we prefer our design to nature's haphazard one, at least for our own yards. If an interloper shows up in the form of a weed, out it goes! Man's design, not nature's, prevails here.

Housewives do the same thing when they garnish and decorate foods to look good. This adds nothing to their nutritive value, but it does make them appear prettier than they would be naturally. The special table silver and linens also add to the overall design of the meal. Even the order of serving and eating the food follows a pattern determined by the human artistic instincts.

Space Structures

The arts, being subdivided into time-sound arts, and space-visual arts, will naturally have two basic areas of structure. Structures based in space will have two or three dimensions and, with the exception of large architectural works, can be apprehended by sight at a single glance, that is, all at the same time. Even in the case of the large structure, an air view would show the basic exterior form, at least.

In painting, the forms (to be defined and investigated in the following chapter) will be found to depend largely on geometrical figures. As a matter of fact, it has been theorized that a painting could be expressed as a complex mathematical formula, colors and all, and programmed for a computer, which would then produce or reproduce it exactly. Two obstacles must be overcome first, however; one, the formula would be of such vast complexity that no human could work it all out; and two, the computer to do the painting would be so costly that nobody could afford to build it. The human brain, coordinated with eye and hand, is still the most efficient "artistic computer" mechanism. It learns more easily, is more adaptable, much more compact, and requires less maintenance! It is worthy to note, however, that computers have been given relatively simple formulas, and with them have produced not only line drawings but original music!

The three-dimensional arts, sculpture and architecture have customarily been cast in either human or animal forms (sculpture) or in geometrical ones. Architectural forms have long been dominated by the building materials used. Buildings are largely right-angled because stone and wood are not easily curved. With builders committed to square-cornered structures, rugs, furniture, and other fixtures follow along to the extent that even if one did build a curving home or office structure (and this is entirely feasible in concrete) the cost of appropriate furnishings would be exorbitant.

Time Structures

Music and literature are totally different in their structures from the visual arts. For one thing, music and literature must develop a plan or organization which exists in time, not space. Instead of being measured in feet and inches, they must be measured in minutes and hours. Instead of being taken in all at once by the eye, they must be absorbed slowly, moment by moment, and held in the memory. It is here, in the remembrance of the work just heard, that the structure is perceived. This is what makes the analysis of music so difficult, even for the musician.

Suppose a viewer were to look at a large painting, not by standing back and seeing the whole thing, but by inspecting it inch by inch in a pitch-dark room with only the aid of a pencil beam of light. The viewer would start at the upper left hand corner, follow the beam of light across, as if reading, then back, across again, back again, until some ten minutes later he had scanned the whole thing, but never all at once. Could the viewer be expected to remember all those yards of painting which passed before his eye, and reconstruct them in his head so he could visualize the whole thing? Of course not, and yet that is the very thing we expect an intelligent listener to do. Surprisingly, it can be done! The ear must be taught to identify the various musical elements and put them together in retrospect, keeping track of what the composer is doing as he does it!

In both literature and music, the fact that forms are set in time rather than space gives them the general character of "events" which happen in sequences. Pictures, statues, or buildings are "just there" but poetry, music and novels have a beginning, a middle, and an end. When the sound ceases, the musical structure vanishes. The literary work disappears when the curtain goes down or the book is closed. But the building, statue or painting are always there, waiting, as much in existence when nobody is looking at them as they are before a gallery of visitors.

Time-Space Structures

A number of ways of combining the arts are known and used. Some very common combinations such as drama and cinema, use not only literature and music but architecture (in the theatre and the sets) and painting. The dance is a sort of moving sculpture set to music, and some sculpture moves of its own volition, as "mobiles" and vibrating sculptures. The automobile has, in its finer designs, been called "hollow, rolling sculpture."

When visual and auditory arts combine, the formal structures of one area generally take a secondary place to those of the other. For instance, in a Shakespeare play there may be music, but it is invariably only a trifling tune which could just as easily be omitted. On the other hand, in an opera by Verdi, where the Shakespearian play has been set to music, the words are mercilessly cut, whole scenes left out, and the plot thoroughly subordinated to the music. Rarely have time-and-space forms been equally balanced. When such occur, their total effect is powerful. Something of this power is felt on hearing a great Bach *Mass* or *Passion* sung in a magnificent Gothic cathedral, with its sculptured interior and glowing stained glass. Here theBiblical words are wed to music and heard in appropriate visual circumstances for an unforgettable artistic experience!

ART PRINCIPLES

The reader, having been introduced to line, color, texture and the other visual art elements, must now learn how these are combined into a visual unity of some kind. Two needs must be met in such a unification of elements; first, certain basic principles must be heeded; and second, a structure or form must be developed.

The Visual Art Principles

Basic principles are few, and those few must be quite broad and elastic. Art textbooks and teachers have advanced many such principles in the past, but succeeding generations always seem to be able to create interesting art by violating the "rules" laid down by the earlier schools and the critics. The principles set forth here are those which seem to have stood the test of time, but none of them is absolute, even so.

I. The principle of *balance* governs many pictures, sculptures and works of architecture. It may consist of:

A. Symmetrical balance -- an even division of "weight" in the picture, statue or building on either side of the center. Such works of art look formal and rather stiff at least to our modern way of thinking. An example of symmetry is shown in the formal balance of the room in Example 17-1. If a line were drawn vertically down the center of the wall, everything on the right would be matched by something of equal size and shape on the left. If you have ever visited homes decorated in the fashion of the earlier centuries, the 1800s or early 1900s, you have undoubtedly seen such rooms. These interiors reflect the personalities of the owners, who were on the whole much more formal than we are. The men kept their coats on in hot weather, the women dressed up to go to the corner grocery store, children stood up

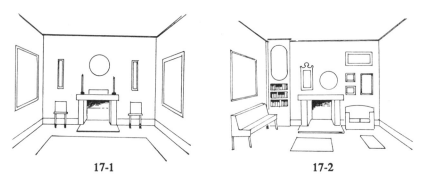

17-1   17-2

when their elders entered the room, and so on. People were careful to get proper introductions, left calling cards, and used first names only with the closest of friends. Now all of that has changed.

B. Occult balance is now the preferred way, with a more casual placement of furniture, pictures, rugs and draperies. If there is a divan on one side it may be balanced by two chairs on the other. A large picture may be counterweighted by two or three smaller ones, and so on. Such a room is shown in Example 17-2.

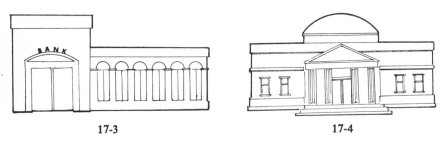

17-3   17-4

This same change has swept over architecture, too, giving buildings a less formal look, making them seem friendlier, if less imposing. This, too, is in keeping with the growing informality of business, which has found it profitable to be on friendly terms with the average citizen, and accessible to all. Note in Examples 17-3 and 17-4 how the first of the buildings balances a large rotunda against a single wing, while the second relies on more formal balance of a symmetrical nature.

In a painting, symmetry is quite readily detectable. Occult balance may not be. The stained-glass window (Color Pl. 5) shows the even spacing and arrangement of figures which mark the symmetrical painting. The "Madonna and Child" (Color Pl. 6) is not perfectly symmetrical; for one thing, the child is not matched by a similar figure on the left. However, there is a kind of balance achieved by the addition of the two figures at lower left so that the interest of the picture is not wholly to right of center. Perhaps closer to symmetry is the watercolor "Singer Building" (Color Pl. 11) in which the central position of the skyscraper is bordered by other structures on either side. Notice how carefully the artist in "The Sacrifice of Abraham" (Color Pl. 7) balances his figures. The angel and the boy to the left of center are counter-weighted by the heavy wing and the basin on the right. The four sides of the picture are carefully kept free of distracting details. Finally we see a good example of occult balance in "The Starry Night" (Color Pl. 9) with its heavy tree on the left balanced by the rising hill on the right.

II. The principle of *dominance* is worthy of study. The idea here is that each picture, statue or building must have one dominating feature. If two features are of equal importance there will be a tug-of-war set up between them which somehow must be resolved. Our own experience confirms this -- when two strong urges or needs pull us in opposite directions we feel downright uncomfortable. We wish we could make up our mind. If we cannot, and the demands on us increase, mental disorder may be one result. Perhaps it is a dominating idea or goal which makes some men successful. They know what they want to do, and nothing distracts them.

Observe the "Young Woman with Water Jug" (Color Pl. 8). The figure of the girl clearly dominates the picture. Although other objects are of comparable size (map, table, window) their regularity of shape, their color, and their position cause them to become secondary in importance. Suppose the picture included another girl, also with water jug, as in the sketch, Example 17-5. The result would be the weakening of the composition, unless one were made to dominate the other, or both were dominated by something more important!

17-5

In "The Sacrifice of Abraham" (Color Pl. 7), the central struggle between Abraham and the angel dominates everything else. Rembrandt has wisely left out all the details of the background so these do not distract our attention from the dominant theme. Picasso has done the same thing in "Mother and Child" (Color Pl. 13). Zorach's sculpture (Color Pl. 12) concentrates on the two faces, the cat's and the girl's, leaving out details of clothing, fur, hair, etc. In Chagall's picture (Color Pl. 14) the man and the cow dominate by their size. Even primitive man knew the importance of concentration upon one central object. It is doubtful that the painter (Color Pl. 1) of the bison would have been capable of sketching in the landscape behind the animal. He was not drawing a scene of which the bison was a part, but was capturing the animal itself! Finally, the medieval artist, Milano, illustrates the same kind of dominance in his "Madonna and Child" (Color Pl. 6) blotting out the background and reducing the subordinate figures to midget size.

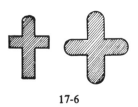

17-6

In architecture, dominance is achieved through several means:

a. Through overall shape. A building is generally found to exhibit a single, easily identifiable shape. The accompanying illustration shows two shapes found in Christian churches, Example 17-6. The left-hand cross-form was developed in Western Church architecture while the other was an Eastern, or Byzantine form. Other buildings may be found frequently in rectangular, circular, oval or square ground plans. Such a simple form as one of these many prove to be the strong dominating feature of a building, everything else being fitted to it.

b. Dominance through structural necessity. Suppose, as was actually the case during Greek times, that a builder had only one

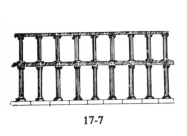

17-7

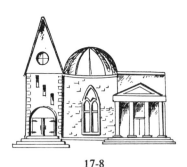

17-8

method of construction available to him, in this case "post and lintel" construction. His buildings would be necessarily dominated by the many columns and horizontal slabs that were used, shown in Example 17-7. This is why such works strike us as unified and coherent, while the style common in the late 1800s of choosing something from all periods and mixing them together (electicism) today seems extravagant and odd. (See Example 17-8).

It was this type of dominance which gave the Gothic Cathedral its tremendous spiritual quality through the pointed arch used everywhere in the building. Such a structure could not help being unified. Note the many forms of the pointed arch in Example 17-9.

     c. Dominance through medium. Today's architect has a bewildering array of building materials at his disposal; brick, stone, steel, aluminum, iron, glass, plastic, wood, concrete, plywood, asphalt, hardboard, styrofoam, cinderblock, tile, and so on and on. Architects of the past had to rely largely on stone for permanence. Their buildings therefore would exhibit a unity or dominance of medium that might not be so automatically obtained today. Our best builders, however, recognize the value of medium dominance and consistently concentrate on one or two mediums in a building rather than make use of them all. While interiors may make use of many materials, exteriors generally do not. Note the Lever House (Color Pl. 4) with its strong emphasis on glass. Notice also the other structures as each concentrates on a single medium.

17-9

     d. Dominance through line. The Lever House concentrates on two kinds of straight line, vertical and horizontal. No curves are used at all. On the other hand, the cathedral at Angouleme, France, makes great use of the semi-circular curve, both outside and inside, as sketched in Example 17-10. In each case, one kind of line dominates the structural pattern.

     e. Stylistic dominance. If one part of a building is Gothic, it would seem self-evident that all parts should be in the same style, yet such is frequently not the case! One sees buildings which exhibit one style in one part and another elsewhere. The "eclectic" school of architecture often chose to mix styles, many times with strange results. But sometimes style mixtures come about when an old building is

17-10

added to at a later date. Then newer materials and methods make possible a faster, better, or cheaper addition, so the earlier style is abandoned. Or it may turn out that artisans and workers in the earlier style are no longer available. Architects of a few recently-built Gothic churches have had great difficulties finding workmen who knew how to cut and fit stone vaulting, for instance!

III.   The principle of *proportion* has to do with the relationships of the various parts of the work of art to each other, and of these parts to the whole. The term "proportion" thus may be applied in two ways; figure proportion and area proportion.

A.   Figure proportion is concerned mostly with the drawing of the human figure which for centuries has been varied in its proportions by painters and sculptors. Egyptian artists depicted one general body shape, early Greeks another, and late Greeks still another, this last proportion being much closer to a realistic human form than any previous one. In the medieval period, however, artists turned again to an unnatural proportion for the human form, making their figures elongated and unworldly looking. A more natural form returned with the Renaissance, and in modern times we have seen a revival of the distorted proportions of the figure once more!

Artists generally agree on an "ideal" proportion ratio for the human body, but of course each artist varies from this as he wishes, distorting the proportions to suit his purposes. This ideal form is shown in Example No. 17-11 with its ratios shown in dotted lines. The body has been divided into eight equal parts, the head taking up one of those parts. The eyes are halfway down the head. Three-eighths of the body length is distributed from the navel to the top of the head, five-eighths

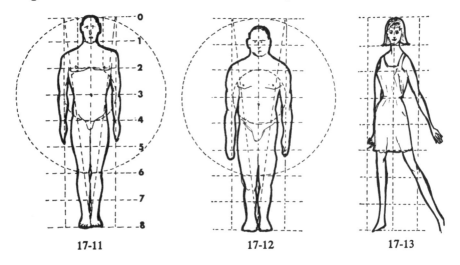

17-11   17-12   17-13

from the navel to the soles of the feet. The navel is midway between the head and the knees. This picture does not show all of the proportional relationships to be found in the human form, nor does it diagram the variations found in children's proportions, or those of women.

The human eye is quick to note deviations from the ideal proportion when seeing living bodies. We immediately categorize a person as short, tall, dumpy, skinny, fat, or disfigured. Very few of us come close to this ideal proportion, and those who do are considered to be handsome or beautiful. When it comes to recognizing distortion of proportion in painting or drawing, the matter is not so easy. We are used to seeing the elongated fashion-ad figures so much that we have forgotten the normal look of the human form! Example No. 17-12 shows how slight a variation from the ideal is noticed.

Fashion artists draw a figure about nine or more heads tall with narrower hips, longer legs, and more slender arms than average. (Ex. No. 17-13) The angular aspects of fashion figures are always accented, too. Models who wish to compete in fashion advertising must possess and retain these characteristics, a difficult task for a young woman of normal health and appetite. In comparison with these models, the girl of average height and correct weight will look plump and short. Each generation and era has its preferences in female proportions, and the currently popular one happens to stress leanness and height. In Rubens' day (1577-1640) the trend was exactly the opposite! Of course, at that time there was no Madison Avenue advertising trade to set standards for the people. Today, most of us are unaware of the extent to which the ads do determine our tastes, not only in products but in design and form of all kinds.

B. Area proportion, as distinct from figure proportion, is concerned with the work of art itself rather than its subject. Here again we find the 3:5 ratio, as one of a series known to students of the sciences as "the Fibonacci Series." This is a row of numbers. the last one of which is always the sum of the preceding two. Thus, in such a series we will find 1,2,3,5,8,13,21,34,55, and so on. In practice, artists will use something close to these ratios (not measuring them out exactly but gauging with the eye) in assigning certain areas of the picture surface. For instance, in a landscape, it is quite usual for the horizon line to

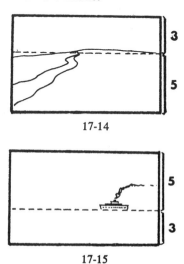

17-14

17-15

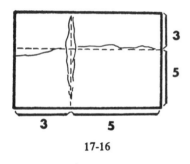

17-16

divide the picture laterally on a **3:5** ratio, as in Examples No. 17-14, 15, 16. Almost never will this line be half-way between top and bottom! In similar fashion, the position of the vertical division line, if there is one, will be in the same ratio. Such a ratio as 3:5 gives, then, a similar ratio between the larger section and the painting itself! (3:5 as 5:8)

We will often see a page of advertising laid out according to the principles of proportion in the Fibonacci series, as in Example 17-17.

17-17

Where the page is longer than it is wide, the division into four segments will result in the general ratio of 5 to 3 in both directions, producing a square and three rectangles of varying size. These are so proportioned as to be both satisfying and interesting to the eye. Color, texture, and other art elements serve to add interest.

One branch of painting, strongly influenced by this idea of area proportion, divides the surface into segments with no thought of subject matter at all! The result is a work of art which must be accepted on its own terms. It cannot be enjoyed for its subject, for it has none. The "Broadway Boogie-Woogie" by Mondrian (Color Pl. 10) is such a picture. The main canvas is square, in itself an unusual feature since artists invariably choose rectangles or other geometrical shapes for their paintings. Within that square are other squares, many of them tiny colored patches, but some are white empty spaces. Rectangles abound, with larger ones subdivided into smaller ones. As one looks at the picture, the abstract pleasures of comparing one area with another, of identifying proportion ratios, and of making mental combinations of various geometric figures, begin to grow. We have all had the experience of lying in bed counting the repetitions of figures in wallpaper, or of staring at a tile floor and making up combinations of the black and white tiles into larger units. Looking at Mondrian's painting is something like this, but much more varied and interesting. If we search for a subject we will be disappointed, despite the title, but if we look at it as intricate pattern-making, we will see it for its true worth.

One art which uses proportional areas most clearly is architecture. The outer surfaces of a building will, unless it is absolutely blank-walled, exhibit some sort of division into smaller areas. An office building (Ex. 17-18) will usually be rectangular in shape, with other smaller rectangles marked off by window mullions, floor divisions and

17-18

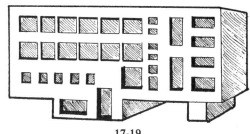
17-19

so on. The French architect, Le Corbusier, has designed buildings which resemble even more closely the irregularity of proportions of paintings. The sketch (Example 17-19) is modelled after a government building designed by Corbusier for India's capital city. When one stops to consider the matter, one realizes that the outer appearance of most of our buildings is strongly influenced by the regularity of the floor-and-room arrangement within. Change this, and the exterior will change, too.

IV. The principle of *rhythm* in the visual arts is followed by repeating a certain "motive." This motive may be any one of a number of things; but the two kinds of motives used most frequently are:

A. Line Motives.

Artists know that any kind of line, if repeated often enough, will set up a kind of repetitive rhythm, as seen in Example 17-20. This is the same principle as the artist used in "Storm on the Great Bridge" (Color Pl. 3) in the slanting rain and the cross hatched lines of the bridge pilings. These two opposing line types add a great

17-20

17-21

deal to the feeling of hurry and urgency of the people running across the bridge. In Van Gogh's picture (Color Pl. 9), the short, thick brush-strokes set up a rhythm of driving force and urgency. In Example 17-21 we see the same picture in outline form. Without that line rhythm, it looks dead and static, but with it, the picture throbs and pulses with life and movement.

B. Shape Motives.

In the picture "I and My Village" (Color Pl. 14) the artist has repeated an oval shape many times. We see it in the eyes, the cow's ears and snout, the large central oval line, the fruit or flowers at the low center, and so on. These pleasant shapes help make the fantasy a pleasing rather than a scary one. On the surface, the picture should by all signs be a horrible nightmare -- a man with a green face and blank eye staring at a huge animal not two inches from his nose, people and houses upside down, menacing black sky, and so on. Yet by clever repetition of the playful fast curve and oval shape, the artist has convinced us that this is a kind of humor and joyfulness. We see a rhythm of window shapes in the watercolor "Singer Building" (Color Pl. 11) which gives a feeling of pattern and orderliness to the upper part of the picture contrasting with the violence and confusion of the street level. Note in the picture of the Lever House (Color Pl. 4) how the rectangle of the building itself is repeated in the thousands of windows, in the spaces between the ground floor pillars, on the terrace flowerbed, and again in the patterns of the sidewalk. Buildings in the background show similar window rhythm, and the one at the lower right includes a rhythm of short-arcs along its cornice and a kind of medieval-fortress crenelation along the very top. (Example 17-22.) Certainly there would be no use for such fortification in downtown New York. Yet it does serve as rhythmic repetition to give an otherwise undistinguished facade something of elegance. The observer will notice this sort of repetition on many old houses, especially about the front porch and door.

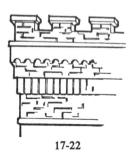

17-22

SUMMARY:

Our discussion of Art Principles has included only four; balance, dominance, proportion and rhythm. Books on art structure will reveal other factors, each supported by excellent reasoning and example. The purpose of this discussion, however, is not to make an exhaustive study of art structures, but to introduce the idea to the reader that visual arts *do* have underlying principles which govern the placement and use of the art elements. Once interest is aroused, it is hoped the student will make a lifelong practice of looking for those hidden factors in art which go so much deeper than the mere surface appearance of the work.

PROBLEMS:

Problem One: Apply the five levels of understanding, as well as you can, to one space-art work, and to one in the time arts. Write out whatever you can find concerning each level.

Problem Two: Give at least five instances you have personally observed (other than those in this textbook) of people creating some kind of order or plan out of raw materials for no other reason than the joy of doing so.

Problem Three: Note existing visual art forms in your town. Make a list of the general types and shapes of paintings, statues, and buildings. Note the address of each one.

Problem Four: List the advantages that an artist would have over a computer even if the latter could produce "original" works of painting or sculpture.

Problem Five: What other evidences besides right-angled corners and straight sides do we have that outdated materials still dictate the shapes and arrangements of our houses?

Problem Six: If a grasp of musical form depends so strongly on the memory, suggest several ways of improving one's musical memory.

Problem Seven: Practice your memory retention by writing out the exact sequence of scenes, and the actors in each, after the next movie you attend. Check your list against a classmate's.

Problem Eight: At the same movie, note any differences between the visual, dramatic, and musical structures which you are able to hear and see. Do musical and visual climaxes occur at the same places as the dramatic ones?

Problem Nine: Make a list of examples around your home, school or town which show different kinds of balance. Look for symmetrical and occult balance in rooms, houses, pictures, furniture, clothing, etc.

Problem Ten: Find the dominant line, color, and texture in things you see. Start with nature, (landscapes, trees, animals) and go on to man himself. What are your own dominant features? What about your home, your neighborhood, and your town?

Problem Eleven: Practice drawing the human form in two ways. First draw as realistic a standing figure as you can, and then measure it to see how closely you come to getting "ideal" proportions. Next, draw the proportion lines (as in Example 17-11) and fill in the body according to where each feature is supposed to be. Compare your two figures.

Problem Twelve: Measure the proportions of the following kinds of figures; (a) comic-strip characters; (b) high fashion models sketched for newspapers or magazines; (c) photos of beauty queens and "Mr. America" male models; (d) mail order catalog models; (e) real photographs of people you know. Make up a chart showing varying proportions you discover.

Problem Thirteen: Find a picture which illustrates good area proportion. Make a sketch of it and chart the proportionate divisions of the picture surface around the borders.

Problem Fourteen: Note the use of shape repetition in buildings, interior decoration, fashion, automotive design, and classroom furnishings.

Problem Fifteen: Find rhythmic motives repeated in the houses of your neighborhood, the downtown "street furniture" (lamps, parking meters, etc.) and in paintings.

CHAPTER 18

SPACE STRUCTURES—
PAINTING & SCULPTURE

Visual art structures may be viewed in two ways, as pre-determined forms and as individual forms. It may help to compare these two kinds of structures to that of the human body. If you were to walk into a classroom of a large medical school or art institute, you might see several skeletons hanging from brackets, placed there for study purposes. Aside from differences in height, all of them would look very much alike. It would take an expert to determine which had been young or old, male or female. And yet in life, the people whose skeletons these were must have looked quite different. Some were dark, some fair, some wrinkled and others beautiful. Our skeletal structures are predetermined on a fairly rigid common plan, but our flesh-and-blood forms may vary greatly according to how we wish to "clothe" that skeleton. Some will overeat and turn out to be all curves. Some will acquire a deep tan. Some will dye their hair, grow a beard, or even have plastic surgery to alter their appearance. All will use cosmetics to some degree, arrange the hair in patterns, clip fingernails and wash off dirt. We can not resist changing our outward appearance but we can do nothing much about our skeletal forms, unless we are willing to undergo rare and costly bone surgery.

Upon examination, we find that paintings and statues may have certain pre-determined forms, too. These are forms which have been worked out over the centuries by artists in the past, and are now common to works of art. They fall into several distinct categories:

1. *Rectangular forms.* These are commonly found in both painting and sculpture where the main figure is either standing or lying down, or the main scene is vertically or horizontally oriented. Thus, in Example No. 18-1, we find a landscape which turns out to be a series of horizontal rectangles as shown in Example No. 18-2, much resembling the forms and proportions seen in non-objective paintings.

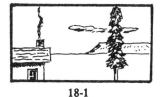

18-1

In Example No. 18-3, the figure

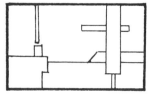

18-2

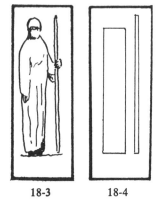

18-3   18-4

forms, in effect, a series of vertically oriented rectangles, as shown in Example No. 18-4. Look carefully at the "Stela of Dedu" (Color Pl. 2) for the vertical rectangular shapes which the artist has used as a major part of his composition. The woman's body, her arm, the man's arm and both legs are elongated rectangles. Even a lock of her hair and his tiny beard are rectangles, as is his staff.

Basically the statue "Child with Cat" (Color Pl. 12) is rectangular in form. Within the overall shape, one finds the rectangular body of the cat, and the smaller shapes of her fingers. The three prominent rectangular areas of the wise men (Color Pl. 5) give this stained-glass window a feeling of height and verticality, even though it is actually square! Note also the strong vertical bars creating horizontal rectangles. These, however, cannot compete in interest with the figures, and hence are not noticed. A final example is the vertical structure of the "Singer Building" (Color Pl. 11),with its dominating central rectangle rising out of a welter of conflicting lines.

2. *Triangular forms.* Structural arrangements feature many kinds of triangles ranging from the nearly vertical to the nearly horizontal. One of the most used types is the "right-triangle" which contains one angle of 90 degrees. This allows the composition to have a vertical, a horizontal, and a diagonal line. The still life sketch, Ex. No. 18-5, gives a clear sense of triangular form, in this case the right triangle. In the next sketch, Ex. No. 18-6, the triangle has no vertical line but instead, two diagonals. The third example No. 18-7 is an inverted triangle, apex pointing downward. Triangles of these and other general types will be found in many pictures. Note the central triangle of Picasso's "Mother and Child" (Color Pl. 13) which almost completely fills the painting surface. Compare this with the taller,

18-5

18-6

more slender "Madonna and Child," Plate No. 6. Then look at the complex series of interlocking triangles which make up the central figure in "Young Woman with Water Jug," (Color Pl. 8). Each triangle is different, and each picture conveys a different sort of mood. The pre-determined structures are alike but the way each artist has chosen to fill out these structures makes each work unique.

18-7

3. *Circular and Oval Forms.* These, as you might suspect, are based upon enclosed curves, and seldom are actual circles but will elongate frequently to oval forms. Many of Raphael's madonnas are conceived as circular.

The structure of the picture, whether oval or triangle or anything else, is always the division of the picture surface itself. Thus, the two sketches, Examples No. 18-8 and No. 18-9, are both derived from the same basic form. One surrounds empty space in an oval shape, the other makes the oval a solid object. Both divide the surface in the same way. The "Bison Lying Down" is clearly an oval shape with irregularities around the edges (Color Pl. 1).

18-8

18-9

4. *Radial Forms.* These are marked by lines which radiate outward from a central point as in Example No. 18-10. In Da Vinci's famous "The Last Supper" there are perspective lines seen radiating from the head of Christ outward in all directions. These at first glance do not seem to center on the head but rather somewhere out in the garden to the rear. Lay a straight edge along any of these lines, however, and you will find that it does point directly to the head of that central figure as seen in Ex. 18-11.

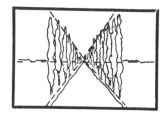

18-10

Such radial forms will serve to concentrate attention on the central point from which they radiate, and for this reason often

18-11

serve for pictures with one strong center of interest. Such a form is seen in "I and My Village" (Color Pl. 14) with lines and spheres grouped around the central point of the cow's mouth and nose! The sprig of flowers points to it, the man's nose forms a radial line from it. Everything seems to revolve about that point.

In sculpture, one may see a radial structure in a human figure with legs outstretched and arms flung upwards, Ex. 18-12.

5. *Combined Forms.* While there are many paintings which exhibit these simpler forms just mentioned, many more are combinations of forms. One section of the painting may be in the radial form while another may show triangular, or any other combination. There may be smaller sub-sections within larger ones, each with its own individual struc-

18-12

ture. Michelangelo's Sistine Chapel ceiling is such a complex form. In Example 18-13 we have a simple sketch showing the possibilities of multi-forms in a single picture. Note how pole and fence divide the picture area into quarters. Each section repeats a different geometric form.

18-13

Visual art forms make use of simple geometric forms from time to time, but more frequently the structures are more complex ones, combining these into a larger, more intricate design.

A good example of combined form is seen in the Rembrandt etching, (Color Pl. 7). The central point of interest is, of course the

heads of the angel and the patriarch, faces almost touching. These are at the hub of a series of lines radiating outward—the wings and the arms together with the shirt front. Below this eye-catching form is the less spectacular form of the kneeling son and the father's robe. The two together form a sort of circular area. Completing the structure is a broad rectangular platform of rock, basin and basket. No single form, but a combination of them make up this intricate picture, as indicated in the sketch, Ex. No. 18-14.

18-14

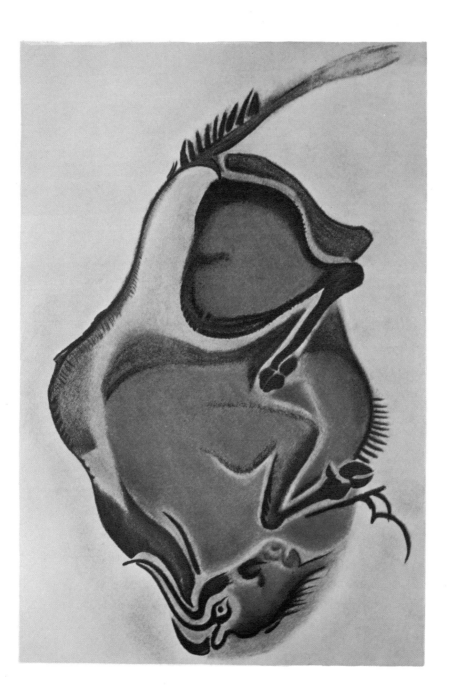

PLATE NO. 1
CM.-197 PUBLISHED AND PRINTED BY
BARTON-COTTON, INC., OF BALTIMORE

BISON LYING DOWN
Prehistoric — Cave Painting

ALTAMIRA, SPAIN

STELA OF DEDU

THE METROPOLITAN MUSEUM OF ART, NEW YORK
(ROGERS FUND, 1916)

PLATE NO. 2
CM-189   PUBLISHED AND PRINTED BY
BARTON-COTTON, INC., OF BALTIMORE

STORM ON THE GREAT BRIDGE

Hiroshige, 1797-1858

THE LEVER HOUSE

PARK AVENUE, NEW YORK
ARCHITECTS: SKIDMORE, OWINGS, MERRILL
(© PHOTO BY JOHN LANGLEY)

PLATE NO. 4
CM-232 PUBLISHED AND PRINTED BY
BARTON-COTTON, INC., OF BALTIMORE

**THE WISE MEN GOING BACK INTO THEIR COUNTRY
AFTER THEIR VISIT TO BETHLEHEM**

CHARTRES CATHEDRAL
(©JAMES R. JOHNSON)

PLATE NO. 5
CM-153 PUBLISHED AND PRINTED BY
BARTON-COTTON, INC., OF BALTIMORE

MADONNA AND CHILD

Giovanni da Milano, 1349-1369

PLATE NO. 6
CM-184 PUBLISHED AND PRINTED BY
BARTON-COTTON, INC., OF BALTIMORE

ACADEMY, FLORENCE

THE SACRIFICE OF ABRAHAM

Rembrandt Van Ryn, 1606-1669

THE FOGG MUSEUM, CAMBRIDGE, MASS.

PLATE NO. 7
CM-199 PUBLISHED AND PRINTED BY
BARTON-COTTON, INC., OF BALTIMORE

YOUNG WOMAN WITH WATER JUG

Jan Vermeer, 1632-1675

THE METROPOLITAN MUSEUM OF ART, NEW YORK
(GIFT OF HENRY G. MARQUAND, 1889)

PLATE NO. 8
CM-170 PUBLISHED AND PRINTED BY
BARTON-COTTON, INC., OF BALTIMORE

THE STARRY NIGHT
Vincent Van Gogh, 1853-1890

PLATE NO. 9
CM-195 PUBLISHED AND PRINTED BY
BARTON-COTTON, INC., OF BALTIMORE

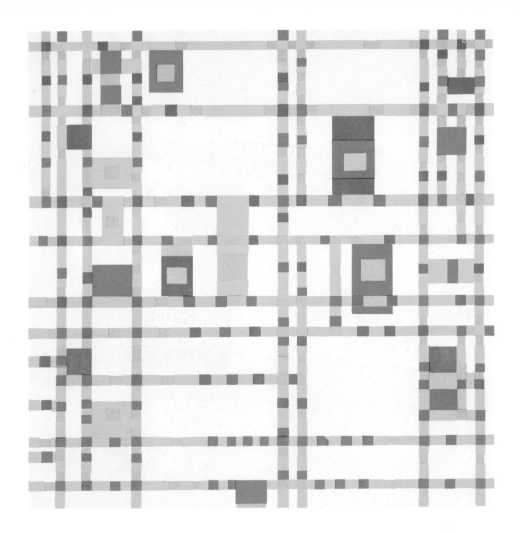

BROADWAY BOOGIE WOOGIE

Piet Mondrian, 1872-1944

PLATE NO. 10
CM-230   PUBLISHED AND PRINTED BY
BARTON-COTTON, INC., OF BALTIMORE

THE MUSEUM OF MODERN ART, NEW YORK

SINGER BUILDING

John Marin, 1875-

MUSEUM OF ART, PHILADELPHIA

PLATE NO. 11
CM-231 PUBLISHED AND PRINTED BY
BARTON-COTTON, INC., OF BALTIMORE

CHILD WITH CAT

William Zorach, 1887-1966

MUSEUM OF MODERN ART, NEW YORK

PLATE NO. 12
CM-187 PUBLISHED AND PRINTED BY
BARTON-COTTON, INC., OF BALTIMORE

MOTHER AND CHILD

Pablo Picasso, Contemporary

THE BALTIMORE MUSEUM OF ART
(CONE COLLECTION)

PLATE NO. 13
CM-151 PUBLISHED AND PRINTED BY
BARTON-COTTON, INC., OF BALTIMORE

I AND MY VILLAGE

Marc Chagall, Contemporary

MUSEUM OF MODERN ART, NEW YORK

PLATE NO. 14
CM-165 PUBLISHED AND PRINTED BY
BARTON-COTTON, INC., OF BALTIMORE

MANCHESTER VALLEY (1914-1918)
Joseph Pickett, Contemporary

MUSEUM OF MODERN ART, NEW YORK
(GIFT OF ABBY ALDRICH ROCKEFELLER)

PLATE NO. 15
CM-154   PUBLISHED AND PRINTED BY
BARTON-COTTON, INC., OF BALTIMORE

REVOLUTION OF THE VIADUCTS

Paul Klee, 1879-1940

HAMBURGER KUNSTHALLE, HAMBURG

PLATE NO. 16
CM-254 PUBLISHED AND PRINTED BY
BARTON-COTTON, INC., OF BALTIMORE

Van Gogh's, "The Starry Night" (Color Pl. 9) also presents a multiple form. Triangles form the hill, tree and steeple. Circles and curves dominate the sky. The cypress tree seems to be the connecting link between earth and the heavens, sharing both the angular and the curvilinear features, as shown in Ex. No. 18-15.

18-15

Finally, Vermeer's "Young Woman With Water Jug" (Color Pl. 8) shows perhaps the most intricate structure of the three mentioned here. The basically triangular figure of the woman is set amidst a number of rectangular forms which serve as a kind of framework. The woman herself is a series of triangular forms one on top of the other. Smaller triangular spaces are seen in the lighted and shadowed areas around her. (Ex. No. 18-16).

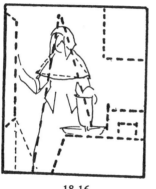

18-16

SUMMARY:

The underlying order which is found in most visual art works is largely a matter of bringing a geometric relationship into the various elements of line, shape, color, texture, and the like. Such relationships provide the work with a kind of "meaning" apart from the one provided by its subject, if any. It is this orderliness which has appealed to something in the viewer's mind which demands it. Normally we do not like works of art which impress us as "chance" happenings, but instead try to find reason, logic, and plan in the arts.

PROBLEMS

Problem One: Find three kinds of trees whose trunk and branch structure is alike but which look different when their leaves are out.

Problem Two: Take a picture of a landscape from a magazine, and laying a sheet of onionskin or other transparent paper on it, sketch the main areas, reducing them to simple geometric forms where possible. Analyze the resulting structure.

Problem Three: Find a painting or advertisement art-work that can be classified as having a rectangular structure or form.

Problem Four: Get a group of your friends together and pose them for photographs using rectangular, triangular, oval or radial forms. Remember that objects other than people can contribute to the total effect. Have prints made and analyze these for form as you would a painting.

Problem Five: On a sheet of paper, draw a "picture frame" and within it a dotted line triangle, fairly large. Now try to fill that triangle with a composition, as in Example No. 18-5, 6, & 7, using different subjects, of course.

Problem Six: Find at least five pictures of statues, and analyze each from the standpoint of its basic structure.

Problem Seven: Examine one wall of your living room, looking at it as if it were the surface of a picture. Make a diagram of the forms and shapes found on that wall, analyze the present "form" of this arrangement, and suggest in a second diagram what could be done to make that side of the room more attractive.

Problem Eight: Find advertising illustrations showing combined form. Indicate these form-areas with dotted pencil lines on the advertisement.

Problem Nine: Analyze the use of the rectangle in Color Plate 15, "Manchester Valley."

Problem Ten: What similarities in structure may be found in Plates 10 and 15, and in Plates 7 and 14?

CHAPTER 19

SPACE STRUCTURES—ARCHITECTURE

The art of architecture cannot be separated from structure. A work in this field *is* a structure. The average person knows more about structure in architecture than he ever will about structure in any of the other arts. He can tell a skyscraper from a warehouse, or a ranch-style home from a Victorian mansion. He must have considerable advantage in this art as compared with opera or ballet, for instance, where his experience has been limited.

Types of Construction

Architecture may conveniently be divided into several basic types. Among them are the wall, the opening, and the shelter.

1. *The Wall.* Since earliest times man has built walls. The simplest kinds were made by piling stones in long mounds such as are still seen in New England where rocks from the field are tossed out onto the edges. Such walls as Example 19-1 (top) are not effective as barriers -- animals or enemies can too easily climb over them. If the stones are cut out and shaped with flat sides, however, the wall may be made steeper, and will offer much better protection. It will stand longer, look better, and serve as a very effective barrier. Such shaped stone is known as "ashlar" masonry, seen in Example 19-1, (bottom).

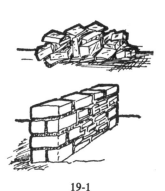

19-1

Walls have been made of many materials. The early American forts were palisades of sharpened logs, but these could too easily be burned or battered down. There have been walls of mud and other kinds of earth but traditionally the stone wall was the best, longest-lasting, and sturdiest medium.

2. *The Opening.* When a wall was built, a way through it had to be left open. This presented serious problems. Enemies could get in if suitable measures were not taken. Mumford suggests that walls

were often built around ancient cities to keep the people in! Control of the gates would, then, be even more important. Several solutions might be offered:

a. The gap opening. One could simply leave a large gap in the wall, but this would be an open invitation for enemies to charge in and to attack. It would be a weak spot in the city's defenses. (Example 19-2)

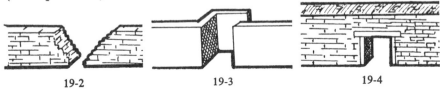

19-2   19-3   19-4

b. The corridor opening. This type of gateway would make defense a lot easier, and slow down any headlong charges, but would also hamper the city's own troops in coming out rapidly, as can be seen in Example 19-3. Furthermore, trade wagons would have a rough time getting in and out.

c. The post and lintel opening. This was actually used for many wall openings (Example 19-4) and had the advantage of offering quick exit and entrance when the gate was open, and equally rapid closing of the gate in danger time. Disadvantages include the fact that a wooden lintel (cross beam) will sag, burn, rot or suffer from termites, causing the wall to collapse. A stone lintel, while resisting these dangers, has to be relatively short; gateways of the post and lintel variety must, therefore, be comparatively narrow.

d. The propped-slab opening. (Example 19-5) This type of opening is a kind of post and lintel in stone but the lintel is now slanted and propped so that it cannot break as easily. The doorways however seem not to have been used widely, possibly because of the rather precarious balance of the slanting stones.

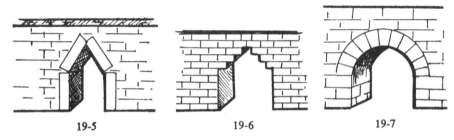

19-5   19-6   19-7

e. The corbel arch opening. In this (Example 19-6) type of construction each layer of stones is projected beyond the one beneath it, much as children build stacks of dominoes. The corbel arch is weak at its center, however, and is not usually extended to ample widths.

f.   The round arch opening.   This was the first successful wide opening which could be roofed over and protected adequately, seen in Example 19-7. The round arch worked because of its wedge-shaped stones which were kept from falling inward by mutually pressing on one other. The arch was later given many forms by medieval and baroque builders. We see in Example 19-8a the lancet arch, 8b the segmental arch, 8c the keyhole, and 8d the trefoil arch. There are many others.

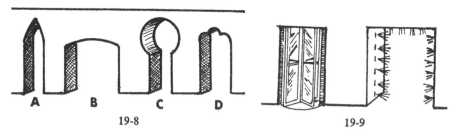

19-8   19-9

g.   Recent openings.   In modern times we have seen many openings built into the "framework" of the wall, a type of construction explained at the end of this chapter. Usually such openings are filled by the customary wooden, glass, or metal doors, but now and then we will find an "air" door which allows people to enter but effectively shuts out dust, cold, insects, animals and noise. (Example 19-9) Air doors are used in stores more than in homes. The revolving door at the left of the air door has been widely used as an effective means of having one's door open and closed at the same time.

3.   *The Shelter.*   Undoubtedly many kinds of early shelters were made by primitive man where he had no caves to live in. These would range from the lean-to in Example 19-10 to the skin-and-frame tepee of Example 19-11, but in no case would these constructions be durable enough to be considered permanent. Without permanence, of course, little architectural development and refinement is possible, so when man wished to build for posterity, he turned to stone for a suitable material.

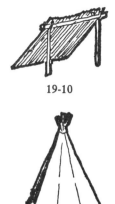

19-10

Here, architects were forced to use post-and-lintel methods because of stone's vulnerability to certain kinds of stress. In order to understand this, let us examine three main kinds of strengths that building materials possess.

19-11

a. Tensile strength is the ability of a material to bend without breaking and to return to its original position again. Stone lacks this strength almost completely. The moment stone bends, it cracks. Wood is much higher in tensile strength, and steel is higher still.

b. Compressive strength allows a material to stand up under heavy vertical pressure. Stone has this strength in abundance and so has steel, but wood has it only in moderation.

c. Shearing strength in a material resists a cutting edge. Roll a heavy piano on metal casters over a wood floor, and you will get "tracks" where the pressure has cut into the wood. Stone or metal possesses more shearing strength than does wood.

19-12

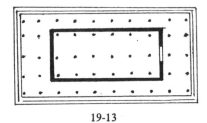

19-13

Because of stone's low tensile strength, it was used at first in post-and-lintel construction. Great numbers of upright posts or columns were required to hold up the stone roof of a building, and this severely limited the interior space. The rooms inside a Greek temple, for instance, would be dark and crowded, of no use for large gatherings or congregations. (Examples 19-12; 19-13). Greek worship was held either individually inside the building or, if in larger groups, on the steps outside. The accompanying drawings show the numbers of columns needed to support this type of building. In example 19-14 we see a compromise between the need for interior light and the need for close-set supports. A building could be constructed with an open inner court, and thus all rooms might have light and air. Fortunately the Greek and Roman climate was mild enough to make this sort of building feasible!

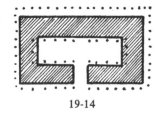

19-14

Architecture was given a great thrust forward by the Romans. Their builders discovered how to use the arch for other purposes than just gateways in walls. Their innovations took three forms:

1. *The arcade.* It was well-known to all builders of ancient times that the arch stones exerted a great outward pressure. If an arch were set on pillars, or even if its base rested on the ground, and if its

sides were not heavily propped or "buttressed," it would fall in. In Example 19-15 we see the typical Roman triumphal arch, a single arch used for victory parades and monuments. Note the heavy sides, necessary to keep its arch from collapsing. The arch at 19-16, lacking side props, is falling in.

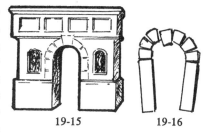

19-15   19-16

The Romans reasoned that a pair of arches on either side of a central arch, each pressing on its side, would effectively serve to keep it from falling in. A long line of such arches was called an "arcade," and could be used for a bridge, aqueduct, or wall. Of course, the arches at either end had to be buttressed by some heavy wall or perhaps a hillside. The Romans built many of these, perhaps the greatest being the "Pont du Gard" aqueduct which carried drinking water for 60 miles to a Roman city in

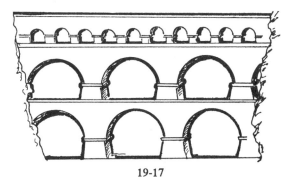

southern France. From stream bed to the top it rose 160 feet in height, with individual arches 60 feet high! (Example 19-17) All that remains of this great architectural marvel is that portion which crosses the Gard River. All the rest has been dismantled

19-17

centuries ago and used to build medieval castles, forts, churches and roads! Another form of arcade lies in a complete circle. (Example 19-18) In this way each arch supports the ones on each side of it, and no buttressing is needed. This clever usage is still popular in stadiums and sports arenas. The famous Roman Colosseum is built in this general fashion.

2. *The vault.* Romans also found a way to use the arch for roofing over a building. By placing a series of arches one in front of the other, they achieved tunnel-like chambers which had the great advantage of requiring no supporting posts, such as earlier Greek buildings of the post-and-lintel style needed. (Example 19-19)

19-18

19-19

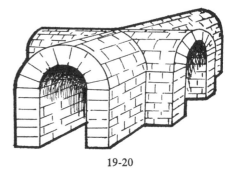

19-20

A later development (Example 19-20) added a second vault crossing the first at right angles. This allowed the original "barrel vault" to be made brighter inside from light entering along its sides. It also permitted more than one directional axis for the building. This new development was called the "cross vault" or "groin vault."

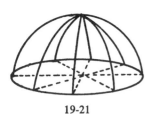

19-21

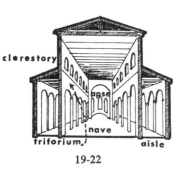

19-22

3. *The dome.* Roman engineers found that if a series of arches were built with their foundation stones arranged in a circle, and with one common top or "crown" the result would be a dome. This, too, afforded an excellent roof for a large area, allowing free open space beneath it. Domes as large as 150 feet across were built by the Romans. (Example 19-21).

When the Roman empire was replaced by a succession of patchwork kingdoms which finally led to the Holy Roman Empire of medieval times, architecture was advanced to new heights by the church builders. The first step was the establishing of a kind of early Christian church style known as the "basilica."

(Example 19-22) It had to be easy to build, and comparatively inexpensive because the early church was an infant organization still, and had little funds. On the other hand, there was a constant demand for new buildings. The basilica had a simple barn-like form. Its central "nave" was flanked by arcaded aisles on each side. The altar sat at the far end. The open space above the aisles let in light, and was called the "clerestory," a "clear-story" in fact. The ceiling was made of wooden beams and the roof of tile. Walls were of stone.

As the Roman church grew larger and developed a more elaborate ritual, the basilica grew more elaborate, too. The far end was pushed back and given a rounded shape. This "apse" now contained enough space for more elaborate ceremonies in the worship service. Added space on either side was created by "transepts" which extended cross-like arms from the main body of the church. (Example 19-23).

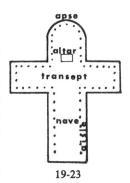

19-23

As builders sought to achieve better churches, they felt the need to get rid of the beamed ceilings and replace them with permanent, fireproof stone. The Roman vaulted ceiling was too heavy and expensive, and demanded very thick walls for support. Builders hit upon a lighter method called "ribbed vaulting." (Example 19-24) In this kind of ceiling, four heavy columns or "piers" were erected, and arches were extended both laterally and diagonally to interconnect them. The space between the piers was known as a "bay." After the rib arching was complete, a filling of stone and plaster was used to fill in the spaces between the ribs. The basilica could now have a permanent ceiling and roof, without the costly, thick walls and heavy supports necessary to earlier construction.

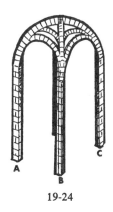

19-24

Out of this ribbed arching technique came the dramatic and beautiful pointed arch, which has come to be known as the "Gothic" arch. When engineers built the ribbed arches, they soon became aware that the diagonal arches were longer and hence higher than were the lateral ones! In Example 19-24, the arch from A to B is not as long as that from A to C. Since both arches are semicircles, the longer one will be higher, too! Builders had two choices, leave the ceiling with irregular heights of arches, giving it a somewhat wavy look, or increase the height of the shorter arches. In Example 19-25, both arches have the same base measurement. If we are to make B taller than A, it can only be done by pointing the arch center.

Gradually arches grew more pointed still, as builders discovered that the greater the point, the less the outward thrust, and hence the lighter the walls could be. As this "Gothic"

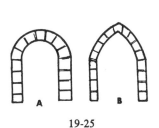

19-25

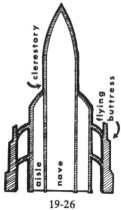

19-26

style developed, (Example 19-26) the buildings grew higher and higher, with weight and thrust carefully channeled downward through arching and buttressing to the ground. Such a building could be described as a stone skeleton with glass between its ribs. It would be light, graceful and tall. Gothic cathedrals soared up to heights of 300 feet, with ceilings of more than 100 feet! All of this construction was stone, of course, with no metal or concrete to help. The stones were held in place solely by pressures!

Although styles in architecture changed after the 1400s, no new advances of the kind we have just seen took place for many centuries. Only in recent times have new building methods again been introduced. These had to await the coming of the iron age! Metal was, of course, available in small quantities from ancient times but it never was cheap enough to use as a building material. The Pantheon, a great domed temple still standing in the city of Rome was said to have a porch built of bronze beams, a unique construction in ancient architecture. So valuable was metal to the ancients that these were later removed and melted down for coins or weapons!

19-27

With the coming of the "industrial revolution" in the mid-1800s, mining and smelting produced metals in quantity. Bridges were made of iron, and architects learned iron-frame techniques from engineers. Gradually the metal-frame building was developed, the first really new construction technique in centuries. (Example 19-27)

With a strong and light skeleton framework, a building could be built to almost any height because its walls were not required to hold it up. Instead, these "curtain walls" were merely hung on the metal framework. This new frame-and-skin technique was basically much like the old Indian tepee! At first, the architects did their best to hide the frame beneath encrustations of Greek columns and Roman arches. In the early 1900s the "eclectic" style permitted architects to draw from many styles of the past in working out the details of their buildings. These older structures are fascinating to study because the practiced observer can pick out details of this or that former civilization incorporated into the building.

One of the first architects to break away from the past, and design buildings which revealed their metal frame construction was the American, Louis Sullivan. His Wainwright Building in St. Louis, Missouri is a landmark in architectural progress and, although built in 1891, remains surprisingly up-to-date looking today. (Example 19-28)

With the modern age many new building techniques were developed. They include the following:

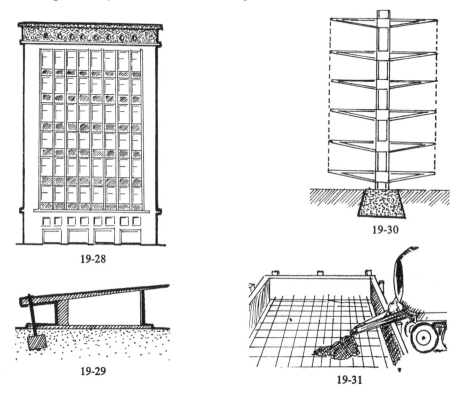

19-28

19-30

19-29

19-31

1. *Cantilevering.* The great tensile strength of metal, especially steel, could be used to extend it unsupported over a considerable span. This allowed builders to design homes with great glass walls as in Example No. 19-29 or buildings whose floors were suspended from a central spine like branches on a tree trunk. (Example 19-30). Such buildings are excellent in places where earthquakes form a hazard. They will shake but not topple.

2. *Concrete and Metal.* The Romans had a kind of volcanic ash mixture which would harden to a rocklike substance if properly mixed. Today's builder has the great advantage of being able to supplement the stone-like compressive strength of concrete with the tensile strength

of iron. He does so by pouring the cement over a metal mesh-work, embedding the metal in the concrete, as in example 19-31. Driveways and streets always have metal in them to prevent cracking. In Example 19-32 we see the mold or form for a concrete post or pier which will hold up a building. The iron rods will give the concrete tensile strength while the concrete will stiffen the softer metal. Thus each material helps the other with the result that a strong, inexpensive constructional method is possible.

3. *Prestressed Concrete.* In this concrete-and-metal combination, the rods are no longer of soft iron but of high-grade steel. These steel rods are stretched in a heavy form until there is a lot of tension on them. (Example 19-33) Concrete is then poured into the form and as it hardens, the tension on the rods is released so that it compresses the concrete into a much harder compaction. The result is a concrete beam of great strength capable of supporting a heavy roof or floor. The added strength comes from the pressure of the rods just as one can pick up a number of books off a desk by squeezing them together from both ends. (Example 19-34). A similar situation exists if you thread buttons on a strong string and tighten it. You will have a kind of "button beam" or rod because of the interior tension of the string.

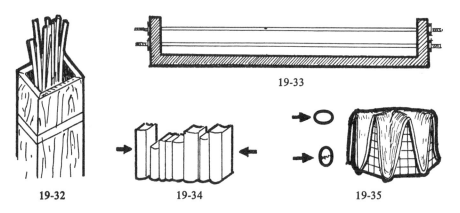

19-33

19-32   19-34   19-35

4. *Shell Construction.* Engineers have long been fascinated by the great strength of the egg shell. Though fragile when squeezed along its sides, it is exceptionally strong if the pressure is put on its ends. Try breaking an egg by pressing it endways between your hands. Most adults cannot break an egg this way! The secret of its strength lies in its shape. Architects have copied the eggshell shape in structures like Example 19-35 which can be built with amazingly thin concrete, yet retain great strength. Notice that there is no traditional dividing line between walls and roof.

5. *Folded Construction.* The strength of a thin material is greatly enhanced by folding it so that it contains a number of parallel creases. In Example 19-36A, we have a simple sheet of notebook paper. If any weight is placed on the edge, the paper will collapse. But fold that sheet repeatedly, as at "B," and you will find it able to support several pounds of weight! This principle has been successfully used in the construction of roofs, as shown at "C." It is also a familiar source of rigidity in cardboard boxes, "D."

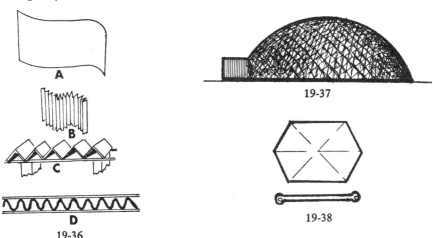

19-37

19-36

19-38

6. *Geodesic Construction.* One of America's leading contemporary architects and engineers is R. Buckminster Fuller, inventor of the geodesic dome. His structures are seen throughout the world, and are the largest, lightest, cheapest and strongest yet invented (Example 19-37). Fuller's domes are basically made from two components, metal rods and hexagonal plates. (Example 19-38.) By bolting the rods together in a certain pattern, and joining the plates into the rod network, a group of relatively unskilled builders under the supervision of an engineer can erect a Fuller dome in a fairly short time. This makes the structures ideal for backward countries not yet possessing an advanced technology. The domes apparently have no size limitations. Their inventor claims he could roof New York City's Manhattan Island if given the funds!

A few older building techniques were omitted from the previous pages because they required wood rather than stone as building material. Wood has seldom been the medium of great architecture, yet certain things were learned in its use which today have been applied to metal construction. One of the early uses of wood in building was the "post-and-beam" method so reminiscent of Shakespeare's England. The more permanent shelters in our own Jamestown Colony were built in this fashion, as were houses in Boston and other early seaboard cities. (Example 19-39) This method shares many features with the post-and-lintel construction used by the Greeks, but with one important

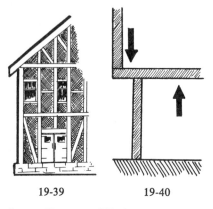

19-39   19-40

addition. The beams do not just sit on top of the posts but are pegged to them, as are the triangular braces. The whole wooden framework is interlocked to make a fairly rigid structure. Stone could scarcely be used in this way because of its low tensile strength. In actual construction, the heavy posts and beams were carefully cut, notched, holes bored and pegs shaped. Then, with the aid of many helpers, the framework was put together. Afterwards, the walls were filled in between the wooden beams, windows and doors set in, and a roof added. In early America, barns were built in this way, and neighbors were brought together by the prospect of a "barn raising" with its fun and feasting. The manpower was needed to lift the heavy timbers into place!

Pictures of early post-and-beam houses often show the upper story wider than the lower one. Various theories have been advanced to account for this, but the most logical is that by extending the beam out beyond the post on which it rested, and adding the weight of a wall and roof, this beam would receive a corresponding upward thrust inside the house. This would aid greatly in preventing floor-sag, and in reducing the necessity of a supporting post in the center of the room somewhere. If this theory is correct, these early builders were already acquainted with the working principle of the cantilever! (Example 19-40)

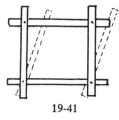
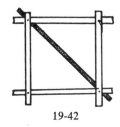
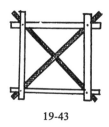

19-41   19-42   19-43

Another technique of wood-engineering has to do with the "truss" brace. Any young boy who has ever built with wooden laths knows that a square of such strips is an unstable figure. Any slight pressure can flatten it out. (Example 19-41) The easiest way to brace it is to put one diagonal in it, creating two triangles. (Example 19-42) Now it is much harder to collapse. A second diagonal in the opposite direction will create 4 triangles and add strength. (Example 19-43) We see this sort of truss bracing in bridges and beams. (Example 19-44) Often it can be seen in basements as one looks at the underside of the upstairs floors (if the basement ceiling is unfinished).

19-44

This same sort of construction may be found in the attic of the house, but with an important difference; the attic often contains usable space, and so special kinds of roof bracing have been developed to permit that space to be used.

At first (Example 19-45) a single center-brace (the "king post") strengthened the roof by making two triangles where one large one had been before. This seriously cut down the usefulness of the attic, so the king post gave way to two "queen posts." Now there were three triangles and, in addition, open space down the center. (Example 19-46)

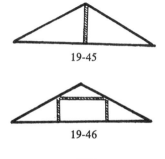

19-45

19-46

19-47

Seeking ways to enlarge this, builders hit upon the idea of conforming the roof to the larger attic area, and the popular "gambrel" roof was born. The three triangles are still there but the attic room is much larger. Barns often use gambrel roofs for added storage space. In a house, the side triangles make excellent storage closets. (Example 19-47).

PROBLEMS:

Problem One: Locate any free standing walls (not in buildings) in your general area. Find out what they are made of, and how they are made. Include fences of all types, comparing and contrasting them with walls in a number of ways.

Problem Two: Look up some of the famous walls of history (Hadrian's Wall, the Walls of Jericho, etc.) to find out their construction and function.

Problem Three: Find several types of openings in walls, noting their constructional features, purposes, effectiveness, advantages and disadvantages. Consider special problems of entrance and exit for theatres, schools, prisons, submarines, cars, homes, and so on.

Problem Four: Find traces of early architectural features in or on buildings in your community. Sketch these, identify their location, and tell what style each represents. Use doorways, windows, corner masonry, cornices (roof caps), porch moldings, etc., for your clues!

Problem Five: Illustrate (by sketching a real example you have seen) the three types of building material strengths. Show examples where each strength failed, causing resultant damage.

Problem Six: Find out more about how the Romans built their great aqueducts, their domes, arches, and vaulted rooms. Pay special attention to dimensions, comparing these with large structures you are familiar with.

Problem Seven: Find, if you can, the location of any nearby vaulted ceilings, arcades, domes, or colonnades. Examine them carefully and compare with pictures of the original usage of these by ancient builders.

Problem Eight: Try to find a nave, apse, transept, clerestory, or other features of medieval church construction in some local churches. Compare the local example with the original styles. What accounts for the differences?

Problem Nine: Find a local building which has a metal skeleton framework. You may never see the actual metal -- it will be hidden beneath brick facing. How does it reveal its underlying metal frame?

Problem Ten: Find examples locally of cantilevering, prestressed concrete, or folded concrete construction. Show how these methods were superior (in each case) to more ordinary use of the same materials.

Problem Eleven: Find cement being poured (foundations for a new home, driveway, pavement, etc.) and watch to see how and when metal is used to strengthen it. Report on your observations.

Problem Twelve: Look for wood or metal truss construction. Sketch the pattern of triangles, and find out the function of each such instance.

Problem Thirteen: Explore your attic and basement, noting constructional features of your house. Sketch and explain each in a short paper.

Problem Fourteen: Experiment with folded paper and glue, making rigid constructions which will support heavy loads. Or use balsa wood and airplane glue to make miniature bridges, towers, etc. A scientific weight-testing experiment will be convincing proof of the truss technique's strength. (Example 19-48)

19-48

CHAPTER 20

TIME STRUCTURES—MUSIC

Music comes to us by way of our ears, which receive a flood of highly elaborate sounds lasting for sometimes many minutes. We are expected to make some sense out of all this, having stored it up in our memory and subjected it to some kind of mental analysis. Fortunately for us the difficulty of this seemingly hopeless task is greatly reduced by the practice of composers writing in certain well-known patterns. When one is familiar with these, he has a much better chance of analyzing what he hears. He may become temporarily confused, but can recognize a familiar landmark and re-orient himself. He is like the person who has a fairly good map of the city committed to memory. Put him anywhere within the city limits and within a few minutes of driving he will cross a main road, sight a well-known building, or otherwise get his bearings. Without his mental map he'd remain lost much longer. The purpose of this chapter is to provide several of the most useful musical "maps."

Popular Music Forms.

1. The popular song contains probably the most used form in music, the so-called AABA form. Each letter stands for a section of eight bars or measures. Three of these are virtually identical, with one slightly different. Millions of popular tunes have been written on this pattern, including the one in Example 20-1.

Note the popular song form invariably has sixteen measures to it. You can count your way through it knowing confidently that on bar five you'll hear the opening tune again, at bar nine will come the "bridge" or B section, and the original refrain will be heard at bar thirteen once more.

2. The Blues is another type of form with which we are all familiar. Instead of having four sections this simple musical structure has only three. Example 20-2 shows this simple blues form, and also presents the invariable chord pattern which accompanies it. In popular songs many different chords are used; in the traditional, only the I, the IV and the V, and always in the same pattern. Simple and unvarying as this form is, it has provided many composers with the framework

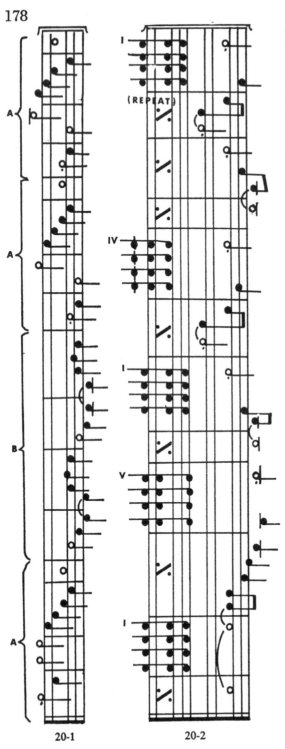

20-1   20-2

on which to hang some exciting and memorable music. Notice the "syncopation" pattern in the rhythm which is found in the second measure and other places. The second note of the melody must be played before the second chord in the left hand. Try practicing this by tapping both hands on your knees. The left hand on the left knee goes along steadily, like the ticking of a clock, setting up the important "beat" of the music. If popular music or the blues lacks this steady meter, it's not worth much. The right hand on the right knee taps out the varying rhythms of the melody. This takes coordination and practice.

3. Sectional Forms. The popular songs and the blues are two kinds of sectional forms. There are many other kinds, some of them quite lengthy and elaborate. Among them are:

a. Marches. As you listen to a march, you will often hear several well-defined sections, each one repeated. This makes marches easy to listen to, which is one reason people enjoy them. The structure of a march looks something like this:

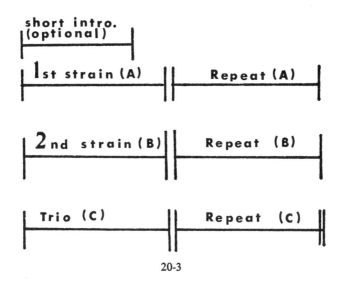

20-3

This pattern of repeated sections may be rearranged slightly by the composer from one march to the other, but will serve as a guideline for listening. The "Trio" section is often marked by a change of key (it is built on a new scale) and is also softer, at least the first time it is played. Sometimes a fourth strain is added.

b. Dances. In the days of royal courts, gentlemen in knee breeches, and ladies in powdered wigs, many dances were popular which have since been almost forgotten. The music for these dances has survived, however, in the "Dance Suites" of the 17th and 18th Centuries. Such dances as the *Allemande, Sarabande, Gavotte, Minuet,* and *Gigue* had music composed for them by Bach, Handel and others. The Dance Suites consisted of usually five or six separate, short pieces each of which has the same structure, shown in Example 20-4.

```
|    (A)    || (A) Rep't ||    (B)    || (B) Rep't |
|            V ||          V ||V         I ||V          I
 I            V   I          V   V         I   V          I
```

20-4

It is interesting to compare the makeup of a Dance Suite with that of a suite of furniture, since both are collections of matching things. In a bedroom suite of furniture one looks for similarity of materials, colors, lines; in the musical suite all the dances will have similar forms, will be played by the same instrument or instruments. There will not be one dance for harpsichord, another for organ, a third for orchestra, etc. In furniture one wants matching styles; in music a suite will not have some old-fashioned dances and some modern ones mixed. The furniture must be matching in size, and so must the music. There will be no very long or very short pieces in the Suite of Dances. The furniture in a bedroom suite is similar in purpose -- there would not be a kitchen table included. In the Dance Suite all the pieces (with the possible exception of a short introduction) will be for dancing.

There is one area today where a kind of dance suite is still used, and this is in square dancing. The old formal dances have been speeded up but still exist in the prescribed patterns and geometric figures of this style of dance. Square-dance callers, in fact, still use some of the 18th Century terms. When the call "element left and promenade" is heard, dancers begin a kind of interweaving step which goes back to the original Allemande. The term "element" is really "allemande" in modern form. Another term "do-se-do" comes from the French "dos-a-dos" meaning "back to back." The dancers make a turn with their backs to each other. Square dancing is the only dancing left today in which prescribed patterns are followed by all the dancers on the floor at the same time. Its attraction is possibly largely due to this fact.

Listen to 18th Century Dance Suites by Bach, Handel, and others. They sometimes go under the name of "Partitas" but are the same forms. Note the exact repetitions and unvarying forms of these pieces. Then compare them to the square dance music of today, and many formal similarities will be found.

    c.   Hymns.   The hymns used in our churches are made up of short musical sections; many repetitions, and simple formal structures. As the verses are sung, the form is repeated over and over. Some hymns may be in AABA form, others in ABBA, ABCA, and so on. Hymns offer a fascinating variety of easily discovered structures.

In many hymnals, there is a numbering system used which classifies all hymns according to the number of syllables in each line of the verse. Thus, Isaac Watts' poem, *"Joy to the World"* has the numbers 8.6.8.6. to indicate alternate lines of eight and six syllables. Fortunately, the composer who set those lines to music, Handel, elected to follow quite another pattern with his music (see Example 10-5), which transformed a sing-songy poem into a great hymn. This sort of hymn setting is highly unusual, however. Most tunes follow the verse patterns so closely that any hymn tune carrying a certain numbering may be switched with any other of the same numbering. Thus it would

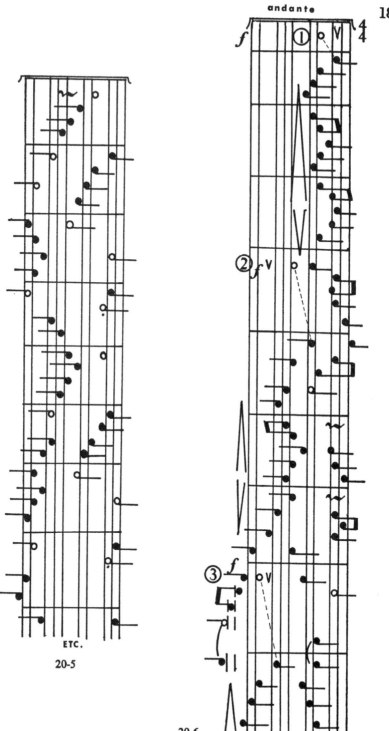

ETC.

20-5

20-6

be possible to sing the words of *"Joy to the World"* to the tunes we now know as *"Amazing Grace," "O For a Thousand Tongues to Sing," "The Lord's My Shepherd," "Awake My Soul," "There is a Green Hill,"* and nearly a hundred more hymns! It would, of course, be possible to sing the words of these hymns to the tune of *"Joy to the World,"* but with rather startling results! Handel's tune is too individualistic to fit most other verses.

4. Contrapuntal forms. The term "counterpoint" has long been used to designate a kind of music featuring two or more semi-independent melodies or parts of melodies which are sounding at the same time. A lot of the popular songs we hear consist of one tune accompanied by chords. Contrapuntal music features several competing tunes. The essential difference is that of a conversation in which one person does all the talking and the others agree with him, and a conversation in which several people argue, offer opinions, generate contrasting thoughts and ideas, and so on. The latter will be harder to follow but may be more interesting. The former may be interesting, too, if the single speaker (or melody) is good enough. In Example 20-5 we have the familiar tune from Example 20-1 set against another tune in simple counterpoint. Now, instead of just one melody to keep track of, there are two. Some popular songs will have a first part sung by a boy and a second part sung by a girl. Then the two parts are put together to form interesting counterpoint. In essence, this is one of the attractions of the jazz style known as "Dixieland." A tune is selected which all the players know. The band usually plays this tune together several times, and then the various players take solos in which they "improvise" their own versions of the same tune. Meanwhile the "rhythm section" (which is really a *meter* section) keeps the steady beat and plays the underlying chords of the tune against which the soloists are improvising. Instruments in this section are usually piano, bass, drums and guitar. When the soloists have had their turn, the final climax features all the melody instruments playing individual solos at the same time, creating a kind of four or five-part counterpoint. The trumpet will be sounding the melody, the clarinet is improvising fancy runs and trills above him, the trombone is playing a "countermelody" down lower, and so on. This contrapuntal climax still is based on the original blues, or the AABA form, and still follows the original chord progressions. But the style is that of counterpoint.

a. The Canon. Although counterpoint can be written within the framework of a sectional piece, it is often featured in separate forms of its own. One of the most common is the "canon," in which the original melody chases itself about in the fashion of a "round." We have all sung rounds in such tunes as *"Row, Row, Row Your Boat"* and *"Three Blind Mice."*

b. The Fugue. This is a more elaborate kind of contrapuntal form, something like a complicated round, in which the melody follows itself along, but changes keys as it does so. In a complete fugue, we find more or less distinct sections, so that the form diagram looks somewhat as follows:

A. Exposition:

> *Theme (melody).......(counterpoint to Theme)....*
>
> *Theme (in new key)...........*
>
> *Theme (in first key)......*

B. Development:

> *Parts of the theme and its counterpoint are mixed together and "developed" for some time*

C. Restatement:

> *Theme heard again more or less as at first ... ending.*

One can usually spot a fugue by the fact that the theme is heard all alone, and is then joined by a second version of itself, and possibly a third and fourth later. Example 20-6 shows the same familiar tune as it might be used if it were the beginning of a fugue.

5. Variation Forms. From music's earliest days, the variation has been a popular way of lengthening a musical idea. We hear this most often in jazz music where different players "take choruses," that is, improvise on the original tune. As each player presents his version of the melody, a set of variations comes into being, albeit by a group of "composers" rather than just one.

An individual composer setting out to write a series of variations has a number of techniques at his disposal for varying the tune. Taking the familiar melody of Example 20-1, the writer might decide to place it in a "minor key," giving it a somewhat melancholy sound, as heard in Example 20-7. Another variation technique consists of simply adding more notes to the melody, being careful not to obscure the original tune. This method was popular for brass instrument solos a few generations ago, and is still heard occasionally. In Example 20-8 we see the melody given this treatment, with arrows pointing to the tones of the original tune.

Popular though this "ornamental" style of variation was, it became too obvious for the more sophisticated audiences of the later era, and was gradually replaced by more subtle techniques. In these, most generally the old melody was transformed into a series of new ones,

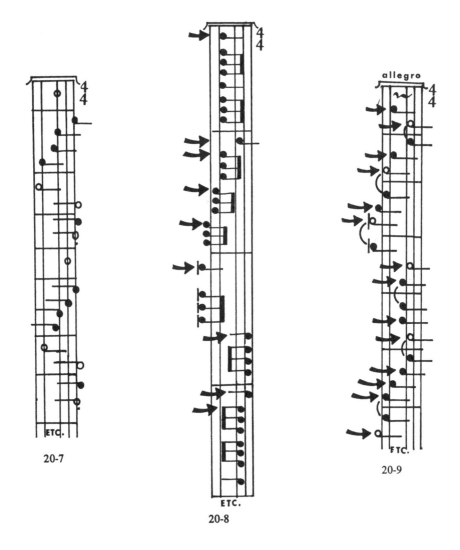

20-7

20-8

20-9

rather than being retained clearly in each succeeding variation. Example 20-9 shows one way in which this might be accomplished. Here we see the original tune marked again with arrows, but it has been syncopated and changed rhythmically until, though it still keeps the notes of the original melody, it is scarcely recognizable.

Variations might also be made by changing the basic meter from the original four-four to something else, such as three-four, five-four, or perhaps six-eight. Composers of the 1900s became quite adept at deriving new melodies from old, and in changing the total style and character of a melody while still retaining some connection with it.

The idea of variations is not, of course, confined to music. It has been used in literature and the cinema, to name two other art areas. In each case, the basic idea is the same; start with a theme, and "develop" it through a series of short episodes, each of which is connected in some way with the original. Musical variations will contain more separate numbers in one set (sometimes upwards of thirty or forty) than literary or cinematic ones. Even the visual arts are not immune to the fascination of variation forms. The suburban housing development, with its myriad look-alike houses employs some slight variation in choice of front doors, paint colors, positioning, and so on. A much more valid kind of variation would be that of the painter of abstractions who, like Miro or Picasso, creates dozens of variations on a single still-life arrangement. It is interesting to look at several of these side-by-side, and see the many devices which the painter uses in creating different variations on a single theme. A study of visual variations will reinforce one's understanding of musical and literary ones, and vice-versa.

6. Sonata-Allegro Form. The musical forms discussed up to this point are all similar in that they deal with only one distinct melody at a time. To be sure, the sectional forms may employ different tunes in different sections but these are kept compartmentalized rather carefully. The contrapuntal forms play one melody against itself so that it sounds like several but is not. The variation forms develop new melodies from old but here again the source is a single tune to start with.

The Sonata-Allegro form is different from the others because it employs two or more themes, contrasting and comparing them in what can only be called a dramatic fashion. Just as a play with conflicting characters is more exciting than a monolog, so a Sonata-Allegro form with its contrasting themes has more dramatic possibilities than a single-melody composition.

In the Sonata-Allegro form we may begin with the slow introduction. If the music does begin slowly, we will know that we are hearing the introduction. When the music speeds up, or if it starts at a moderate tempo, we are hearing the opening theme.

This first theme is followed by a second one, contrasting in nature. If the first is vigorous, the second is likely to be gentler. If the first leaps and skips, the second will probably stick to scale passages. The second theme often is in a different key from the first. The section featuring the two (or more) themes is called the "Exposition" as in the fugue, and is sometimes repeated note for note, except for the introduction.

In the "Development" section which follows, the themes are varied, explored, taken apart and worked with in various ways. The first theme may get most of this development, especially in Sonatas written before 1800. As later composers began to develop themes more fully, whole groups of themes were introduced and extended. It was as if a playwright began using larger and larger casts of characters, working them all into his plots with equal emphasis!

At the close of the Development section, the composer takes us back to the two themes again, often in reverse order; that is, presenting the second theme first and the first or main theme last. He may end with a short final section called a "coda."

The total form looks in diagram like Example 20-10.

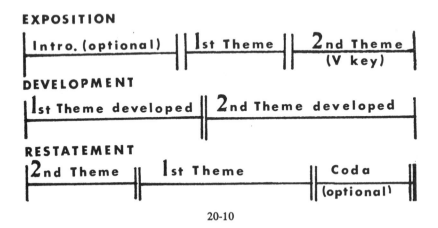

EXPOSITION

| Intro. (optional) | 1st Theme | 2nd Theme (V key) |

DEVELOPMENT

| 1st Theme developed | 2nd Theme developed |

RESTATEMENT

| 2nd Theme | 1st Theme | Coda (optional) |

20-10

The theme which has been used throughout this chapter would possibly be more suitable for a second theme of a Sonata-Allegro form. It is simple, lyrical, of not great consequence. A first theme is generally more dramatic, and would likely show greater rhythmic vigor, such as is seen in Example 20-11.

The short, abrupt repetitions of this theme will offer contrast to the smoother melodic line of the other. In the development section, this first theme can be easily broken up into its component motives, which may be developed separately. The rhythmic motive A, the leaping motive B, and the upward pattern of C are all capable of being extended indefinitely. This is the kind of "playing around" with parts of a theme which composers have used so frequently for development sections in music. It is to be found in sonatas ranging from the short, simpler works of Haydn (1732-1809) to the longer compositions in this form by Beethoven (1770-1827) and Brahms (1833-1897). Composers are still relying upon this method for developing their themes.

There is some confusion in terms regarding this musical form. What we have illustrated is, actually, the first piece or "movement" in a larger structure known variously as the *Sonata* (when written for a solo instrument), the *Quartet* (for a group of two violins, viola, and cello), the *Symphony* (when written for orchestra or band), and the *Concerto* (when written for solo instrument accompanied by orchestra or band). We have often heard of "a Mozart Sonata" or "a Beethoven Concerto," or the "F Major Symphony." All of these are compositions which begin with a piece in the Sonata-Allegro form, the "first movement." The second movement would likely be of a slow, song-like nature. A third movement would be lighter, more dance-like perhaps, and the fourth movement would be lively and vigorous, perhaps using the Sonata-Allegro form again. It is not unusual for one of the movements of a sonata to be a Theme and Variations, an ABA form, or a Minuet, especially in works written before 1800.

20-11

In summary, we might compare our full sonata with a four-act play. The acts offer varying settings, contrasting moods, different characters, yet all are related. In later sonatas of the 1800s it is not unusual to find the same themes showing up in all four movements, just as characters in a play. The complete form (especially in its full orchestral version, the *Symphony)* was able to sustain the listener's attention for up to an hour of uninterrupted listening. The variety and logic of this form has made it a great favorite of composers since it was perfected in the middle 1700s.

7. Program Music. Although program music is not a formal structure in the strict sense of the term, it is a kind of logical way to make the music have meaning for the listener. Program music is music which has a subject. Just as a painting may either be with or without a subject, so music may be written to tell a story or describe a scene, or it may have no relation to things other than itself at all. Most music is non-objective. Its beauty comes from its tones, rhythms, harmonies, timbres, and so on. But from time to time generations of composers have rediscovered music's ability to suggest and describe things.

One such period of composition began in the early 1800s and lasted until around 1900. This was the age of the industrial revolution, which produced such vast wealth and brought into being a great middle class with money and property. With money came more leisure time and a desire for cultural advantages. Composers who formerly had been patronized by the nobility now found their source of income in this growing middle class, and began writing music of a less reserved, less intellectual style. The new "Romantic Era" of the 1800s stressed the emotions, featured large and extravagant orchestras, dashing virtuosi pianists who cultivated exaggerated styles and played the most difficult music to show off their technique, flamboyant "grand operas," and anything else which would attract attention. In the midst of all this ferment and showmanship the many excellent composers of the time wrote enduring music with solid craftsmanship and great talent.

Program music, like any other kind, can be good and it can be bad. Like painting with a subject, however, music with a subject can fool people into thinking it is good when it isn't. They follow the subject so intently they may forget to listen to the music at all. As one example, take the fantastic career of one Monsieur Jullien, a French conductor who brought an orchestra to America in the early 1800s. Although he played some fine music, his chief attraction was an unbelievable piece of program music called *"The Fireman's Quadrille"* which described a sleeping village in which a fire breaks out in the middle of the night. Bells are heard, the tempo quickens, horses' hoofs can be heard galloping, the fire engines are brought up, and so on. At the climax of this noble work Jullien arranged for a real fire to break out in the stage curtains, at which time scores of real firemen would rush in to put it out. The composition finished with the firemen beating time with their axes on anvils ranged around the stage while the orchestra played the closing strains of the music!

Americans of that day and age flocked by the thousands to hear this piece of music. Its vivid story made it understandable where a much better piece might have been over their heads. On the other side of the Atlantic, at about the same time, another Frenchman, Hector Berlioz, was to write an equally strange work called *"The Fantastic Symphony."* Its story concerns a young man who is in despair over a love affair. He has highly emotional daydreams about his sweetheart, which are described with great effectiveness by the music. He wanders out into the country, listens to shepherds piping, experiences a thunderstorm, wanders about and finally in a fit of depression tries to commit suicide by an overdose of opium. In his drugged dreams he sees his sweetheart at a ball but doesn't get to dance with her, apparently. Then, all of a sudden, he discovers he has killed her and is on trial for his life. The death sentence is pronounced, and he is guillotined as the music vividly portrays his march to the scaffold and final thoughts. Berlioz spared no details, and even depicts the victim's head bouncing off into the basket! As if this were not sufficient, the final fifth movement brings our hero down to hell where a tremendous celebration is in progress complete with hideous screechings and wailings. The climax comes when the Queen of Hell is brought in, and who should she be but the beloved sweetheart, now greatly transformed.

Program music, attractive as its story may be, is only as good as its musical ideas and construction. *"The Fireman's Quadrille"* has long since been forgotten. *"The Fantastic Symphony"* is still played regularly because it is well written, and story or no story, is worth listening to.

The reader should not think that these are the only forms or structures music possesses. So long as composers write, new forms will be invented and used. Others which have been used were not mentioned because they may have been little used in recent times, or because they are closely related to the ones chosen for explanation in this chapter. All music has some type of form. This is one of the joys of listening, to be able to find that form and know how the composer has made use of it.

PROBLEMS:

Problem One: Make a survey of tunes which are currently popular, listing their forms in letter-fashion (ABC, etc.)

Problem Two: Write a popular song in AABA form. Make up your own words, and harmonize it with I-IV-V7 and other chords.

Problem Three: Write a blues tune. For words, use two lines of iambic pentameter, repeating the first line as the music repeats. Other poetic meters may be tried, too. Use traditional blues chords.

Problem Four: Listen to some band marches, writing down the pattern of sections in the music. If possible, watch the music at the same time.

Problem Five: Listen to an old-time dance suite, comparing the musical forms with those of square-dance tunes.

Problem Six: List some interchangeable hymn tunes and verses. Note the numeral designations, the indexing, and the way in which the composer handles the word rhythms and music rhythms. Write a short paper on "forms of hymns."

Problem Seven: Find a record of Dixieland music. Analyze the counterpoint in it, pointing out the kinds of parts played by the soloists on the final choruses. Read something of the history of this style.

Problem Eight: Chances are that one of the popular songs you sing could be handled as a "canon" or round. Try out some of these to find out what a tune must have to make an effective canon.

Problem Nine: Listen to a fugue of Bach, and practice counting the times the theme enters. Many entrances will be hidden in the inner or lower voices, and will require sharp attention to identify them.

Problem Ten: If one of your classmates is preparing an instrumental solo, check to see if it might not be in the variation form. If so, get his cooperation in analyzing the basis for each variation. Why would a vocal solo not be in variation form?

Problem Eleven: Listen to several versions of popular music on records. As soloists play the same tune, describe the variations on it made by each one.

Problem Twelve: Find a recorded work in the Sonata-Allegro form. Listen to it until you can find and point out the Exposition, the Development, and the Recapitulation sections. Be able to identify the first and second theme (or more, if present) and explain how they are treated in development. When you are able to explain the movement, do so in class.

Problem Thirteen: Find a piece of recorded program music. Follow it once for the story or program. Then forget about that aspect, and see if you can figure out its form. Write or explain what you have been able to find.

CHAPTER 21

TIME STRUCTURES--- LITERATURE

The problem of form differs in each of the two time-arts, music and literature. To a composer, form is of great importance. It helps in keeping the attention of his audience fastened on the abstract qualities of his art. Music has little of the imitative about it, and its subject matter, when it has any, is necessarily vague to the listener. If a composer is dealing with a given subject, let us say "Romeo and Juliet," he can only hint at episodes and vaguely suggest personalities and events. The listener who does not know the subject will be able to hear that the music is dealing with something emotional, that there is excitement, unrest, strife, love, and other changing emotions, but these might just as easily be descriptive of Abelard and Heloise, Napoleon and Josephine, or Caesar and Cleopatra, for all the listener can tell. The composer, therefore, dealing as he does with an almost wholly abstract medium, has to rely heavily on the formal patterns he creates.

It has often been noted that music repeats itself much more often than literature. Look over the musical examples in the earlier part of this book, and the frequency of straight repetition will be easily seen! Literature rarely repeats a sentence or phrase twice, especially not without intervening material. The repetition that is accepted and needed by the music lover will not long be tolerated by the person who is reading a story or an essay. To understand the reasons for this difference, we must examine the nature of literature.

The Nature of Literature.

Literature is made up of sounds or of signs for sounds in the form of words. These words are, in turn, names of ideas or, if you like, pictures which we form in the brain. Now it is this double identity of words as sounds and also as ideas that gives literature an added dimension over music. Where, in the latter art, a tone or a chord is just a sound, in the former art it is also an idea. "Silent Night" ends on an E flat chord which has no particular significance otherwise. The poem, "Silent Night" however, ends on the word "peace." As a sound, this one-syllable word has a rather softly explosive beginning, a bright-vowel middle, and a sibilant ending. But, unlike the chord of E flat, it also contains an idea, or rather a whole train of ideas. One of these may be a dove with an olive branch; another, the armistice in 1945; a third, the appeasement of Hitler, or the headlines on November 11, 1918. With this great richness of ideas and mental associations on tap, an author can quite easily forget about literary form and simply go ahead and use the words to tell a story. What he says is more interesting to the average reader than how he says it. This is not to say that form is not important in literature. It does say that form is not so necessary to hold the interest of the reader. We listen to hundreds of hours of conversations each week and the lack of any formal pattern in it is not particularly bothersome to us. Could we endure the same amount of formless, unorganized musical material? Probably not. Again, it is the ideas in literature which hold the attention of most of us, not the sounds themselves.

TYPES OF LITERARY FORMS

In every literary effort, there is some arrangement of ideas. These may be the strictly logical marshalling of facts in an essay, or the free flights of fancy in a love poem. There may be a train of thought leading from the particular to the general, or vice versa. There may be chains of paired comparisons or the opposition of contrasting ideas. Narrative works may run on a straight chronological sequence or can start with the present and move backward. One story will be told through letters, another by diary entries, a third with eye-witness accounts.

In each of the cases above, the interesting point is that the author deliberately selects a way of arranging his words and ideas, and this selection amounts to a kind of formal structure. No author includes all the material which real life contains. The many necessary meals, hygienic chores, useless conversations, or hours of sleep are always left out unless they play some part in the story. Likewise, many interesting incidents may be omitted because they do not further the story or cannot be given room in the poem. The more rigid the form is, the less place in it for extraneous material. Here, the sonnet stands in a special place -- its fourteen lines limit poets to few if any unnecessary words or ideas. A novel, on the other hand, can accommodate almost any amount of writing. Those of Thomas Wolfe are, for instance, huge affairs which take in what seems to be almost the whole range of human experience.

Literature, as has been said before, is dual in nature; it is made up of sound and meaning, both the actual noise of the word as spoken, and the meaning which we assign to it. The sound components of words have been discussed earlier. Now let us consider how it is that the author deals with the sense meanings. We will illustrate with a number of examples.

Scientific Meaning.

One kind of meaning relies upon scientific fact -- the kind of knowledge which can be tested in laboratory conditions. In the following excerpt, we are using this sort of knowledge:

> *On a warm summer evening, the air above a lake will cool faster than the body of water which retains its heat longer. This phenomenon produces a layer of warmer air next to the water and cooler air a few feet higher. Sounds coming across the water seem louder and clearer for two reasons: first, there are no obstructions to absorb and reflect the higher frequencies and, second, there are no convection currents of hot air over the water's surface to impede the flow of sound waves, carrying them astray in 'elevators' of rising air which are so often found on land during the summertime.*

Notice that the words convey only factual content -- there is no attempt to add that necessary ingredient of literature, human emotion. Without the latter, we cannot turn fact into literature any more than we can turn a calculating machine into a thinking, feeling human brain.

The Essay

The closest literary form to the scientific example just quoted is the essay. Here, the purpose is to describe, point out, observe, and explain. Yet the essayist subtly turns scientific knowledge into literature while he does these things. Note how he manages to add the human element:

> *Have you ever been out on a calm lake on a warm summer night? As you drifted idly along in your canoe, you may have been surprised to hear conversation from the shore some hundreds of feet away or music from a portable radio at a great distance. You've noted how beautiful such music sounds and may have wondered what caused this. The answer lies in two acoustical terms, "refraction" and "reflection."*

Following this, the essayist could illustrate with suitable observations and examples just how the sound waves travel across water but note that he has introduced such ideas as "drifted idly along in your canoe" and "how beautiful such music sounds" neither of which is necessary to the explanation. These begin to turn cold scientific language into literary exposition.

There are types of essays just as there are types of any other literature. Sometimes the essayist will choose to describe something he has seen; he may engage his powers in giving directions for doing something; he may even analyze, compare, or contrast to get his points across. In our example above, the essayist could compare the sound waves coming over the water with a flashlight beam or a flat stone skipping. The bending of sound in the cool air layer might be likened to the optical "bending of a spoon" in a glass of water. He might compare sound across a lake to sound heard over a field, through woods, or in a city. He might contrast sounds heard on cold days with those heard in the summertime, daytime sounds with night noises, and so on.

The Story

If the author were to take the bare scientific facts of the original illustration and make a story of them, he would first of all have to add people, or perhaps animals. We are not going to be very much interested in a story which has no possibilities for action -- just the concept of sound waves crossing water is not enough. This may be interesting from a scientific viewpoint but not from a literary one. Neither will the personal touches of the essayist satisfy us. We want characters, action, plot, setting, a point of view, and an underlying theme or idea. Let us begin by adding characters, action, and setting.

> *As Helen and Roger drifted idly along in the canoe, Lake Louise grew calm and quiet. The sun had gone down more than an hour before and a warm mist was rising into the cooler air above the water. Roger laid the paddle across his knees and took out a cigarette. Far off to the left they could hear the radio on the dock playing "Ah, Sweet Mystery of Life." The sounds were almost beautiful even though both hated the tune. It had been sung at their wedding last winter.*

In this short paragraph (which still keeps the essential facts of the essay) we have established two characters, Roger and Helen. We have the setting, a dark, misty lake on a warm, calm evening. We have some little action -- the canoe drifting, Roger lighting a cigarette. We have even a little character development in the fact that they are married and that they dislike their wedding song. Perhaps they dislike each other.

What must we do next? One important step is to work out a plot -- what is going to happen next? In order to do this we must select an overall theme. We could use the idea that high-school age people are too immature in judgment to get married. Roger and Helen

are both 17 and after six months of married life, they have discovered
that they can't keep from quarreling. In following up this theme, the
author will construct the plot and develop the characters so as to bring
out the idea he wishes to put across. Helen will scold Roger for smoking
too much. Roger will accuse Helen of penny-pinching, and so on. The
original event, the canoe trip on the lake, may end in a tragedy or it
may be only the opening scene in a long novel that ends many years
and many pages later with both Helen and Roger middle-aged, unhappy
parents of a teen-age son who is planning a high-school marriage
himself. Of course, the theme could just as easily be the opposite;
that high-school age people *are* responsible enough for marriage. In
that case, the author would have different kinds of events, characteriza-
tions, and so on.

Point of View

Every story is told from some point of view -- sometimes from
more than one. The author can tell his story from the viewpoint of
a minor character as follows:

*My name's Ed Stuart -- work down at the Sandy Beach
Lodge on Lake Louise. Well, sir, one night last summer, a
couple of youngsters -- couldn't have been much more than
16 or 17 come down wantin' to rent a canoe. She looked
scared and he looked mad. I asked him to sign the book and
he put down "Mr. and Mrs. Roger Garen." I was a mite
surprised and musta looked it because he said real snappish,
"Want to see our marriage license?" I said no, and they took
off sorta clumsy like and headed for the middle -- I could hear
them arguin' as plain as if they was still on the dock the way
sounds travel over water on a hot summer night, so I tuned in
my radio to drown them out.*

The author could tell the story from Roger's point of view:

*Helen never did understand me. She always argued
about little things and knew just what to pick on that would
make me sore. Like the night we went for a canoe ride on the
lake. It was real great out there with mist and moonlight -- so
calm and peaceful -- and then she has to make this remark
about the music.*

Or, being the author, he can even tell his story from "inside"
either or both of his characters.

*Helen looked at Roger -- saw the match flare up and
illuminate his scowling face, a frown on his handsome fore-*

head. "How like a little boy he looks," she thought. Roger was thinking too. "She's beautiful -- if only she would just relax and not say anything at all." He took a drag on the cigarette. "There's that lousy Sweet Mystery of Life tune again." Helen was thinking the same thing.

If an author wishes, he can cut his own part to a minimum and let his characters speak. He does not interpret their thoughts nor enter their minds. The reader must do this for himself on whatever evidence he can get from the story.

"Let's rent a canoe and go out on the lake" said Roger as they saw the sign.

"It'll cost too much," replied Helen.

"No, it won't -- we'd still have money enough to get back to Chicago."

"Do you really want to?" she said.

"Don't you?" Roger took out a cigarette.

"I guess so, if you want to." Helen frowned. Roger slammed the car door and started walking towards the dock. Helen followed.

Here we watch the action from the outside, as it were, getting our clues from a few words and actions. Can we tell why Helen is frowning? Is it the setting sun in her eyes or is it Roger that is making her frown? These and other points are cleared up as the action develops but they take time, unlike the earlier examples where the author interprets his characters' actions.

The Play

From the last example, we have but a short way to go to reach the play as a literary form. Here the action is all external -- that is, the author shows us his characters from the outside only. We are left to judge by their words and actions what sort of people they are. In a play, the author must establish a setting by stage directions first:

On the left is the boathouse, a door with a sign over it; "Canoes for Hire" with five or six canoes lying upside down on the dock. Dock projects halfway across the stage. A path approaches from the right. Pine trees are seen overhanging the stage from both sides. It is early evening. Ed Stuart, a handyman of about 55, dressed in overalls, and smoking a pipe, is seated in a chair reading a paper. Beside the chair is a portable radio. A car door slams off right.

> *Helen:*   *(offstage right) It'll cost too much to rent one.*
> *Roger:*   *(offstage right) Don't you want to go?*
> *Helen:*   *(nearer) Do you?*
> *Roger:*   *(coming on right) C'mon -- don't be a piker all your life, Helen. (he scowls)*
> *Helen:*   *(angry, following him on) Somebody had better watch the money in this family!*
> *Ed:*   *(rising) What can I do for you folks?*

Now the author must again decide on his main theme, plot, and so on. Whatever he decides to do, it will be carried out through speech and action. Only rarely will we get any direct information about what's going on in the minds of the characters. We have to guess this in a play just as we do in real life, and perhaps this is one reason why a play often seems more real to us than the book on which it is based. Only rarely does the author of a play give us any direct information about what's going on in the minds of the characters. We have to find this out for ourselves although sometimes the author may make a character reveal, through his speeches, what he is thinking.

> *Roger:*   *I'm sorry, Helen, but when you made that crack about our wedding song, I thought you really were making fun of me. And then I remembered how you'd looked at Bill that night at the dance and I figured you really hated me.*
> *Helen:*   *And I thought you were mad at me for trying to save a little money.*

Other plays from earlier periods of time contain special passages in which characters could reveal their inner thoughts. The famous soliloquy in "Hamlet" is such a device and it allows Shakespeare to reveal the character's thoughts. Not many people in real life talk to themselves but in a play we accept it as a convention useful to the author and to the advancement of the story. A similar, but cruder device is the "aside" used by characters in the melodramas of the 1890's.

> *Roger:*   *(aside) Little does Helen know that I, Roger Garen, am plotting to steal her father's formula, throw her out of the canoe, and escape to Canada where I can live the life of a wealthy man.*

SUMMARY

In the foregoing examples and discussions, we have established that prose forms are governed much more by the way in which the author handles ideas than by the form in which he puts them. We expect the novel to be longer than the short story but we do not expect that it will have a radically different form. The same emphasis upon characters, plot, setting, action, point of view, and so on is maintained. When it comes to poetry, something additional takes place.

THE FORMS OF POETRY.

When we say that something additional occurs in poetry the reader will quickly guess what that addition is. It is, of course, "sound", the sound of the words themselves. However, when focusing attention on word sounds -- on consonants, vowels, syllables, rhymes, and all the rest of the sound elements of our language -- we do not abandon the elements of prose mentioned earlier. Indeed, it is often as important to a poem to have characters, point of view, setting, action, and all the rest as it is for a story to have them. We might take the same incidents as were used in the story and try our hand at turning these into various forms of poetry.

The Couplet.

One of the simpler patterns of sound in poetry is called the couplet. It is simply two lines of equal length which rhyme. When they are iambic pentameter, they are given the term "heroic couplet."

> *The boy and girl got in the old canoe*
> *And drifted slowly out into the blue*
> *And misty waters of the evening lake.*
> *Then Helen sighed as if her heart would break*
> *To see the worried frown on Roger's brow;*
> *That scowling frown she knew so well by now.*

Here the original thought has been preserved and we are relating the story from Helen's viewpoint. There is action, character, and all the rest but, in addition, the words are used for their sounds and syllables, not only their meanings. The couplets give the words some added force --- even if read to someone who did not understand English, they would hold some kind of interest, exhibiting a pattern of rhyme and meter which does not depend on understanding of word meanings.

The Ballad Stanza.

A somewhat more complex system of arrangement of rhyme and line is that of the ballad stanza, found in a good many poems. Each such stanza has four lines of iambic meter. The first and third lines are tetrameter and the other two are trimeter. The rhyme scheme is ABCB.

The music came across the water
Sounding soft and clear.
The memory of her wedding day
Touched Helen's heart with fear.

"Ah, Sweet Mystery of Life,"
The song's prophetic verse
Had changed her to a wretched girl
Who lived beneath a curse.

This rather melodramatic example shows another way to organize the elements of sound to produce a poem dealing with the same subject as before.

The Sonnet.

Perhaps the most intricate and beloved of poetic forms is that of the sonnet. In its fourteen lines, the poet tries to encompass the whole story by dividing it into two sections. The first eight lines, called the "octave," contain the essential plot and action or the particular details. The last six lines, or "sestet" generalize upon the earlier section. In the example below, the sestet contains the "point of view" which was so important a part of the story illustrated earlier. It still must be considered in poetry.

The boy and girl got in the old canoe
And drifted slowly out onto the lake
And Helen sighed as if her heart would break
While Roger scowled and smoked. The silence grew
Oppressive, darkness fell, the lake was blue
With mist. Across the surface like a snake
The sound of singing coiled and in its wake
The silence shaped a wall between the two.

And so it always is when youngsters wed
Before they're old enough to know their mind.
The little walls of silence grow, and fed
By immature reactions and unkind
Words the wall gets higher and instead
Of love, distrust and hatred make them blind.

Notice here the use of such poetic devices as simile (sound coiling like a snake) and alliteration (surface -- snake -- sound -- singing -- silence -- shaped). In this example, as in most sonnets, the lines are iambic pentameter with a rhyme scheme of ABBAABBA for the octave and CDCDCD for the sestet. Other arrangements, however, are often seen, among them the English or "Shakespearian" sonnet.

Blank Verse.

Iambic pentameter seems the most natural speech-like meter for English language poetry, and it is widely used. Blank verse contains more or less regular lines of this meter and length but the ends of the lines do not rhyme.

As Roger lit his cigarette, he scowled,
And seeing this, his bride remembered how
He looked in some forgotten photograph
Of boyhood days; a stiffly-posed, dressed-up,
Unnatural, small-boy look, as if he knew
He ought to be quite natural, yet would not.
"He's acting out a part" she thought, and he
Was thinking, "Wonder if she's angry, too?"

Blank verse is not to be confused with free verse in which the poet sets his own meter, or lack of it, and conforms to no predetermined line length, meter, or rhyme.

Free Verse.

Free verse and prose are often confused, which is understandable. There is no regularity of meter or line length to identify the free verse, and if the verse were set in serial form as prose is, one could scarcely tell the two apart. What, then, is the final deciding point? Wherein are the two different? Their differences lie largely in the type of language they use. If one were to tell the story "prosaically" it might begin, as did the original example:

As Helen and Roger drifted idly along in the canoe, Lake
Louise grew calm and quiet. The sun had gone down more
than an hour before, and a warm mist was rising into the
cooler air above the water.

This is fairly factual with little of the poetic about it. Something closer to poetic language might be:

Helen and Roger, like two idle dragonflies in the sum-
mer evening, sailed effortlessly here and there over the glassy
calm of the lake. The sun had left the lake to them, and the
warm mist was rising to wrap them in its embrace; a soft,
white cotton blanket that waved the stars away from their
private world.

The effect has been exaggerated to show clearly the difference between straightforward prose and something like the poet's language. Now let us try to set these same thoughts in free verse:

1   *Two idle creatures,*
    Useless as dragonflies in the summer sun;
    Purposeless as the moths that alight in the warmth;
    Effortless as planing falcons --- or vultures that watch
5   *Endlessly for food from their circling heights --*
    Two young people drift.

    Drift without purpose in the evening sun,
    Heedless of a mist that rises to shut out the stars;
    Unmindful of the coolness of the evening descending;
10 *Careless of the wending path they take*
    on the misty lake.
    Two idle creatures --
    Drift.

Now the literary language of the previous example has been given a more conscious formal structure. There is repetition in lines 1, 6, and 12. The two stanzas or sections are linked by the word "drift" repeated. Lines 2, 3, and 4 all begin with similar construction, as do 8, 9, and 10. Line 5 contains the alliteration, "for food from." Lines 10 and 11 use "take" and "lake" for a more obvious rhyme while lines 9 and 10 contain an internal rhyme, "descending" and "wending." The first and last lines of each stanza begin with the same word, "drift." The last word in each section is this same word also. So we see that free verse, though it does not conform to any textbook pattern may have a form all its own, and sometimes this is as intricate and difficult as any other.

SUMMARY

To sum up the formal aspect of poetry, one can say only that poetry is the use of language for its sound and rhythm as well as for its sense. In reading poetry we must always be aware of these elements for they add much to the enjoyment of the poem. This gives poetry that "added dimension" over prose; while prose can set forth ideas, delineate character, detail actions, plots, and settings and be fascinating in its complexity, poetry can do these things and more. Poetry can also fascinate by the arrangement and sound of the words.

It should be clearly understood that the few examples of form in poetry given above are only a few of the possible ones. Actually, any good poetry handbook will list dozens of forms which have been developed in the past and which are found in many of our most beloved poems.

PROBLEMS:

Problem One: Compare the amount of repetition found in hymn music with that found in the words to those same hymns.

Problem Two: Although musical sounds generally have no meaning, as word sounds do, there are a few musical phrases or combinations of tones and rhythms which have come to carry a "meaning." One example is the tune "Taps" which often signifies death, sadness, sorrow, "the end," etc. List as many others as you can find, telling what each one stands for.

Problem Three: Select a short news item from the paper, and proceed to develop it first as an essay, then as a narrative in first person, one in third person, and finally a story told from "inside the characters." What will be the main "conflict" in your story? What are the characters like? How can you depict each one by his actions, words, setting, etc.?

Problem Four: Select a short story, and begin to write it as a play. Make sure that the essentials of the original are acted out for the most part rather than simply related by one of the characters.

Problem Five: Go to a movie or watch a television drama. Jot down notes on the scenes as they unfold. What does each scene do to help the plot along? From what angle, distance, and viewpoint is it taken? What particular camera work makes it more effective? How did the scene begin, and how did it end?

Problem Six: Try your hand at writing various verse forms (not only the ones covered in this chapter) whose subject is the same news item chosen for problem three.

CHAPTER 22

MEANING THROUGH SYMBOLS

Much of the meaning of art is conveyed through the use of symbols. Poetry, as we saw in the previous chapter, uses sound to convey far more meaning than the poet can put into words. If the poet had to explain everything he meant, his poem would be far too long, and would lose all the beauty of sound, rhyme, meter and other elements which poets know how to use so effectively. Symbols are equally effective in the arts. The essential key to their success is always the reader's or viewer's understanding. If the symbol is unknown to him, it is not effective. As always, the consumer of the arts has an obligation to try to understand what the creator is getting at. Thus, symbols become part of the student's training in learning to appreciate the arts.

Signs and Symbols.

Right at the outset, a distinction must be made between "signs," which are simply directions, and "symbols" which have deeper meaning. The notes of music, for instance, are signs. In reading musical notation, we are merely following a set of directions which tell us what the composer wants us to do. A set of architect's plans are drawn in a special "sign language" which must be properly interpreted by the builders. The letters of the alphabet are also signs, telling us how a word is to be pronounced. A flashing red light is a sign of danger. A skull and crossbones on a bottle label is a sign of poison. A nod of the head is a sign of affirmation while a shake of the head, at least in our society, is one of refusal or negation.

Symbols go deeper than signs. One might say that we react to a sign, whereas we *respond* to a symbol. If we are driving a car, and see the familiar color and octagonal shape of the stop sign, we will react automatically. We may be talking to a companion and never be conscious of actually going through all the mechanical steps necessary to stop and start up again. We obey the sign from force of habit. Suppose while we are driving along we happen to see a big eagle soaring over the hills and valleys. This bird symbolizes freedom, fierceness, strength, and solitariness. We may envy him his freedom, his lofty view of the men below who have to struggle and accept all sorts of humiliations just to make a living. The eagle takes what he wants, fears no man, is inaccessible in his rocky nest, completely independent. The bird is a symbol, and we respond with our emotions as we watch him soaring against the clouds. Actually, of course, it is ourselves who have endowed the eagle with all of these great qualities. He is obliged to live in precisely the way he does, or he would die. Eagles, in fact, are dying out in many parts of our country, while sparrows flourish. Perhaps the latter is really the freer, more independent bird! Man does not, however, cherish that kind of bird as a symbol -- he cannot respond to it emotionally, unless one calls annoyance an emotion! So the eagle has taken on symbolic meaning while the sparrow anonymously goes on multiplying right under our feet, so to speak.

Types of Symbols.

1. Visual symbols may take several forms, as objects, as actions or as elements.

a. Objects have been used as symbols from time immemorial. The Christian religion has furnished us with great numbers of these. A partial listing would include the following:

Symbol Meaning	Symbol Meaning
Cross—Suffering, self-sacrifice	*Lilies—purity*
Crown—reward	*Rock—steady faith*
Anchor—faith, steadfast-ness	*Alpha—the beginning*
Dove—peace, hope	*Omega—the end*
Rainbow—promise, convenant	*Cup—life*
Ship—the church	*Lamp—learning*
Fish—symbol of Christian faith	*Olive Branch—peace*
Lamb—Christ, purity	*Sword—war*
Serpent—evil	*Halo—holiness*
	Weeds—sin, evil
	Grain—goodness, good deeds

b. Actions often become symbolic. The hand-shake, the tipping of the hat, opening a door for a woman, rising as an older person enters, bowing the head, clasping one's own hands over his head, all of these symbolize some kind of feeling or indicate an attitude. The same action could be interpreted both as a sign and as a symbol. Suppose you saw a young man suddenly toss his hat high into the air. Such an action would probably symbolize high spirits, youthful exuberance, and so on. However, suppose he had arranged for a race to start when he threw the hat. This action would then be a sign, a signal giving directions. In the first case the observer responded with emotions of his own; in the second, the reaction was more or less automatic, a signal to do something.

c. Among elements of visual art which become symbolic, colors are probably most frequently seen in this usage. Yellow has come to stand for cowardice, red for bravery, and white for purity. Red white and blue have a special symbolic meaning for Americans while some other colors would carry meaning for citizens of other nations. School colors become symbolic during a part of our lives, then gradually lose their meaning as we grow older. Purple has long been a symbol of wealth and noble rank because the dye in ancient times was so rare and costly that only a king could afford to use it.

Other visual art elements may acquire meaning. Black, or low value close to it, symbolizes grief, death, sadness or mystery. Scenes of sadness in movies are often shot against gray, low-valued backgrounds. Of course in real life it doesn't get dark just because we are unhappy. Our greatest moments of grief might come on a brilliant day in summer when everything is in full color, but for art's sake a painting conveying this emotion will have to mute those colors, tone them down, and darken the picture.

Perspective and volume may take on a kind of symbolic meaning, too. We use vast open spaces as a symbol of freedom of spirit, though in real life a person living out on the plains might be as mean and petty as one living in a city. Churches attempt to have their congregations worship in a lofty room with a lot of space above the people's heads. Night clubs and bars generally have low ceilings. We equate small thoughts with small spaces, noble thoughts with large ones. (See Examples 6-13 and 6-14)

Even some kinds of lines have taken on a symbolic meaning of sorts. The absolute straight line is used to indicate unbending rigidity, honesty, or an uncompromising stand. The curve stands for, at least in some pictures, a pliant, more gentle attitude. One can easily imagine a picture in which a stern, severe father is lecturing a wayward child. The father's figure will be erect, dominated by vertical lines, probably carried out in dark hues. The child will be all curves and diagonals, a confusion of lines at different cross-purposes. In real life, of course, many strict parents are short and stout, and many lenient ones are tall and straight. Only in art do our symbols remain consistent.

Several paintings in this text make use of symbols. Look at the Wise Men (Color Pl. 5), noting their crowns and staffs. These are symbols of office, rank, and power. A recent TV commercial had a crown suddenly appear on the head of the lady who chose a certain brand of something-or-other. She had become elevated to the rank of "queen of the household." The staff is a symbol with a long history. Its latest manifestation is the baton which army drum majors use, and its cousin, the twirling baton so popular across the country. There is also a star shown in the stained-glass window. From the stars on our flag to the sheriff's star, this symbol has been popular for a great length of time. We even speak of stars of television, movies, the stage, and in sports. One might even consider the beards as symbols of age and authority. At different periods of time, the beard has become a symbol for various things. At some times, it is a symbol of conformity. Later, when styles have changed and men are all clean-shaven, it becomes the symbol of defiance, non-conformity, and revolt.

Symbols may also be seen in the "Madonna and Child" (Color Pl. 6). The overhead arch symbolizes the church, sacred things, and heaven. The gold, red, and blue are symbolic colors for royalty, wealth, honor, etc. The halos around the heads of the mother and child symbolize holiness, and came to be symbolic in a strange way. Very early statues of saints and the deity were protected from the elements by flat plates supported by rods. As painters copied the statues, they tended to copy the protective plates, too. In early Christian paintings, the halos are solid discs. Later on they changed to circles of light, and became symbolic.

Notice also the gleaming stars which appear as a regular pattern in the robe, and the rays which extend in all directions from the central figures. These are symbols, too.

Symbols in Architecture.

If we are used to identifying the customary visual symbols of painting, it may be hard at first to get used to the idea of architectural symbols. After all, architecture has no "subject"; nothing imitates anything else. How then, can there be symbols which do stand for something other than themselves?

Let us look at some of the drawings of buildings in this book, imagining each to serve the function of a courthouse. Would you think that Examples 17-19, 19-28, 19-35, or 19-37 would serve well in this capacity? How about Examples 2-1, 17-4, or 19-12? Most people would unhesitatingly choose the latter group because these "look like courthouses" somehow. We feel that the latter group represents justice, wisdom, law and order, while we don't know what the first group represents. Obviously, either style could serve functionally perfectly well, but *symbolically* we have come to associate the Greek-Roman style with government and law, and our symbols are very important to us.

It is for the same reason that most congregations stick to the older styles of church architecture when choosing a plan for a new church. The church and law, as well as education, often take a strong conservative role in a community. How opposite we are when it comes to fashions and cars. If we were as conservative in these areas, we would be still wearing high button shoes and riding in cars with running boards, cranks, and side curtains!

Architectural symbols then, include certain stylistic features which have come to have special meanings. These features include the arch, dome, column, steeple, pediment, and so on. Many times such features no longer have any practical value at all. They are only used for their symbolic meaning. Long after an interior iron framework was customary to support a building, the exteriors of such buildings were covered with the remnants of former styles, now no longer needed for constructional support. Even as late as the mid-1900s, the Federal government built the great Supreme Court building in the style of an immense Roman temple. The symbol still is a powerful factor.

Ordinary symbols in architecture include such commonplace features as doors, windows, chimneys, steps, and so on. Let us explain:

1. Doors as symbolic features are quite common. Almost every house has a front door which is more elaborate than the back door. Why should this be the case? Both serve the same purpose, to allow entry to the house. But in addition, the front door has a symbolic meaning as the guest entrance, and it must be more elaborate for that purpose. It is the point at which a formal entry is made into the family circle. Deliveries are made to the back door because, of course, the delivery man is not being admitted to the social circle of the family but is merely attending to its physical needs. It takes a fairly high-ranking service to rate front-door treatment such as medical service, and nowadays, the TV repairman!

2. Steps often aid the front entrance by transforming it into a "portal" rather than just a means of entering. On most government buildings there is an imposing flight of steps leading up to the main doors. The long climb (the nation's Capitol Building is a case in point) only makes the entrance more special, and the visitor feels a bit like a mountaineer who has finally reached the summit; his efforts have brought him to the threshold of something very special. On the other hand, for the employee who works there, there are always unobtrusive doors along the sides where one can slip in to take the elevator.

3. A window can become a symbolic feature, and in recent decades we have seen the "picture window" establish itself as a strong symbol of modern affluent living. At first, modern pioneers in domestic

architecture broke with the older tradition of the "house of boxes." The older house had been a collection of rooms brought together under one roof, and living in it was often compared to moving from one box to another. In protest, the "modern" architects of the 1920s and 30s sought to open up the interiors with larger, interconnecting rooms such as we have today. They also sought to blend the inside of the house with the outdoors through use of patio, screened breezeway, and glass walls. In the ordinary house, this glass wall became the "picture window" for reasons of economy. Not remembering that a picture window should look out onto a "picture" of some kind as a landscape, woods, or lake, builders use the picture window today as a symbol of urban status. Every house has to have one, although the majority only look into the neighbors' picture window!

4. The chimney, as a functional feature, is today only a heat vent in most houses, for the gas or oil furnace. Homes heated by electricity need no chimneys at all. Yet the chimney and the fireplace have made a strong comeback as a status symbol, as is mentioned in Chapter 26 under the functions of houses.

Audible Symbols.

22-1

a. Music has a few symbolic sounds, largely certain conventional motives which we all recognize as carrying some particular meaning. In Example 22-1 we have the well-known phrase which signifies "the end" in a humorous manner. In Example 22-2 the phrase has come to symbolize melodrama and phony mystery. It also has comic implications. Various musical sounds have taken on a meaning outside themselves, so to speak. There is a kind of music which has come to represent the busy city street. We hear this music during opening shots of movie scenes, where the action is laid in the city. The brisk tempo, the style of accompaniment, and the peculiar tones of the xylophone mark this unmistakable musical symbol of urban life.

Bells are often symbolic sounds, causing us to respond with thoughts of church (if deep toned and slow) or fire (if higher pitched and fast) or Santa Claus (if very high pitched and rung in a certain rhythm). Drums symbolize war and the military. The oboe, if played lyrically, has come to have a pastoral meaning, and the French horns often symbolize woods and hunting.

b. Literature contains a vast amount of symbolism. We have already discussed some of it but there

22-2

is a good deal more to be found elsewhere. An author can, of course, make use of the same kinds of symbols that are found in visual arts. He has only to describe or mention the religious symbols listed earlier, and his meaning will be conveyed to many people. As a matter of fact, quite a few of these objects have become parts of our idiomatic language. We often hear about someone who has "a heavy cross to bear," or we say that somebody "has earned his crown" by a good deed he has done. A dependable athlete is an "anchor man," and a day-dreamer is "always chasing rainbows." We wait for our "ship to come in," and when others' children are quarrelsome or fussy, our child "behaves like a lamb." An evil person is a "snake in the grass" while a strong and steady one is a "rock in the raging flood." His help can be counted on "from Alpha to Omega" and so on and on. Literary symbols are everywhere, and are used to give the story, poem or play additional depth. When a symbol is used, the writer does not need to explain in detail. His idea is conveyed in the fewest possible words.

Outmoded symbols are often found in older works of art, making them quite difficult to understand, sometimes. The stained glass and sculpture of the Middle Ages, for instance, was often used as a means of educating the illiterate. The various scenes portrayed in glass and stone told stories, illustrated morals, or conveyed some Biblical message. Very often a figure could be identified by some symbol, such as the keys caried by St. Peter. Whenever we see a statue or painting of this time in which one character bears a key, we know whom it represents. St. Luke's symbol is the physician's staff, or perhaps the mortar and pestle. St. Mark is the winged lion, and St. Matthew the eagle. These symbols are quite frequent in church glass, even today, though many do not know what is being represented.

In an earlier day, the one book which everyone knew was the Bible. Many people who knew it well had read only a handful of other books during their entire lifetime. Thus, the stories and passages from the Bible formed a great reservoir of symbols from which to draw. For one raised in the 20th Century, where so vast an amount of printed material exists, there are few universal literary symbols in the sense that Biblical symbols used to be. We still use certain phrases like "be a good Samaritan" or "they're a regular tribe of Philistines" but we may not really be familiar with the originals of either phrase. If we accuse someone of being " a Jonah" or "a Judas" there's more likeli-hood that the symbol will be understood. But how about the once useful symbols of Ananias and Sapphira, or Sisera and Jael? Who knows what the "Gadarene swine" stood for, or the four horsemen of the Apocalypse? In this poem by John Milton, numerous symbols from a second favorite source, Greek mythology, are scattered throughout the lines. It makes very little sense when their meaning is not known. One must have a thorough knowledge of Greek names and places to get the sense of Milton's verses.

> ---*not that fair field*
> *Of Euna, where Proserpin gathering flowers*
> *Herself a fairer flower by gloomy Dis*
> *Was gathered, which cost Ceres all that pain*
> *To seek her through the world; not that sweet grove*
> *Of Daphne by Orontes, and th'inspired*
> *Castalian spring might with this Paradise*
> *Of Eden strive; not that Nyseian isle*
> *Girt with the river Triton, where old Cham,*
> *Whom gentiles Ammon call and Lybian Jove,*
> *Hid Amalthea and her florid son*
> *Young Bacchus from his stepdame Rhea's eye;*
>
> ---*from "Paradise Lost"*

Some of the stately majesty still resounds, but without the symbolic meaning, the former effectiveness has been weakened.

In one of the greatest literary feats ever attempted, James Joyce uses a vast and comprehensive network of symbols in his novel *Ulysses*. Set in modern Dublin, the events of one day in the life of the "hero," Leopold Bloom, are made to parallel events in the adventures of the Greek hero of the *Odyssey*. A newspaper office is the modern symbol for the original cave of the winds, and some barmaids symbolize the irresistible sirens of the ancient tale. The symbolism of the Joyce work is so intricate and hard to grasp that it has become the subject of much scholarly detective work. Several books have been written to assist the reader in identifying these double meanings, but once the symbols have been at least partially pointed out, the story takes on a fascinating double life -- everything one reads can be viewed in several contexts, giving the book a richness of meaning scarcely paralleled in fiction. Many critics may not approve of this obscure and devious way of handling the English language, but all will admit that Joyce's work has greatly changed the scope of writing, and strongly affects his generation.

SUMMARY

It is obviously impossible to treat the subject of symbolism anything like exhaustively in so short a chapter. Let us only remember that the basic idea of the symbol is a widely used feature of all kinds of works of art, and that if we look for symbols, we shall find our understanding of the arts greatly enriched with their presence.

PROBLEMS:

Problem One: Show how the following things might serve *both* as signs and as symbols:

A fire siren   Wiping sweat from one's forehead
A red flag   A police-whistle blast
A wink of the eye   A skyrocket
A yellow caution light   A dog barking
     Sunrise

Problem Two: Find ten symbols which have been created by advertisers to help people identify the product. Analyze each one to see why it has been effective.

Problem Three: Find ten visual symbols in paintings, and tell what each stands for.

Problem Four: Find five symbols which your school uses to identify itself to the people of your community. What sort of image or idea of the school does each symbol convey?

Problem Five: Find five symbols you, yourself use about the house or on your person -- things which really stand for something else.

Problem Six: Ask a musician if he knows some musical phrases or tunes which have some extra meaning for another musician? List or write these out if you can, and tell what they stand for.

Problem Seven: Look about your community for symbols in the public buildings. Think carefully about features which are not really functional, or features which would be equally functional but less expensive if carried out in another manner. List such features together with what they symbolize.

Problem Eight: Look about your home for objects which are symbolic. Do not confuse the symbolic object with the merely decorative one, though some objects will be both! List these, and discuss what they stand for.

Problem Nine: Find symbols in literature for five or more of the following:

Birth	Honor	Riches	Temptation
Life	Old Age	Marriage	Faith
Death	Evil	Divorce	Happiness
Sorrow	Success	Failure	Hope
Shame	Suffering	Weakness	Dissipation

Problem Ten: Look up the Greek names in the excerpt from Milton's "Paradise Lost." You will need a good encyclopedia, atlas, and dictionary of mythologia to find some of them. See how much more meaning you can bring to the poetry by this method. Write an explanation of it.

Part Six

EXPLORING NEW AREAS

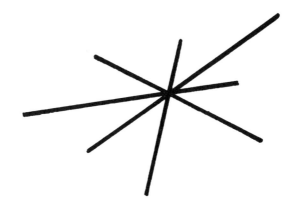

CHAPTER 23

PRODUCT SALES AND DESIGN

Probably no sector of our American economy has grown so rapidly in the past quarter century as the area of design and sales. Not much more than a hundred years ago, a manufacturer designed something to fill a certain need, announced that it was for sale, and placed it on the market. If it was well made, word got around and people began to buy it. If it had serious flaws, people gradually discovered them, and sales slowed, forcing the manufacturer to revise his product or lose money. What little "salesmanship" the manufacturer employed was directed at the retail dealers. The company's salesmen went from store to store persuading dealers to stock their products. Only a few salesmen approached the public directly, and most of these were the door-to-door salesmen about whom many stories were told. Just about the only others were the medicine show "doctors" and the carnival "barkers" or "pitchmen" whose activities usually seemed to have something slightly improper about them.

In the period following World War I, American businessmen became gradually aware that there was an alternative to waiting for the public to buy their products. This alternative was the daring concept that a demand for the product could be created by advertising. If a buyer could be made to feel that he *needed* the thing that was for sale, he might buy it whether he really had that need or not. Several approaches could be made. The seller could:

1. Point out a real need which the buyer had not yet recognized. This might be done by a manufacturer of toothbrushes whose advertising stresses the hidden dangers of neglecting one's teeth. By making the public aware of these dangers, he not only sells his product but serves the public welfare. Some of the finest advertising campaigns have alerted the nation to various neglected health perils.

2. Stress a desirable quality or emotion, and suggest that the use of the product will bring this with it. "Youth" is a quality which most buyers either want to keep or wish they had. Many products are advertised with phrases such as "that young look" or "youthful feeling," and feature photographs of teen-agers or young adults. Every-

thing from soft-drinks to automobiles has been promoted in this way, and very effective such an approach is, too!

3. Picture a famous personality using the product, and hope that his use of it will induce others to follow suit. The "halo effect" is seen anytime a sports star is shown using a certain brand of soft drink or shaving cream. We all know he was paid handsomely for the testimonial, but we still somehow believe and buy the recommended brand because "he" used it. Even when there is no advertising present, a star can promote a product unintentionally. In the late 30's when Clark Gable was shown taking his shirt off in a movie to reveal a bare chest, sales of men's undershirts dropped off noticeably. Since then, advertisers have tried diligently to get actors to use or wear certain products in films, often with the desired results of increased sales for those products.

4. Make the buyer feel ashamed if he did not purchase the product. Various approaches in the past have made the man-on-the-street feel unpatriotic (war bonds), old-fashioned (late model cars), neglectful of his family (insurance), or ignorant (encyclopedias). He feels that he is mistreating his children if he hasn't provided them with the latest model of television or hi-fi set. He is made to feel guilty about overworking his wife if the modern appliances are not in her kitchen, and so on.

5. Create a "good image" of the company, thus getting people to buy its products out of friendship and respect. Auto firms stress their father-and-son workers' teams, oil companies sponsor charities and sports groups, paper companies stress our American heritage, and foods corporations work with communities to help solve local problems. Nowhere else in the world do great corporations devote so much time to helping others; and not all of this is purely to stimulate sales. The concept of the manufacturer as a responsible member of our society has rapidly grown until today the old idea of the ruthless businessman has virtually disappeared. Instead, we tend to look upon our great businesses as friendly, helpful members of our community.

No matter how diligently the advertiser promotes the product, he must have something to sell which can compete with other products, both in price and dependability. The better his design is, the more it will attract the eye of the buyer. The design is therefore a kind of advertising which the product itself does. By looking good, it helps sell itself.

This kind of reasoning has led to the establishment of design departments in most of the major manufacturing companies, and to independent firms of designers for the businessman who doesn't have his own design staff. It is such departments which are largely responsible for the changes in automobiles, appliances, furniture, and almost everything else we buy except raw foods. Even here, designers work on attractive egg cartons and fruit boxes, meat packaging and potato sacks. Nowadays, if a product does not look good, other better-designed and packaged products will outsell it.

One advantage of widespread attention to design has been to simplify and beautify many appliances until today's ordinary household devices are unusually good to look at.

How do design workers arrive at a product which will both fit the needs of the customer and will look good, too? Generally speaking, some fundamental principles are followed:

1. *Very careful thought is given to the product's use.* This is more difficult than it might appear at first, because we are so used to certain products that it is hard to consider their real shortcomings and strong points. Sometimes the simplest products require the most penetrating thought. A case in point is the change in design of silverware in the past few decades. For centuries, tableware had held to virtually the same patterns. Then, in the 1950s, designers began to ask questions. "Why does the fork need such long tines? The food gets stuck between them and they are hard to clean. Nothing we eat requires that much metal to stab through it! On the other hand, the fork leaks when we try to eat something semi-liquid. Why not make some changes?" The obvious answer called for a fork with a spoonlike bowl and short prongs, widely spaced. Why didn't we think of this a century sooner? The knife was re-designed to eliminate the long blade which was not needed and the short handle which didn't fit the grip, to just the reverse. Only the spoon keeps its original shape; it was already well designed.

23-1

Perhaps an even greater innovation was brought about by the man who first conceived a new way of improving the traditional eyeglasses. They fell off, got lost, disfigured the looks, steamed up, were next to useless in sports, hurt the nose, and generally were a necessary nuisance. Even with all these inconveniences, who among us would have thought to take the lenses out of the frames and *put them in the eye!* This took careful thought, indeed.

In thinking of the product's *real* uses, we have to forget about the customary ways of doing things and let our imaginations roam freely. Let's say we begin by trying to improve the wrist watch. If we seek only to make it lighter or smaller, we will be approaching the problem from the wrong end. We must find out what the watch's purpose is.

Actually, it is to let its wearer know what time it is any hour of day or night. It is cumbersome, inaccurate, expensive, easily damaged, and has other disadvantages. The ultimate solution might be something so unheard of as a very tiny radio receiver in the ear or on a finger ring, which when pressed, gives the time signal from a local station. The present small transistor radios are beginning even now to approach this size and function.

2. *Certain practical considerations are carefully worked out.* The following sub-points are adapted from a list supplied by the Canadian Institute of Design and added to by Joseph Broadman.

a. The product must be strong and well-made. This goes without saying, but how is one to find out until he purchases it? Fortunately, there are several independent professional groups established for just such purposes as testing products and evaluating them. These groups buy appliances from stores just as any customer would, take them back to their laboratories, and give them as thorough a test as they can devise. Usually groups of products from different manufacturers are tested together, and then compared. The results are published in magazine form, and the corporation makes its profits from the sales of its magazine.

b. The product should be easy to maintain. This includes such daily maintenance as cleaning, in addition to repairs. In the first place, today's housewife wants appliances that can be wiped clean with a damp cloth, furniture with non-stain upholstery, floors that won't show dirt, silverware that stays untarnished. Her husband insists on an easily polished car finish, shoes that never need shoepolish, shirts that can be hung to dry without ironing, and trousers with a permanent press. The old days of inexpensive help in the home are gone, at least for the present. Today's manufactured item must almost maintain itself.

In the second place, if the item does need repair, then it should be easy to fix. If only a small part is broken, one should not have to replace some larger unit containing that part. Possible sources of trouble should be easy to get at, which has been less and less the case with automobiles in recent years. It used to be possible for the motorist with some mechanical ability to repair his own car. Nowadays only a trained mechanic with a shopful of parts dares attempt this. Many hours of work are often necessary just to get to the source of trouble, to say nothing of repairing it!

c. The product should be safe. If it is to be touched in its use, the surface must be appropriately shaped and treated. Sharp corners or edges should be eliminated where possible. In Example 23-2 we have two gas ranges. To all intents and purposes they look alike, yet there is one difference which makes one of the stoves much safer than the other. In stove A, the controls are up front where children can reach them or where they might accidentally be turned on by brushing against them. Dangerous enough in an electric stove, such positioning could be lethal in one which uses gas. Yet many stoves of type A were made by unthinking companies and sold to unsuspecting buyers!

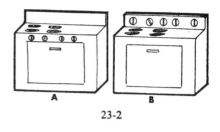

23-2

The lack of awareness of the safety factor on the part of the American consumer is nowhere more apparent than in the case of automobiles. If as many as 500 of us died some year from exploding hot water heaters or from vacuum cleaners which electrocuted us, there would be great alarm, demands for safer products, investigations on all sides, and a tremendous slump in sales. Yet automobiles contribute directly to some *50,000* deaths each year and nothing significant has been done to improve the safety factor until very recently. Apparently the consumer doesn't care! We suffer an injury in an auto accident, and a short time later we are back on the road in a newer car which, if anything, is less safe than the one we had before! Here is surely an area in which the American consumer needs to become design conscious!

d. The product should utilize a basic style which will not become outmoded rapidly. A well-designed object must not only function well for a number of years, but retain its visual appeal all those years, too. If it is over-ornamented to cover up a basic design which is poor, it will look old-fashioned very quickly. Again we turn to the automotive industry for an example. There is no other object for which we pay several thousand dollars knowing in advance that we will become dissatisfied with its looks in three or four years! Occasionally a car is so well-designed that it becomes a kind of collector's item, with enthusiasts holding onto their models for many years. The vast majority of cars, however, end up on the used car lots, superseded by others which, though new, will be destined to fall from favor in a few years also. One aspect of styling is the forthright use of material to its best advantage, not making it imitate something else. Wood has been painted to imitate marble, and asphalt shingles designed to resemble brick but in general this is poor use of material. Wood has its own great natural beauty, so why should it have to imitate any other material? Asphalt, if used for exterior house siding, should create its own patterns, not follow those of the bricklayer. The first plastics were often used to imitate leather, but we know now that plastics have their unique beauty and it should be put to use.

e. The product shall not have wasted space. For many years it was the practice to put "feet" on bathtubs! There never was any use for the space beneath the tub but there it remained for years and years. Finally, designers saw that this place was only a dust catcher and re-designed tubs to eliminate it. Equally useless, and hard to clean is the space behind the toilet stool. It has taken designers much longer to raise this fixture up off the floor and improve this problem.

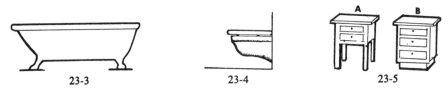

23-3   23-4   23-5

Early refrigerators often stood on legs, too, but now have either a motor or a drawer in that space. Many office-appliance tables used to look something like Example 23-5A with much of the space wasted. Now they have been redesigned for much greater efficiency, as in 23-5B.

f. The product should be easy to mass-produce. This is one requirement which has caused our latest designs to tend toward simplicity. As parts are stamped from metal or extruded in plastic, they carry less and less ornamentation and intricacy. The emphasis is more and more on good lines, proportions, and shapes. Greater ease of production results in lowered cost per unit, a factor which is greatly sought by manufacturers. If a worker in one of the great auto companies can figure out a way to save just twenty-five cents in the making of a $2500 car, his discovery may save the company more than a million dollars per year! Naturally an easy-to-make part is much preferred over one which is difficult to turn out.

3. The buyer is carefully studied. "Market research" has become a fixture of business in our age. Scarcely any product is put on the market without a good deal of testing to find out the consumer's prefer-ences. New breakfast foods are tested in the factory kitchens, then on selected housewives, and finally in certain parts of the country before being released for nationwide consumption. TV producers constantly poll the viewing public to try to find out what it wants to see. Fashion designers have various ways in which they "sense" the readiness of the public for a style change.

Market researchers know more about our buying habits than we do ourselves. They know what color attracts us most (red) and which one repels us (mustard yellow-green). They know that most people tend to turn in a certain direction when they enter a store, and will put harder-to-sell items there. They know that buyers are attracted to products advertised as "giant" and "super" so that if there are three sizes of the same toothpaste, they will be named "large" (the small size), "giant" (the medium size) and "super" (the largest size). Even the stores themselves are sometimes named in this fashion, so that one may see the strange title of "Superette" over the door of a local neighborhood grocery.

4. *A compromise is reached.* In the case of many products, the item you purchase is not the best or cheapest which the company is capable of making but is a compromise between efficiency, design, and consumer desires. It has been repeatedly demonstrated that clear, white fog-lights are superior to the yellow kind, yet motorists insist on the latter, so manufacturers keep making them. In the case of something as complex as an automobile, the compromises between engineering and body design are many. The designer might like to have a radiator pointed like a jet plane's nose but the engineers know the car cannot be cooled efficiently, so a compromise is reached. Engineers may demand heavier door hinges but the design department fears they will ruin the looks of the car, so again a compromise is reached. The end product is not the safest or most thrifty car that could be made -- it is the one which we will buy the most readily. In a sense, then, we are to blame for some of the weaknesses and dangers of cars today. We continue to buy, apparently satisfied with the product being offered for sale.

PROBLEMS:

Problem One: Find old magazines or newspapers, and note the kind of advertising used. Compare ads for similar products today. Write down the differences you find.

Problem Two: Find an example in your own experience of an advertiser "creating a demand" for his product. Try to analyze just how this was done. What sort of appeal was made, and how?

Problem Three: Find advertising which points out unrecognized needs. Get as many examples as you can find and list the areas in which the needs are found.

Problem Four: Find advertising which ties the product in with a quality or emotion you would like to possess. What products are thus advertised? Which ones are *not* sold in this way? Why?

Problem Five: Find examples of the "halo effect" in advertisements. Make a list of personalities featured. Comment on the likelihood of these people actually being competent judges of what they sell.

Problem Six: See if you can find examples stressing the "shame" approach. For this, search out some of the cheaper periodicals. Why is such advertising frowned upon by many people?

Problem Seven: Select examples of "good image" advertising, listing the companies involved. What kinds of firms are likely to use such ads? What might the results be?

Problem Eight: Find pictures of old and new appliances. Make a list of the improvements you note. Are there some desirable features of the older models which have been eliminated? List any you find.

Problem Nine: Think of ways in which some of the following might be better designed:

Beds	Crutches	Drinking fountains	Fishing rods
Lamps	City streets	Fountain pens	Envelopes
Men's suits	Alarm clocks	Parking meters	Key chains

Problem Ten: Rate ten products found in your home on the six "practical considerations" mentioned earlier in the chapter.

Problem Eleven: Ask a local merchant for information he may have on market research including pricing, loss leaders, placement of merchandise, competition of products for shelf space, packaging, etc. Report to the class on what you find.

CHAPTER 24

THE DANCE

In studying the other areas of the arts we found the raw materials which we all know so well in their common form can be transformed into beautiful patterns by the artist. Stone, wood and steel can become a magnificent church when put into new combinations by the architect. Ordinary words can be used together in ways which create great depth of feeling, emotion, and insight. Clay can be moulded by the sculptor, and tones can be organized by the composer.

We have also learned that such patterns of organization can range from the very simple works of a beginner to the complex designs of a master artist. In both cases, however, the raw material will remain much the same. A great poet does not use harder words than the beginning writer; a famous painter has no secret colors which the apprentice lacks.

In the field of the dance, the "raw materials" are something we all possess, body movements. We have all used these raw materials, furthermore, in simple creations of our own. As children we skipped, and as youngsters we have danced to music, so that the area of the dance is already familiar to us. The great question is, what sorts of things does the mature creative artist do with organizations of body movements that we cannot do? How are these raw materials handled by the professional dancer? What does he do that makes his dancing an art, while ours remains at the beginner level?

I. Elements of Movement

Our body motions have three aspects. They take place in a given *space*, they last for a certain amount of *time*, and they possess a given level of *force*. As a simple illustration, consider a person walking. He may take long strides (space), move swiftly (time), and step out vigorously (force). On the other hand he may shuffle along slowly, with short steps, exerting little energy.

These three elements, space, time and force, are good indicators of our feelings. When we are angry, our movements tend to be more vigorous, wide-ranging, and tense. When we are at ease, our movements generally are more relaxed, cover less space, move slower, are not , so abrupt, and so on. Some people get quite expert in judging the moods and feelings of others by watching their motions.

It is possible for motions to produce moods, too. We have all had the experience of being mentally tense and worried. Someone tells us to "relax, take it easy," or we may tell ourselves to do this. As we relax, we find some of the tension and worry draining away. Sometimes exercise which relaxes our bodies will also relax our mental tensions at the same time. If we are depressed, vigorous action such as a brisk walk or a swim will help set us in a more cheerful frame of mind. This is perhaps one of the greatest benefits of social dancing, the mental release it affords.

Each of the three basic elements has subheads which are important to our understanding.

A. Space

1. *Line* -- The body can be so placed as to suggest various kinds of lines. These lines are not unlike those used in the visual arts area of painting and sculpture, in that horizontals still indicate rest (A) and verticals, poise (B). The curves suggest grace (C) and the diagonals, action (D), shown in Example 24-1.

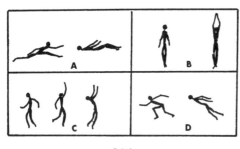

24-1

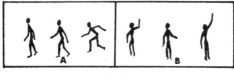

24-2

2. The lines of the body motions also have *range*. In Example 24-2, we see three types of forward motion at (A), short steps, normal stride, and vigorous, wide gait. The movements are alike, yet vary in range. At (B) a man is waving in three variations of range. A simple act like the waving of a hand tells so much. A child will jump up and down, waving vigorously at someone he likes. The bored adult will barely make a motion. Actors can convey a great deal about the character they are portraying by the range of movements they make on stage.

3. The motion also has *direction*. If a person is seen slowly entering a dark doorway, and a moment later is seen backing out of it, his movements may be the same but their direction has changed the whole meaning we give to the situation. Dancers will often create a

pattern by repeating a certain step, and then doing that same step in a different direction.

4. *Level* of the various movements is yet another factor in the space element. The horizontal line created by the dancer's arms may be of a high level, a medium, or a low level, shown in Example 24-3. A particular movement may be carried out at these different levels also, sometimes with quite widely different effects. A man with a clenched fist held high overhead is in an attitude of defiance, perhaps against fate. The clenched fist lowered to chest level

24-3

is a belligerent defensive gesture. The fist held down at the side would indicate a struggle for self-control. Think, too, what a great difference is made when the hands are clasped overhead, and at chest level!

5. *Body facing* in a movement is another means whereby the dancer expresses his ideas and emotions within "space." The direct approach, for instance, with the body facing straight ahead, will indicate openness and confidence (unless other movements set up some different feeling at the same time). In contrast, a movement in the same direction but with the body facing to one side will indicate fear or uncertainty. Notice how actors use this simple device. The hero walks fearlessly forward, while the cowardly villain "sidles" and shifts his body as he walks. Body facing can indicate much to us in other people's actions. The feelings expressed by a man moving away from dangers are quite different if we see him facing it and backing off, and if we see him *turn around* and move away.

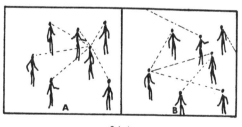

24-4

6. *Eye focus* in the dance, as in painting, can be a powerful directional force. If there are ten dancers on stage and nine of them are looking at the tenth, we will look at him, too. He will become the focus of our attention as well as theirs. This kind of focus is illustrated in Example 24-4A, and the lack of it in 24-4B. When each dancer is looking in a random direction, our own attention wanders. But let them all concentrate at one point and our focus of attention is directed there as well. It is the same old trick of getting two people on a busy street corner to gaze up into the sky. Very soon everyone on that corner will be focusing on the sky. We can't help following someone else's gaze.

B. Time

This basic element is the same one we have studied in connection with music and poetry. It consists of three sub-sections.

1. *Tempo* -- the speed of the body movement. We can control the speed of most of the movements of our bodies, and those over which we have no direct control (heartbeat, eye dilations, etc.) are not visible to the point where they are useful in the dance.

As we alter the speeds of our motions, we also alter their meaning. A very slow nod of the head conveys a gracious, majestic, or even condescending approval, while a fast nod could show over-eagerness. A slow turn of 360 degrees is quite different from a fast whirl-around. Raising one leg to a forward horizontal position *slowly* is a graceful movement, but at a fast tempo, the same motion becomes a kick, which could even be vulgar!

2. *Meter* -- the basic "beat" of the dance. Social dancing and square dancing have this basic beat in abundance. The dances we do in the ballroom are mostly "double" meter, with few in "triple" meter. We do not, for some strange reason, dance to a quintuple meter, even though we use a decimal system for many other kinds of counting.

The dance as an art form makes great use of meter, too, but may be done without it. Expressive movements of the body need not be made in time to a beat, any more than expressive words need meter in poetry, but when a motion is carried out in a metrical fashion, it often acquires a certain power and impressiveness. As a simple experiment, try walking to an even beat as you silently count 1-2-3-4, 1-2-3-4, Then, keeping at the same pace, try switching to a 1-2-3, 1-2-3 meter. Notice how different you feel. For an even greater effect, try *not* to walk in a steady meter of any kind. Make your steps of uneven length.

24-5

Notice how hesitant and unsure you feel, an emotion which will soon convey itself to others. Simply taking the meter away can change the effect of the motion entirely!

3. *Rhythm* -- the duration of individual movements, either within the framework of meter, or without it. To illustrate the relationship of rhythm to meter; walk at a steady pace and clap your hands each time a foot strikes the floor. Your feet are marking the meter, and your hands echo that same meter. (Example 24-5) But now change so that on every foot step, you clap twice. In Example 24-6 we have marked the hand claps and also shown the new rhythm pattern with long and short lines. At the extreme left, the conventional rhythmic notation is seen. Many other rhythmic varia-

tions, some of them quite intricate, may be made. When one considers all of the possible combinations of different bodily movements, together with all the rhythmic permutations, the possibilities are endless. The dance has an inexhaustible source of material just in body rhythms alone!

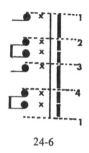

24-6

C. Force

A movement may be executed not only within a certain space and time but also with a certain degree of force. The playful punch which we throw at a friend is far different from the one struck in anger, even though they travel through the same distance and at the same speed. This feeling of force expended on the part of the dancer communicates itself very directly to the observer, who often experiences a sympathetic feeling in his own nerves and muscles. When we see a football player hit with a smashing block we feel something of what he is feeling. The vigor with which a dancer moves can invigorate us as we watch him, and at the end of a particularly demanding dance section, we are limp with relief when the dancer can finally rest.

II. Qualities of Movement

All of the foregoing factors dealing with Space, Time, and Force are, of course, seen in combinations rather than singly. One can never see a leg movement which does not show some degree of speed and force as it moves through space. This is the same in music; we never hear a pitch without also hearing duration, timbre and volume. One separates these elements in theory, in order to study them separately, but in actual art they are never separated.

Putting together the space, time and force elements, then, we end up with a number of kinds of movements to which we can give simple names. This is a lot handier than having to refer to space-time-force descriptions. For instance, a motion which covers a given space at a steady time-rate, and with equal force at all times would be called a "continuous" motion. The following chart shows the elements which go to make up various motions of the body: (Example 24-7)

III. Structural Principles

Thus far we have only dealt with the different elements and movements which the dancer may use to create his dance. We have not seen how he combines these into a work of art of some kind. In order to

ELEMENTS OF MOTION

24-7

Name of Movement	Space	Time	Force
"ABRUPT"	Can be large or small; often small.	Sudden beginning, rapid acceleration or deceleration.	Usually from medium to maximum.
"CONTINUOUS" or "SUSTAINED"	May be large or small; often large.	Longer time-span; steady tempo.	Medium, usually cumulative expenditure of force builds up.
"SWING"	Often large.	Meter felt, pendulum-like division of time. Rate of speed alternates as swing proceeds.	Minimum force at either end of swing, maximum in middle.
"VIBRATORY"	Small, as a rule.	Rapid pulsation may be metrical.	May be considerable, but it is wasted in sustaining the vibration.
"SUSPENDED"	None, or only that occupied by the body.	Little or none felt. Cessation of meter, rhythm.	Zero, complete lack of energy, or stored if a position of balance is obtained.

understand this phase of his work, we must recall some of the elements which go to make up a work of art.

A. *Unity and Variety.* All works of art, whether visual or auditory, need to "hang together" in some way, so that we feel that each part of the work belongs to the rest of it. On the other hand, if it is too unified, the result will be monotony. A dancer *could* come out on the stage and merely do one step over and over. But very soon we would get tired of all this unity and want him to do something different. When the dancer plans out the different things he must do in order to keep his dance interesting and meaningful, he is directly involved in creating the form of his dance.

B. *Repetition.* One of the dancer's most useful "ingredients" in making up his dance form is straight repetition. If it were not for his ability to repeat a movement a number of times, and if we were not willing to watch the movement repeated, the dance would be a far different art. Many an intricate-looking dance is not much more than four or five basic steps repeated in different directions, positions, and levels.

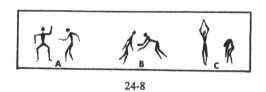

24-8

C. *Contrast.* There are many ways in which the basic idea of contrast may be brought about. In just the element of space alone there could be contrasting lines (A), directions (B), levels (C), and so on, as seen in Example 24-8. There could also be contrasting tempos, rhythms, and energies. There is the basic contrast of male and female, and frequently the costumes of the dancers are designed for contrast of color and style.

D. *Climax.* In the time-arts, each composition, whether it be a piece of music, a novel, a movie or a dance, builds up to a climactic point. This point is usually found somewhere towards the end of the work, but seldom at the very end. (Example 24-9) If the work is twelve minutes in length, there may be several sub-climaxes before the main one is reached. A long play or movie usually has a number of passages building up to points of tension before the principal peak of excitement occurs.

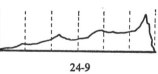

24-9

In the dance composition, the climax may consist of all the dancers making long leaps at a fast tempo and in opposing directions, with the greatest vigor. Sub-climaxes would perhaps involve fewer dancers, less space, a slower tempo, and so on. Quiet passages building up to the climax points would make use of slower tempos still, gentler movements, more relaxed and smaller motions. Of course, the music would greatly enhance the impression which the dancers made by means of its dynamics, timbre, pitch and duration. The musical composition and the dance form would be mutually helpful.

IV. The Ballet

A word should be said at this point about the ballet as a special kind of dance. "Dancing" is a general term which, as we know, consists of body motions organized into some kind of pattern with which the dancer expresses himself. Ballroom or social dancing touches on self-expression. So does the traditional square dance, but there the patterns are almost too "set" to allow much individual expression. The more expressive dance areas are the so-called "modern dance" and the ballet.

Ballet is an old, established, traditional kind of dancing whose performers must spend years in perfecting the techniques necessary to perform the steps flawlessly. The ballet dancer must begin as a child to build up the muscle control and strength which he will need as a mature artist. The girls strengthen their toes, feet and arches for the weight they will have to bear as they dance on tiptoes. The male dancer never dances in this way.

As a part of their training, ballet dancers learn the traditional foot positions and steps which are used in ballet compositions. Knowing audiences look for these, and judge dancers on the skill and technique shown in the various positions and footwork. Somewhat the same situation exists here as with the figure skater or diver who is judged on the perfection of his required figures or dives.

There are many great works in the ballet field which have been handed down from one generation of dancers to the next. This has been necessary because the dance, up to our times, has lacked that one ingredient so needed to make a time art more widespread -- the means of writing it down! Only recently have dancers been able to put down on paper the complexities of body motion so that other dancers could read and re-create them. The new notation system is called Labanotation, and uses a system of figures running from the bottom of the page to the top, on a "dance staff" a little like the music staff used in this book. The various geometric signs stand for kinds of body movement, direction, and so on. In Example 24-10, for instance we see the set of signs which give us the direction of movement. If one is not moving in any direction but simply "marking time," the rectangle is used. For any other direction, the sign points the way. Since movements in dance may be done at a high, middle, or low level, these signs are marked to indicate this too, as at Example 24-11. The combination of direction with level results in such signs as shown in Example 24-12.

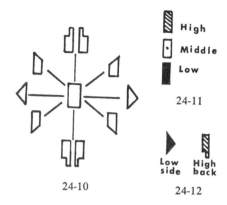

24-10

24-11

24-12

The dance staff, like the piano staff, is vertical, but reads from bottom to top. The length of the sign on the staff indicates its time length, just as in the examples of music we have seen. In reading the Example 24-13, remember that all signs on the right side of the staff denote movements of the right leg, and those on the left show left leg movements. No movements of arms, head, etc. are shown here.

We begin with feet together (rectangular side by side). At the count of one, the left leg moves in place, followed by the right leg, the left, the right (marching in place, not lifting high). In the next measure, the leg movements become much higher, like a drum major strutting, but still in place. The new level is shown by the striped signs.

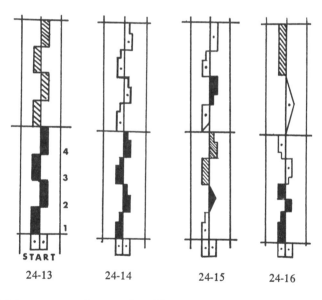

24-13 24-14 24-15 24-16

In Example 24-14 we get a forward walk at a low level (as one would walk on a paved sidewalk, followed in the second measure by a higher level forward walk, as if going through wet grass.

In Example 24-15, the steps occasionally move to the side or back, at various levels. In Example 24-16 steps of different lengths are shown, some for a full count, some for half-counts, and so on. Although we have only used notation for foot movements, the complete Labanotation staff has lines for leg gestures, arm and hand motions, the head, the torso, and so on. Experts in its use say that any movement of the body may be now written in notation. See Example 1-4 for an illustration of complex dance notation.

V. The Modern Dance Composition

The dance routines which we see in movies, television, and in musical shows are really works of art which are constructed from the raw materials of body movements through space and time. These compositions in dance vary greatly just as do musical compositions. The composer of a tune for a musical comedy tries to write something which will appeal instantly to the tastes of a mass audience. It has to be catchy, not too complicated, and fairly short. On the other hand, the serious composer who is writing for an audience of his own musical stature will write a much more difficult, complex and lengthy piece as a rule.

Dance compositions, too, range from the popular to the complex and difficult-to-understand. There is a great difference between the sort of dance worked out for a "television spectacular" and the dance composed for a troupe of professional artists who devote their lives to interpreting man's ideas, emotions, and designs in dance form. This is not to say that one level of dance composition is "better" than the other. Both are needed, and both can be well or poorly done. But if we are acquainted with the dance only in its popular form, we will never know how much can be done when the dancer turns from entertainment to serious thoughts.

Let us imagine we are composing a dance. Here are some of the problems we will have to solve.

1. What will be the *idea* which we wish to express in this dance?
2. What *music* will be suited for accompaniment?
3. What *resources* in the numbers and kinds of dancers will we have? What are their abilities?
4. What *time limitations* are there? Can the dance run for thirty minutes, or must it be shorter?
5. What *space limitations* have we so far as a stage goes? Is it large or small?
6. What *budget* do we have for costuming, stage scenery, other needs?
7. What *equipment* is available for special effects such as backdrops, lighting, etc.?
8. What is the *deadline* for the work? A dance that must be learned quickly needs to be simple in construction. The abilities of the dancers to learn new works is a strong factor here.

9. What sort of *audience* can be expected? This will often play a big part in deciding on a dance form and style.

We begin by selecting a "theme" which in this case will be "The American Cowboy." The music could be from such a source as Copland's *Rodeo* suite (already very successfully used in modern dance) or from one of the many other compositions based on Western themes. Our dancers will be four students of better-than-average abilities, but not professionals. Our time limit will necessarily be that of the music. Composers of dances often build their works on pieces of music written for some other purpose entirely. Just as often, however, the composer is hired to write music to fit the dance. In this case, budget costs force us to begin with a recorded work.

We will assume a normal-size stage with good facilities for lighting, and all the necessary apparatus for hanging a scenic backdrop behind the dancers if we want one. Our budget is low, so we will forego cowboy outfits and settle for blue jeans and colored shirts. The dance will be given in six weeks from the time school starts, so we will concentrate on a dance work simple enough so it can be perfected in that time. The audience of parents and students will be there for entertainment, to be sure, but the "success" of the dance will not be dependent on continued ticket sales, so it can be somewhat more daring in its scope than might otherwise be the case.

We begin our composition by listening carefully to the music. We note its changing moods, its fast and slow sections, its rhythm patterns, dynamic levels, and so on. The form and content of the music begins to suggest various dance movements, and a visual picture of the four dancers working on the stage begins to take shape. As we get a clearer concept of what we are going to do, our dance begins to shape itself into definite physical movements, steps, routines. Some of these may be:

1. Opening sequence -- dancers enter rapidly from right and left with long running strides, suggestive of horseback riding. Arms held out and slightly down, hands curled as in holding reins. Heads held high, gaze forward in direction of movement, backs straight. Dancers form a zig-zag pattern on stage, coming forward. As they reach stage front they stop; "dismount" with exaggerated, wheeling movements of right arm and right leg.

2. Square-dance sequence -- to capture the flavor of the Western life, the dancers move into a smaller grouping, faintly suggestive of the square-dance. There will be several "steps" to go through, each one based on one of the common square-dance routines. The tempo is fast, the motions large and vigorous.

3. Lonesome cowboy sequence -- three dancers retire to back-

ground and accompany the fourth who dances a solo interpretation of the emptiness of the desert, the lonely life of the cowboy, the thoughts he has as he gazes on the vast heavens at night and the immense earth by day. The dancer's movements are not vigorous but are wide. His tempo slows down, his gestures are thoughtful. His eye focus is upward or on the horizon. At times he may make small and inward movements indicating how tiny he is in comparison with his environment. But at the close of this section, the dancer has re-established his place in the universe and faces heavenward with arms stretched high, firmly planted on the earth.

4. Climax sequence -- "the chase" involves the dancers slowly awakening from the previous sequence, and picking up tempo and vigor as they move about on the stage. The patterns here might include some of the earlier ones (square dance and entrance patterns) but will go on to faster and faster turns, wider leaps, and most vigorous movements. The climax will have the dancers at their maximum speed, range, and force.

5. Closing sequence will return the dancers to their opening pattern, this time in reverse, moving toward the rear of the stage. At the closing chords, they "dismount" and salute the audience in a gesture similar to that of a cowboy taking his hat off and waving it.

Throughout our dance, we will insist on the bold, front-facing, shoulders-back, wide-swinging motions characteristic of a person who is independent, free, and self-reliant. Only in the introspective "lonesome cowboy" section will these movements be changed in force and scope. The dance itself will cover the whole stage, but we must be careful lest the four dancers "get lost" as they separate in so large a space. Part of this can be prevented by following them with spotlighting. We want the general impression of our dance to be that of vigor, youthful enthusiasm, confidence and a pioneering spirit.

This composition tells no story, but only suggests through its elements the concept of the cowboy, his character, and his thoughts. Its success will depend jointly upon the abilities of the dancers to use their bodies convincingly, and upon the composer to group these movements into meaningful sequences and patterns leading to a climax.

PROBLEMS:

Problem One: Select three or four of the currently popular dance steps for teen-agers and analyze the space, time, and force elements which characterize each. Write a short commentary on the structures and functions of these dances.

Problem Two: Work out a list of various body movements which you use to convey information to other people without use of words. The following will serve to get you started; see if you can add ten more to the list:

Information	Motion
"I don't know"	raise both eyebrows and shoulders, and at the same time open both hands, palms up, fingers spread.
"I have just forgotten something"	frown, and snap the fingers as you move your arm in a descending half-circle in front of you.

Problem Three: Describe the movements of three of your favorite actors or actresses in movies or television. Use the "space-time-force" elements to describe how they walk, gesture, etc. Compare the movements of one with the others.

Problem Four: Watching a movie or television show, observe carefully the amount of information or emotion which is conveyed by movements of the actors rather than their words. Write a description of a scene you have witnessed in which body movement helped convey information.

Problem Five: Make up a dramatic or humorous pantomime scene in which you tell a story and convey moods by motions. Practice it before a mirror until you have it perfected. Then present it to the class. Some scenes will have a story, others may simply be a mood, such as the feeling of being outdoors on the first warm day of spring.

Problem Six: Look up the basic ballet foot positions and learn the meaning of the following ballet terms: entrechat, fouette, pirouette, pas de deux, battement, cabriole, etc. In the next television or movie musical you watch, try to identify as many of these as you can. Even in a modern dance you may see some of them.

Problem Seven: Try to use Labanotation to "write" some simple physical actions, such as hopping on one foot, raising the arms over the head, walking forward, etc.

Problem Eight: Watch a modern dance, chorus routine, or short ballet sequence, and try to figure out what is being done to create a structure or form. Note any repetitions, climaxes, etc. you see.

Problem Nine: Read some biographical material concerning the lives of the pioneers of modern dance; Martha Graham, Mary Wigman, Ruth St. Denis, Ted Shawn, Doris Humphrey, Agnes de Mille, Isadora Duncan and others. Or do the same for some of the great names of ballet; Camargo, Taglioni, Elssler, Nijinsky, Pavlova, Fokine, Diaghileff, etc.

CHAPTER 25

CINEMA AND TELEVISION

People can become so used to having the arts around that they are likely to forget about their aesthetic value. Common examples of this include our houses, schools and churches, which have become so familiar that we forget that they are works of architecture. Another art which has become a part of our life is that of the cinema. In fact, many people would be surprised to learn that it *is* an art. Yet the movies have all of the qualifications needed for an art medium. They are certainly man-made, they involve light, color, movement, sound, and other art elements, and they possess the power of stirring the emotions. For all of this, the cinema has yet to be widely recognized as a form of art, in the same way that painting, poetry, music and sculpture are. Perhaps this is because we in America have grown up with the movies and cannot quite grasp the fact that a new form of art has been born practically in our own era! We still tend to think of "art" as something old and venerable.

When considering the film as an art, it is convenient to think of it in terms of the subjects it covers, the purposes it has, the technical aspects of its production, and the various kinds of music used with it.

Film Subjects

When compared with other literary forms, the film medium is surprisingly versatile. It can cover virtually any subject or can be completely divorced from subject. Films have been made using moving lines, shifting colors, fluctuating shapes and rapidly changing textures usually accompanied by music, but not "about" anything. Even without any subject the patterns on the screen can be fascinating to watch.

When the film makes use of a subject, its range is almost unlimited. Movies deal with nature, animals, and especially man in various situations. These may run all the way from films dealing with only two or three people, to epics involving whole armies. Films can cover a few hours or centuries, can be set in one room or range over all the world. As compared with the drama, movies have far greater leeway in subject. On the stage such events as volcanic eruptions, hurricanes, battles and ship sinkings are difficult if not impossible to show effectively. These events are the life blood of movies, however, and many a poorly acted film has been saved by some such great spectacle. As a matter of fact, a certain type of movie will advertise a "cast of 10,000" or will feature the "costliest set ever built" and so on.

It has been pointed out that literature can deal with any subject. The author can even enter into the minds of his characters and tell us what they are thinking. The cinema art has this same ability. We have all seen movies in which a character is shown on the screen while his voice is heard through lips that do not move at all. This convention is easily recognized as indicating the actor's thoughts. Movies have shown us dreams (usually signalled by a dissolving, wavering image accompanied by a harp glissando) and even have portrayed the human conscience, sometimes by a tiny image of the actor floating alongside his own shoulder and whispering in his ear!

Purposes of Films

The movies have had wide use in our day and age. Their primary purpose is still that of public entertainment and profit but a surprisingly large part of the movie industry is devoted to other purposes:

1. Instruction --- thousands of reels of film are produced for school use and for other educational institutions. Films range from mechanics to the arts, and are used from kindergarten through professional graduate school. Doctors learn new techniques of operating, scientists keep abreast of the latest discoveries, and teachers see classroom procedures on the screen. Many large corporations use training films for their salesmen, and the armed forces regularly employ films for instructional work of all kinds.

2. Sales --- many products are sold today through the medium of the movies. Virtually all network TV advertising is done by film, and even the movies use films to advertise their own "coming attractions." The production of commercial films often includes elaborate sets, especially composed music, casts of actors and even highly paid celebrities. A single 60-second commercial film may cost tens of thousands of dollars to make, and much more in advertising air-time.

3. Religion --- just as the other arts have served the church, the art of cinema now is used for religious purposes. It is quite common for churches to rent and show films dealing with religious themes several times a year, and it is not unthinkable that as film usage increases the worship service might include a filmed presentation each Sunday, along with the anthem, offertory, sermon and prayers.

4. Recording of events --- the film is an ideal means of preserving important visual-auditory events of the past. Think what a thrill it

would be today if we could see on-the-spot films of Caesar's speeches, the crowning of Charlemagne, or Columbus' landing in the new world. Our descendants will be able to view the Allies' landing in Normandy, the crowning of Elizabeth II, as well as many other notable events. With the advent of television video tape, the cost of filming and keeping such events on file has been reduced, and the electronics industry promises us low-cost home cameras for video tape recording soon. Everyone can then make his own home movies for keeping personal records in sound and vision.

Among the different events now being recorded on film and tape are such items as interviews with presidents, statesmen, artists, and other leading figures of our time. Sports events are recorded which will enable people many generations later to compare our athletes with theirs. Certain art works, too, are being preserved for the future, such as dances, and the actual techniques of living artists, seen painting, playing, or acting on the screen. We are preserving architecture on film in a unique way, through the "tour" of a national shrine such as the White House. We can see these places through the contemporary eyes of one who lives there, a kind of historic record which will be even more valuable in the years to come.

Film Techniques

The average movie-goer is almost totally innocent of knowledge in the techniques which go into the making of the films he watches. It is the purpose of this section of the chapter to describe some of these, so that they may be identified and understood.

1. Camera Distance. A picture may be taken from a number of distances, depending on what needs emphasis.

a. The long-shot or distant view will allow the spectator to place the action which follows. A typical opening for a movie may show the vast mountain and desert country of the American Southwest. In the distance, far below, we see a trail of dust made by something moving across the desert floor.

b. The medium-shot narrows our vision down to the general area, and we see the stage coach which has been causing the trail of dust seen in the first shot. It may still be several hundred feet distant in this shot.

c. The close-up shot concentrates directly on the stagecoach which now fills the screen. We can see that the driver is fearfully glancing back over his shoulder, and that his companion is checking the loading of his rifle. We might even be taken inside the stagecoach to see the faces of its passengers, hear their conversation, and examine what they are wearing. We might find the young lady holding a Bible, a fat and perspiring salesman hiding a wallet, and the lean bronzed stranger holding a flat package.

If we had not been shown the two previous shots, our introduction to the occupants of the coach would be less meaningful. We would not know that they were far from any town, passing through rugged country, for instance.

2. Camera Angle. The position from which the camera takes its shot is most important. Notice how the camera seems to jump from place to place during the presentation of scenes, As two people talk, you will see the face of one over the shoulder of the other. When the other person answers, all of a sudden you are seeing *him* head on! Contrast this with the theatre, in which you always see the actors from the same angle and distance, and rarely get the small facial gestures so common in the movies.

The camera can shoot from above the heads of the actors. In a saloon gunfight photographed slightly from above, you will feel that you are observing it from some safe vantage point. But if the same scene is shot from a waist-high angle, it can be terrifyingly realistic, and you become personally involved. A scene shot from a very low angle might be made to appear as through a child's eyes. Or, if the hero has been wounded and is lying on the ground, the villain's approach can be made more realistic if shot from the ground upwards.

3. Camera Position. The movie photographer can allow us to see a scene from many different places. As the stagecoach gallops along, we follow it as if we were flying smoothly alongside. If the heroine is running through the woods to escape the villain, we can watch her approaching, see her running away, look at the scene from up in the trees, or even run with her! In the latter type of shot, the camera is turned on and held in the hands while someone runs through the trees with it, photographing anything that comes into view. The result is a screen view of approaching branches, tree trunks flashing off the sides of the screen, changing focus and crazy angles and tilts. The effect is such that we become, for the moment, that girl running through the woods.

Camera positions have included "hidden" locations, as when the villain robs the bank, and the camera is shooting from between the bars of the teller's cage. The moviegoer feels that he himself is hidden and watching the robbery. Sometimes a view of a cozy domestic scene will be taken from inside the fireplace with flames leaping up between the viewers and the room. We are so used to the magic powers of the camera that we don't even think about the fact that if this were real the cameraman would be burned to a crisp.

4. Cutting. Almost as important as the kinds of scenes shot by the cameraman is the manner in which one scene leads to the next. There are several ways of getting from scene to scene. In our opening stagecoach shot, the distant view of the desert was immediately followed by the shot of the stagecoach. This direct cut indicates to the viewer that this particular stagecoach is the cause of the dust! If the night bank-robbery scene begins with the view from the teller's cage we might hear a creaking board outside, and a direct cut would show us a man walking stealthily alongside a building. By the swiftness of the cut, we would know that the noise was caused by this particular man, and that the building near him was the bank we saw previously.

On the other hand, suppose our cut was made to a scene at a party. We would then assume that the party was going on at the same time that the bank was being robbed. If we made a slow fade from the prowler to the party, we would feel that the bank had been robbed, and that it was now some time later. The slow fade indicates a time-lapse.

    a. The split-view is often used to show two people engaged in a phone conversation. The viewer can be in two places at the same time, a feat which classical geometry has long held impossible. The right half of the screen shows the heroine in her room holding the receiver to her ear, while on the left half, the hero sits in his office speaking on a phone.

    b. The montage is a special cinematographic technique involving rapid fading, overlaying, and dissolving of a number of "symbolic" visions used to indicate a particular sequence of happenings. For instance, the hero takes a long trip to Washington, D.C. The screen does not show him arriving in Denver, St. Louis, Cincinnati, Philadelphia and Washington but instead, the fact of the trip is shown by a rapid blur of train wheels, steamboat paddles, flying horses' hoofs, and a final shot of a train pulling into a large station. We know the journey is finished, and the montage took perhaps ten seconds, accompanied by appropriate "travel music," of course.

Another favorite montage sequence comes after the hero has made his maiden speech in Congress. On the screen is shown a rapid series of newspapers running through presses, phantom newsboys crying, "Read all about it" and telegraph keys clicking and typewriters banging. We know in an instant that the speech attracted nationwide attention.

    c. The fast pan shot is the movie equivalent of the phrase, "---meanwhile, back at the ranch---" and is used to show both a time and place connection between scenes. Suppose the villain has succeeded in robbing the bank undetected. As he divides his loot with the local judge who planned the crime, he says, "Judge, there's absolutely no way in the world that anyone could connect you and me with this crime. The only other person who knows anything is old half-witted Pedro, the cook, and he's too scared to ever say a word." Immediately the camera is swung rapidly in a semicircle (or it looks that way, at least) and as it slows down we see the interior of an office with the U.S. Capitol dome seen through a window. A man speaks. "What word do we have from our Mexican agent, the one who's posing as a cook?" The fast pan shot tells us the conversation in Washington is taking place at the same time, and is related to the one in Texas.

d.   Superimposed pictures are often used to denote a longer passage of time. The heroine is seen standing in front of her little cottage with its shady trees, flower beds, and vine-covered porch. She says, "I hope that Senator Strong won't forget me now that he's living in high society in our nation's capital. He promised to write me every week." She turns and enters the house. The camera stays focused on the scene as the picture dissolves slowly into the same scene without leaves on the trees and vines. We at once know that our story has leaped forward several months. A postman appears, the young lady runs out (we hope with a different dress on), snatches the mail from the postman's hand, and examines it sadly. The Senator has not kept his promise.

5.   Film Music.   No moving picture is complete without music, yet film music remains curiously overlooked in the average movie. Only in a musical show do we pay much attention to the musical portion of the film, and perhaps we are instinctively right in this. It has been said that the most effective movie music is that which goes unnoticed. When background music is too obtrusive, it takes attention away from the visual scene, and robs the film of its primary effectiveness. Film music can be separated into several categories:

a.   Theme music.   Many films, especially the larger, more expensive ones, have themes especially composed for them. This music is often promoted separately from the film, is recorded and sold on records, and is heard at various points throughout the movie, especially during the screen credits. In the past, such movies as *Three Coins in the Fountain, Ben Hur,* and *Lawrence of Arabia* have had widely played theme music.

b.   Music for opening credits.   The somewhat lengthy and boring business of listing the names of all those connected with the making of a movie has always been a problem. Most of the time this portion of the film has to depend on its music for interest, and screen-credit music tries hard to set the mood for the story to follow. Elaborate orchestration is often used, with the musical climax coming with the announcement of the director's name. A comedy will feature music of a fast tempo, while a mystery will be heralded by sinister sounds in the introductory music. Were it not for the music, we would not know what mood to be in as a film began.

        c. Background music. As the scenes follow one another in a film, the music changes with each new scene. A camera shot of the mountains will be backed up by a grandiose, full orchestration of a sweepingly broad theme. A party scene will feature light music in a happy vein. A night scene in the forest will call forth the quiet, low-pitched sounds of the orchestral instruments, and so on. Over the years, several conventional kinds of backgrounds have become established, notably the one always used for big city traffic amid tall buildings and crowds, featuring the ever-present xylophone.

    One of the most effective uses of music for background purposes occurs when the music suddenly stops and the theatre is left in dead silence. All of a sudden we notice the absence of that continuous accompaniment, and the effect can be highly dramatic.

        d. Imitative music. On occasion, there will be a deliberate matching of the music to the actions on the screen. The comedian's walk may be matched to the meter of the background music, for instance. A humorous scene in a boarding house might show all of the roomers eating soup in time to a march. A Chaplin film once showed the comedian as a barber, shaving a customer to the strains of a Hungarian Dance.

        e. Specific music. At times the story of a film calls for music to be included as an actual song. This most often comes in the musical film, where a number of set songs are featured. In this sense, however, it is the music which takes precedence over the film, and the action stops while the set musical numbers are presented. This has to be done skillfully, lest the effect be one of annoyance on the part of the audience. There is always something faintly ludicrous in the suspension of action in a film just to allow the star to sing, especially when the singer is all alone in a boat in the middle of a lake, and is being accompanied by a 100-piece symphony orchestra!

    A second kind of specific music concerns that which is played on the screen. Here a strange kind of process often occurs in the movies, especially movies set in some period of the past. In a film of medieval knights, castles, tournaments and crusades, the director will spare no expense to provide authentic details of clothing, armor, furniture, and weapons. Yet invariably there will be a scene where trumpets or horns are to be sounded, and out of them will come tones which are possible only on modern instruments. Scenes set in ancient Rome are never accompanied by music in an appropriate style to that era, and even comparatively recent ages of man are shown on the screen accompanied by music not heard in that period. To complete the confusion, pictures of modern life are not accompanied by music in the contemporary style. Instead, almost all movie music seems to have settled in the style of the late 1800s. Tschaikovsky, Wagner, Brahms, Grieg and Schumann are the models for today's movie music, with an occasional movie score of a slightly more modern touch here and there. In fact, one Hollywood composer, when awarded an "Oscar" for his work, proceeded to thank "all those who made it possible" and went on to name those five eminent composers with a few more. It has long been apparent that the musical portion of the film art must take a subordinate position to the visual and dramatic aspects. So long as this remains true, our best composers will seek their musical satisfaction elsewhere, and film music will continue to be what it always has been, a background accompaniment for what takes place on the screen.

SUMMARY

It seems safe to say that movies are fully established as a combined art form. Having witnessed their spectacular growth from a curiosity in the early 1900s to a sensitive art medium a half-century later, we can foresee great things in the future. Of all the arts, that of moviemaking possesses perhaps the greatest potential, combining both audible and visual elements into a large form. Films may be cheap or blatant at times, but they cannot be ignored. People will continue to be attracted to this exciting art medium.

TELEVISION AS A MEDIUM OF ART

In the early 1950s television spread across the nation and the world as a new medium of entertainment and education. The novelty of having a continuous source of entertainment in the home swept the nation, and nearly everyone had a TV set within a few years. Television originally had a spontaneous quality about it which the cinema lacked. In the theatre one saw actors in carefully rehearsed performances, but on the TV screen one could see the real play being televised, and some of the excitement of the theatre came through.

In recent years, however, the costs of live television drama, together with the ever-present danger of errors being made and seen by millions, have driven TV drama back to filmed productions. At the time of this writing, local news and late-night commentary are about the only television programs which feature performers in unfilmed, unrehearsed appearances. Even some of these are taped and replayed a few minutes later just to control any unwanted spontaniety that might crop up. One technical factor contributing to this change is the invention of "video tape," allowing for instant replay of anything which one might wish to review or edit. However, despite the growing similarities of cinema and television, there are differences, as follows:

1. The viewing of television is done on a small screen. This makes vast panorama shots somewhat ineffective. Where a wide-screen film can show the Rocky Mountains in all their glory, the same shot on a 17 inch TV screen loses most of its power. The TV film, therefore, concentrates more on smaller views, or at least uses the larger ones less.

2. The viewing is done at close range. One never gets as close to a movie screen as to a TV set. The greater distance makes things more impersonal. Thus, seeing a face view of an actor twenty feet high at a distance of 75 feet is not the same as seeing one lifesize at five feet. The latter view is much more intimate. For this reason, the TV personality becomes a personal friend, while the movie star remains a more distant figure.

3. The viewing is done alone or in small groups. In a movie theatre, one sits in a mass audience and shares mass emotions. If a particular film is funny, one laughs as much at the laughter of others as he does at the film. In the home, the generating mood of the mass audience is lost.

4. The viewing is done amid distractions. There are children, pets, phones, visitors, street noises, and so on to compete with the TV program. In the theatre there should be far fewer distractions, including those ever-present commercial messages of television. This allows a movie-maker to devote more care to subtleties --- the TV director must make his main points clearly.

5. The viewing is done in short periods. Television is broken into half-hour segments with quarter-hour sales commercials. This forces writers for this medium to divide their work into uniformly timed segments. One can notice the difference between a drama written for TV and a regular movie being shown on TV. In the latter, the commercial breaks often come at awkward times, dramatically speaking.

6. The viewing is done with alternatives always available. When one goes to a movie theatre, he is committed to staying through to the end. Rarely does anyone walk out of a movie for which he has paid an admission fee. The TV viewer, on the other hand, can change pro-

grams with the turn of a dial, and if no program suits him, he can always read a magazine or play solitaire! This forces the TV producer to search for a surefire attraction which will keep viewers watching. The usual solution has been a program series based on a fairly simple and standard kind of plot, rather than any attempt at an experimental or controversial sort of program. Anything above a fairly low level of appreciation will lose viewers, and the medium is too costly to entertain any such thought on the part of an advertiser.

SUMMARY

For a time TV was thought to be the medium which would replace the cinema (just as the latter was thought to do away with the stage drama). But the inherent differences in the two soon made themselves felt, and both now flourish as art forms. Television is still hampered at the present by its dependence on masses of viewers and upon commercial advertising. These two factors have kept it from being the art that it could be. It has become, instead, what the newspaper is as compared with the novel, a kind of journalistic-entertainment-commercial venture. Some hopeful approaches are being made through educational television and through pay-TV to offset the above-mentioned drawbacks. Only time will tell, but for an infant art (if we can call it that) television has evidenced surprising growth and vigor.

PROBLEMS:

Problem One: Make a list of all the different subjects you have seen in movies, and try to arrange them into groups or classifications. As you do, place several titles in each group. Notice which categories contain most of the films. What does this indicate about your own taste in movies?

Problem Two: Name the movie you have seen which covered the widest range of subjects, and make a list of the topics, characters, and places it treated. Then do the same for the movies you have seen with the most limited subject matter or range.

Problem Three: Make a list of the ways in which an educational film differs from the kind you see in the theatres. Your list should include as many factors as you can think of.

Problem Four: Make a list of things which you feel should be recorded on film for future generations to see and hear. Consider the things you would like to see from past periods of history as you make up your list.

Problem Five: Take a notebook with you to the next movie you see and write down the kinds of shots taken by the camera in the opening few minutes of the picture, together with a short description of the shot. Note also any unusual camera angles and positions.

Problem Six: Make a list of transitions from one scene to another in the next movie you see, noting what kind of cut is made and how it relates the two scenes which it connects.

Problem Seven: Compare the number of scenes in a movie running two hours with a stage play of the same approximate length. Consider the advantages and disadvantages of rapid shifting of the setting in films. Discuss the resulting differences in the production of films and plays.

Problem Eight: Make a list of requirements for a screen actor that are needed for a theatre actor, and a second list of those required by the stage but not the screen.

Problem Nine: Read an account of the inventions which have aided movie-making since the earliest days. Then discuss the relationship between the inventions and the expansion of the movies as an art form.

Problem Ten: Sit through a movie once with your eyes closed. Then write an essay on the kinds of music you heard, the relationship of music to the other sounds and noises of the film, and to the dialog and plot.

Problem Eleven: Try to determine the historic accuracy of music in the movies you have seen which are set in the past. Check on musical instruments used on the screen, and those heard in the background. Determine whether musical practices in the film are historically correct (such as 15th-Century women shown singing in a church choir) or not.

Problem Twelve: Observe a TV dramatic program, noting what kinds of distance shots, cutting, and vantage points are used. Can you spot instances in which a movie for regular theatre showing would have done any of these differently? Why?

Problem Thirteen: Make a list of suggestions for improving the quality of television programs available in your community.

Problem Fourteen: Consider the whole idea of showing old movies on television. How might this be similar to what is done in the world of music or drama, when we hear music of the past at a concert, or see an early play revived? Might there be any particularly good results from reviving the old movies?

Problem Fifteen: Write a short paper describing the television and movies of the future, using what you know about these arts today as a basis for your "predictions."

CHAPTER 26

DOMESTIC ARCHITECTURE

One of the least studied of all the arts, yet one of the most used and useful of them all is architecture. Within the overall area of architecture, probably the least studied facet of that art is domestic architecture. We live in houses all of our lives but know almost nothing about them as forms of art. In this chapter, we shall explore some of the more common aspects of our homes.

The Functions of Houses

Think how different life would be if we lived in some type of community where all the men and boys slept in big dormitory rooms, and the girls and women in other, similar rooms. All would dress alike, and at mealtimes everyone would eat in a large dining hall. There would be mass recreation centres, large-scale storage facilities, clinics, exercise grounds and so on, much like an army camp. Life would be indeed strange under those circumstances, and most of that strangeness would be a direct result of but one thing lacking, the private home! Because we *do* have private dwellings, we are enabled to do many things and enjoy many privileges which we could otherwise not have. Let us examine this kind of architecture more closely to see what it really does, and how it functions.

1.   *Shelter* is perhaps the most easily identified function of the home, and the only one many people can readily name. When we begin to think about all of the things we need shelter from, the matter is not so simple after all.

a.   Cold and snow are related elements from which we need protection, but are not the same. Cold may be warded off by insulated walls, and adequate heating. Snow, if it falls in great quantities, is heavy, and houses in climates where there is such a heavy snowfall usually feature steeply pitched roofs, as in the Swiss Alps, to allow accumulations to slide off before too much weight is built up. Such a roof is shown in Example 26-1.

26-1

b.   Heat and humidity are also different in the forms of shelter they require. The old Southern mansion shown in

Example 26-2 was designed for a climate where moist heat was the rule. It therefore had a large shaded porch and tall windows through which the breezes could pour. Often the center of the house was an open hall from front to rear which acted as a breezeway. In contrast, the house shown in Example 26-3 is designed for a hot, dry climate. Its windows are small to keep out sun glare. So long as humidity is low, one only needs shade to keep cool. When it is high, shade *and* air movement are required.

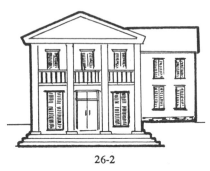

26-2

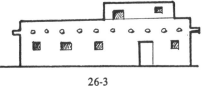

26-3

26-4

c. Rainfall and dampness are related factors. Where annual rainfall is great, as in certain tropical sections, the houses will have wide, overhanging eaves which help drain water away from the sides of the house and offer shelter, as seen in Example 26-4. Windows may be kept open during a shower. Some houses in such climates are built on stilts, an extremely practical design. The ground beneath will be fairly dry for additional shelter for animals. Occasional floods will not hurt the house, and breezes passing beneath it will allow moisture to dry out of the floors, and the house to remain cooler. In some parts of the world the extreme dampness necessitates building homes with heated closets where books, clothes, shoes and other materials may be stored. Without such precautions, many objects will become moldy.

d. Several other shelter factors involve various elements encountered here and there around the nation. High winds in hurricane and tornado areas necessitate houses with specially designed structural features. One of the newest is the "bubble house" found here and there in Florida, shown in Example 26-5. Built of concrete, its construction is novel and inexpensive. First a concrete slab is laid on the ground, just the way a cement driveway or patio would be made. Then a heavy plastic or rubber balloon

26-5

is inflated over this cement slab in a hemispheric shape, just about the same size as the finished house is to be. Over the surface of the balloon is laid a network of wire mesh, and onto this a mixture of concrete is sprayed by air hose. As the mixture sets and is smoothed out, the walls and roof of the house take shape, with openings left for doors and windows. When the concrete has hardened, the balloon is deflated and withdrawn. The house interior is completed, and the owners move in. Advantages include quick and cheap construction, safety from high winds and fire, low maintenance costs, and simplicity of form.

2. *Protection* is often listed as a prime function of the private home. In one sense, shelter is a form of protection (from the elements) but one may think of two additional needs in this area.

a. Protection from animals and insects is built into almost every house in one form or another. We use screens to keep out flies everywhere in our country. In addition, in some areas we must protect against rats, snakes, termites, and other pests. The stilt house shown earlier has excellent facilities for such protection. In addition to the fact that snakes cannot climb the smooth poles, there will usually be metal guards on top of the poles which keep out rats and other non-flying pests. Such a guard-shield is shown in Example 26-6.

26-6

b. Protection from humans is also built into our homes. We invariably have doors and windows that will lock, sometimes with rather elaborate hardware, to foil thieves. City dwellers often have chain guards on their doors, and devices allowing them to lock their windows *open,* so that they have ventilation without fear of inviting burglars. Many front doors will have small peepholes allowing the owner to see who is calling before opening the door. Occasionally a house will be equipped with an alarm system, a safe for valuables, and other protective devices. In certain foreign countries spike-topped walls and metal shutters are not uncommon devices in an ordinary home for protection.

3. *Privacy,* while related to protection, includes many areas not concerned with potential danger so much as with annoyance. We all equip our homes with curtains, shades, and drapes to screen us from the gaze of passersby. Within the home we create areas where we can shut ourselves away from others when necessary. In many American homes the ideal of a private bedroom for each member of the family has been achieved. In more and more homes, each bedroom has its own bathroom, and further privacy is gained by adding a den or study.

Privacy is a luxury, and is not to be found in slum dwellings, in backward societies, or among the poor. In fact, privacy in the ordinary home is a comparatively recent achievement. During medieval times whole families, together with relatives, apprentices, and visitors slept on straw pads spread on the floor of the kitchen-living room-dining room. Centuries later it was still uncommon for houses to be divided into specialized rooms for different purposes. Our American pioneers lived in houses which had one large room with bunks off the sides or in a loft overhead.

Privacy has taken on new significance today when almost every house has a telephone. "Intruders" can now demand our attention day and night, and sometimes can make life miserable for the housewife or her family. Many people in cities find themselves being called a dozen times a day by people with sales messages. Others may find they have become the victims of a prankster, or of an anonymous "hate campaign." The only protection is application for an unlisted phone number, or perhaps giving up the telephone entirely.

4. *Sleeping facilities* may be the most essential aspect of the home after shelter. Other functions of houses have changed, but in no case is a home to be found without sleeping facilities for its owners. In considering what conditions are necessary for suitable sleeping quarters, one finds the following:

a. Light-control is essential in the sleeping areas. One must be able to darken the room for sleeping, keep early morning light out if desired, brighten the room for reading, lower the light-level for watching TV or relaxing without sleep, and so on. If more than one person sleeps in the room, there should be individual lighting for each, in case one wishes to read or study while the other sleeps.

b. Temperature control is equally important, and with modern air-conditioning, heating, electric blankets, fans and other devices, it is easily (though not cheaply) obtained.

c. Sound control is a third essential, but this does not mean that one always wishes sounds to be shut out. On the contrary, there are times when one wants to be sure that certain sounds come in. Parents with young children need to be able to hear them cry out at night, but most other sounds are not desired. One modern way is to equip the sleeping room with an intercommunication device which brings sounds from the nursery directly to the parents' bed but excludes all other sounds.

Sounds of traffic and other outdoors noises are much easier to screen out these days when air conditioning allows closed windows in the summertime. In addition, the hum of the air conditioner adds its own masking noise, helping to make other noises less noticeable.

d. Storage is essential in the bedroom. Space for clothes, linens, and other needed furnishings will be a part of every well-planned sleeping area. Modern houses feature spacious, well-designed closets, built-in shelves, drawers, dressing-tables and mirrors, and so on. Older houses of the late 1800s and before had large wooden "wardrobes" which stood in the corners and held the clothes and bedding.

e. Space is a psychologically necessary feature of sleeping quarters for most people. Actually, one needs very little space in which to sleep. Imagine a "bedroom" equipped with several small cubicles set into the walls, each containing a bed, such as is shown in Example 26-7. All members of the family could sleep in such places, in which they would shut themselves for privacy. The bed spaces would be equipped with individual light, temperature, and air controls, and would be perfectly safe and comfortable, except for one thing. Most people

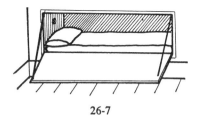

26-7

would get claustrophobia from being shut up in a small space all night. So sometimes the most efficient arrangement is not the one we settle on; there are many aspects of our houses which are not strictly practical but which do suit our temperaments none the less.

f. A final needed feature of the sleeping room is that of communication. There are certain messages we need to receive, and emergencies which might arise demanding our attention. Many people now install a telephone in the bedroom for this reason. Almost everyone will have a radio, a one-way communication to be sure, but useful for news and weather. Television is fast becoming another communication device for the sleeping quarters, and with the use of earphones, it can be as unobtrusive as one wishes.

5. *Food* occupies a prominent place in the function of a house. It is dealt with in three stages:

a. Preparation and storage involves stove, refrigerator, freezer, shelves, bins, sink, and disposal unit. All of this is contained in today's modern kitchen, but in earlier times, food areas had to be divided into cellar (for storing fresh foods such as potatoes, carrots, apples, and so on), pantry (where the utensils and cooking supplies were kept), and kitchen. Often, especially in farm homes, a "summer kitchen" was added to the house for cooking during the hottest weather. It would be set slightly away from the main part of the house so that the terrific heat from the old cookstoves would not make the rest of the home uncomfortable.

b. Cooking, which used to be a full time chore for the housewife, now takes up much less of her time, as a rule. Most foods come prepared for cooking, canned or frozen, so that the housewife need only open the container and warm its contents. Baking is simplified with pre-mixed ingredients, and whole dinners may be popped into the oven and left to thaw and heat. Many a present-day homemaker has never killed and dressed a chicken prior to frying it. Fewer still have ever "cold-packed" fruits and vegetables, or rendered lard from a freshly-killed hog. Today's kitchens reflect the greatly simplified cooking chores in their compactness, efficiency, and automation.

c. A special room for serving and eating the food is seldom found in the average modern home. The dining room gave way to the dining "area" which is often merely an extension of the kitchen or living room. Lack of servant help has contributed to this change in domestic architecture. When the lady of the house has to serve her own dinners, it seems foolishly formal to have a separate dining room where she acts as a maid and hostess all in one. Instead, the whole setting has become more informal, as befits our present way of life. In a larger, more elaborate home, where formal entertaining includes dinners, a dining room will be desirable, of course. There will no doubt be a servant or two to assist at the dinners.

d. Cleaning up after the meal is today done by several labor-saving devices. The automatic dishwasher and the garbage disposal unit have added to the compactness of the kitchen, helped compensate for the lack of servants, and generally made the kitchen into a fairly complex collection of machinery.

6. *Recreation* has become a major function of today's home. From the family room with its television set to the rumpus room in the basement, many parts of a house are devoted to the after-work pleasures of its inhabitants. More and more houses include areas for workshops, hobbies, and sports. Swimming pools are not uncommon in back yards. All of this contrasts sharply with the house of the early 1900s. In those times a husband worked at least 60 hours per week, while today a 40 hour week is standard, and many people work even less time. The modern home reflects these changes in its growing recreation areas.

7. *Prestige* plays a great part in the shape and size of our dwellings. We select the style for a new home by comparing it with the styles of our friends' houses. Frequently we follow fashions in house-building with as little reason as we follow them in clothing. The

picture window, for instance, has become a kind of status symbol in houses. The fireplace, once a necessity, is now a costly luxury and a prime prestige item. In those days after fireplaces were no longer needed, builders of new homes were dead set against having them, and owners of many older homes had theirs bricked over and closed off. It usually takes some time before a feature of this kind becomes old and antique enough to acquire prestige value.

Sometimes certain building materials help the homeowner acquire prestige. Cut stone is preferred over brick, brick over wood, and wood over asphalt shingle siding. At one time "stucco" was a fashionable siding material, and lately aluminum siding is having a run of popularity. Glass, plastics, formica, nylon, and other excellent materials are all being chosen by homeowners today partly because they have been glamorized through advertising, and have thus acquired a prestige value.

8. *Maintenance costs* are often strong factors in determining the shape and structure of one's home. More and more owners put in copper tubing plumbing, electric radiant heat, aluminum windows, and enamelled siding. None of these need attention once they are installed, though their initial cost may be high. Extra time and money spent on waterproofing the foundations pays off in freedom from costly repairs later, and metal basement beams will prevent sagging floors, and resist termites.

9. *Future needs* will also help determine the form of the house. A young couple just starting married life may not need a three-bedroom home but will find it quite desirable a decade later when they have a growing family. There may be a prospect of having one or more parents to take care of in the years to come. A choice of house may be made on the basis of a spare room or wing for such an eventuality. A good, basic design for a house will be capable of expansion. Sometimes this is done by finishing a large basement with tile flooring, plywood walls, and an acoustic-tile ceiling. At other times, the garage may be converted into a room, or an attic finished off.

10. *Interior traffic* must be properly planned. The people in a house in which this has been ignored may find themselves having to cross the living room to get to the kitchen from the front entrance. The traffic to and from the bathroom is always a sensitive problem in the design of a house, especially where there are small children. The kitchen should be so planned that the housewife need take no unnecessary steps in the preparation of the meals. Access to the kitchen from the outside should be as direct as possible, so that groceries may be brought in without trouble and mess. The garage should be attached to the house, making for easy entry when the weather is inclement.

The Choice of a Location

Planning the interior of the house carefully is not enough to insure the owner of a smoothly functioning dwelling. He must also consider the site of his house with equal care. Some considerations will surely include the following:

1. *Climate* will have much to do with the shape of the house, as was seen earlier. The house which is suited for Texas may not be at all good in Maine. If the winter brings icy north winds, the house should face away from them if possible. If hot sun is the rule in summertime, the roof overhang should be at such an angle that the summer sun is kept off the sides of the house as much as possible, but the winter sun is allowed to strike walls freely, as seen in Example 26-8.

2. *Soil* makeup will be a consideration in building a house. Basements are impractical in extremely wet locations, or where the soil is quite rocky. Sandy soil will require a different kind of draining system from clay soil.

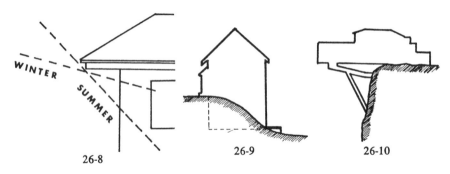

26-8   26-9   26-10

3. *Topography* of the building site will certainly determine the type of house built there. A ranch-type home will fit a flat lot beautifully, but a more steeply sloping one will require some other kind of plan, perhaps a split-level or two-story home set into the hillside, as in Example 26-9. Many lots formerly thought totally unsuited for houses have in recent years become prime locations, and now bring high prices. The house perched on the edge of a cliff, shown in Example 26-10 is an example of such a location. Modern engineering methods of construction make such a feat possible. The view of a city or a valley spread out below makes this a highly desirable building site today.

4. *The zone of a city* in which a building site is situated may have a direct bearing on the kind of house one will build. Some zoning laws will specify the type and cost of a home in a certain area. Others, as stated in the following chapter on cities, will permit various types

of business within or near a neighborhood. This may be a help if the homeowner wishes to run a small business from his house, but it may be a detriment if a business establishment starts up next door and the street is clogged with parked cars or delivery trucks all day.

A prospective homeowner should also consider the directions of city growth when buying a house or lot. Many a family has built a new home in a sparsely settled area only to find themselves surrounded by other houses in a few years, their desired isolation totally lost. On the other hand, building in an area where the city is expanding may cause your lot to rise in value.

A lot may lose value if located on a street bearing heavy through-traffic. The same house on a quiet side-street a block away may be worth a good deal more. A location near a school, church, or market may well enhance the value of a home, while one close to an auto junkyard or an odorous city dump will certainly remain low in value.

With today's increasing traffic, a city lot is valuable if close to a freeway but not so close as to have traffic noise. If one must drive several miles through ordinary city streets to reach the high-speed expressway, the ease and speed of getting into and out of the city will be greatly hampered. Nearness to airports has become a prime factor with the advent of increasingly noisy jet planes. The airport has become the modern equivalent of the railroad line, but with more noise and less dirt. The homeowner should, if possible, select a site away from both.

PROBLEMS:

Problem One: Find an older home like the one shown in Example 26-11, and make a floor plan of its interior. After studying both its outward form and its inner arrangements, write an essay on the relationship between the life of that day and age, and the form of its domestic architecture.

Problem Two: Make a floor plan of your own home, listing the functions of each room. Suggest ways in which each room might be improved, according to its function.

Problem Three: Design a "dream home" of your own, first listing your specifications, and then fitting the floor plan to them.

Problem Four: Imagine a home for some time in the future when the head of the house will

26-11

need only to work for fifteen hours per week, most of which can be accomplished from the house via "visiphone" and other devices. The three children are ages 3, 12, and 17, with the youngest a girl and the other two boys. Design such a home, draw up a set of plans, and write specifications as to size of rooms, equipment, furniture, etc.

Problem Five: Criticize the floor plan of the home shown in Example 26-12 as to how functional the house will be.

Problem Six: Criticize the site (marked X) as to suitable location for a home in a city of 50,000 population, as shown in Example 26-13.

Problem Seven: How could the room shown in Example 26-14 be redesigned to provide the storage space needed? Draw up a set of sketches of alternative solutions.

Problem Eight: Indicate how the house shown in Example 26-15 might best be enlarged. Change the room usage on the interior if necessary, that is, change dining room to living room, and so on.

Problem Nine: Suppose a device were put on the market which would have the following specifications and capabilities:

1. Weight, six pounds. Size, 1 ft by 8 inches by 6 inches (shoe-box size).

2. Self-contained power unit, with rechargeable batteries which will run the device for 24 hours.

3. Costs approximately $1 per day to operate.

4. Exerts a field of force around its "wearer" at a distance of six feet at a strength of about one pound per square inch, sufficient to keep out rain, snow, dust, pests, etc.

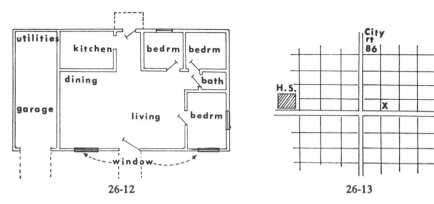

26-12   26-13

5. Control of temperature, humidity, and air freshness with the sphere of force is simply managed through controls.

6. Sphere of force may be made opaque so as to control amount of light entering. Almost total darkness within it is thus possible.

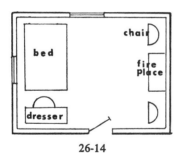

26-14

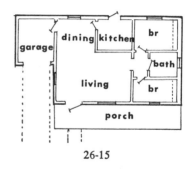

26-15

7. Absolutely safe in operation. Children may operate unit without danger.

8. When several such units are placed close together, the force fields do not combine, but repel each other.

9. Total cost of the unit, approximately $300.

List the possible consequences of such a product on the housing industry , and the effects it would have on architecture in general.

CHAPTER 27

CITY PLANNING

The present generation of men has witnessed a strange new phenomenon; all over the world human beings are gathering themselves together in larger and larger groups until more than half of the world's population now lives in cities. Americans are no exception; in fact, they lead the parade.

This swarming of people to the cities and away from farms and small towns brings with it many problems. As we begin to study what is happening, we realize at once that if this urban growth is allowed to take place without any direction or plan, chaos and disruption will occur. If, however, there *is* a plan, and if that plan is a good one, great benefits may arise from city growth. To the extent that the city is shaped by an "aesthetic" plan, then, it may be considered as a work of art, and the city-planner as an artist. We shall see some examples of this sort of art a little later, but first we must examine the city itself to see what it really is.

The Meaning of the City

Not all large collections of human beings living close to one another can be called cities. Army camps and prison compounds, though possessing large numbers of people at the required density, are certainly not cities. Nor are sprawled out suburbs where the people live who work in the cities. In order to qualify as a city, certain things are necessary:

1. *Numbers* --- there must be sheer numbers if the magical qualities of a city are to make themselves felt. Small towns, no matter how beautiful or comfortable or industrious, lack that exciting atmosphere which seems to be generated when people gather together in hundreds of thousands, or in millions. Almost all of the city's attractions ultimately rest on its sheer size, for out of numbers can come great things.

2. *Specialization* --- when millions gather in an urban setting, there will inevitably be vast differences of skills and interests in evidence. No matter what business you are in, the large city will offer some outlet or point of contact with others in the same type of work.

Even if the business should be such a non-urban one as farming, the city will provide experts, information, and manufacturers of equipment for it. If you have an unusual hobby, the metropolis is sure to contain among its people a club or association devoted to it. You might be a lonely collector of pre-Civil War political buttons in your home town, but in a city there would be others interested in the same hobby.

3. *Culture* --- out of the millions who live in or near a great city, there will be enough supporters of cultural institutions so that a symphony orchestra, an opera company, a large library, a museum and an art gallery may flourish. These are the hallmarks of a great city, and form one of its distinguishing features. It is no accident that our great orchestras are all associated with large cities, that the nation's best art collections are housed and supported by these same cities.

4. *Entertainment* --- like cultural institutions, entertainment facilities abound in major centers of population. The pro football and baseball teams need the financial support which only a metropolis can give. Theatres, nightclubs, racetracks, and other forms of amusement cluster about cities.

5. *Manufacture* --- the city serves as a gigantic processing plant for the region around it. Raw materials arrive by the trainload and emerge as salable goods. It is here that the farm products are shipped to become the packaged or canned food we eat. Here the crude metal becomes the automobile, the raw cloth is transformed into the dress or suit. Only in the city are there the necessary skills and machinery to do this job on the required scale.

6. *Trade* --- in addition to making salable products from the raw materials, the city trades in these products. Its warehouses are the half-way point in the journey from factory to consumer. The "middleman" who distributes the goods occupies an important position in the city. The salesman who promotes the product, the advertiser who glamorizes it, and the TV announcer who puts the message across -- all are "middle-men" to be found in the city.

7. *Finance* --- the city exerts great power over the surrounding territory by its control over the flow of credit and money. The great banks of the metropolitan areas supply credit to the smaller local banks, and thus indirectly control the financial and business structure of an area far exceeding the city limits. There is nothing particularly sinister in this; control flows from the source of wealth, and wealth is naturally concentrated in cities.

8. *Job opportunities* --- nowhere can the job seeker find a greater number of opportunities and a wider choice of positions than in the city.

This is one of the city's most powerful attractions, especially for the young person. Many must "try their luck" at making their fortunes in New York or Chicago or San Francisco, if for no other reason than the sheer challenge of conquering the city, and making one's own place in it.

9. *Stimulation* --- the city is an exciting place to be, of that there is no doubt. It is the place where things happen, and happen fast. Where the small town closes up after 10 P.M., the city remains alive all night long. Where a really important event rarely breaks the calm of a village, the city sees such events take place almost daily. "Big names" live there, others are always visiting, newsworthy events occur almost hourly. Even though the average city-dweller has no more personal contact with all of this than does his country cousin, there is undeniably a sense of excitement in being close by. This fast-paced life is especially attractive to younger people, and many go to live in cities because of it.

The visual and auditory stimulation offered by the city is most powerful. The constant traffic, the noise level, the movement, the multi-colored lights, the kaleidoscopic views of store windows, the parade of fashions, the odors and tastes of a vast variety of foods and cooking styles --- all of these stimulate the city dweller's senses, and attract more and more to city life.

To summarize its attractions (and this short list certainly has not named them all, by any means) it could be said that the city acts as a gigantic magnet which draws people to itself, some for one reason and some for another. By the same token, it repels certain people, and for equally good reasons. People might find the city unattractive for the following reasons:

1. *Danger* --- just as many are drawn to the city for its job opportunities, others are attracted for criminal opportunities. Concentration of wealth, and density of population tend to concentrate crime in a smaller area. This means that more crimes happen closer by in a city. Many people who have lived in a city with perfect safety still become apprehensive at the fact that crimes occur within a few miles of them.

2. *Slums* --- most cities contain densely packed areas of under-privileged people whose congestion tends to breed the very ills that forced them to live there in the first place. As such areas grow and spread, those near them tend to move out, many to leave the city altogether.

3. *Traffic* --- undoubtedly cities prove hazardous to the motorist and almost impossible for the pedestrian. Traffic jams and the search for parking space make the driver's life unpleasant. The commuter

faces the weary ride to and from work. The pedestrian must try to dodge this traffic as he scurries across the street between lights. Most American city-dwellers have lost the freedom of driving without undue tension which the rural motorist still possesses. Many leave the city for just this reason.

4. *Air pollution* --- few cities can say the air breathed by their inhabitants is healthful. Smoke, fumes and smog have proved definitely harmful to the health. Many people prefer the fresher air of the non-urban environment, and move away from cities.

5. *Dehumanization* --- the almost inevitable result of so many many people in so small a space is the building of personal barriers between man and man. In a small town, everyone knows the latest gossip about everyone else, while in a city most people are strangers to one another, and anonymous. This dehumanization sometimes goes so far that city dwellers can pass by a person lying collapsed on the sidewalk without stopping to see whether he needs help. In a small town this would be unthinkable.

6. *Bureaucratic complexity* --- the administration of the great city's affairs has become bewilderingly complicated. Suppose the cover is missing from a manhole in the street which runs past your apartment house. Do you notify the police, the street commissioner, the traffic department, or the Bureau of Public Safety? Perhaps it should be referred to the Department of Sewers and Sanitation, or the City Engineer. At times the citizen finds himself trapped in a maze of red tape as he tries to find his way through the complex organization of metropolitan bureaucracy. The contrasting simplicity of affairs in smaller towns is often an attraction.

The City as an Art Form

All cities show evidence of some kind of planning, but usually the plan is haphazard, made up of bits and pieces, and put together without any long-range goals in mind. All too often the only planning is that of each individual who has built whatever he likes wherever he chooses. Such a situation is contrasted with that of a city which is pre-planned before it even starts! This type of city is not uncommon today in America, and is usually the brain-child of a real-estate developer who buys up all the necessary land, calls in a city-planning expert, and designs the city in its entirety before selling lots to those who will live there. Such cities may allot land to parks, schools, churches and other public centers so that it can never be sold for private use. Roads may be laid out to funnel traffic around residential areas rather than through them. Factories are given space in an "industrial park" close to adequate rail, highway, and water facilities. Even the type and cost of houses may be prescribed, so that the end result is harmonious. Here we have the totally designed city, as against the haphazard one which "just grew." Perhaps neither is the ideal, but something in between, something that grew naturally but within a general guiding plan to keep it in bounds. For a city, unlike a painting or statue, is a *living* work of art. Its materials are not only bricks, steel, and stone but people. It is not only a static three-dimensional object, as in a building, but it moves and grows. It develops through a time-span and is, thus, a combined art existing in both time and space.

The Development of Cities

Although the city of five to ten million inhabitants is a modern development, the institution of the city itself is an ancient one. As far back as history goes there were cities, and it seems likely that men banded together into something like community life long before that. The student of urban development will be able to pick out certain types or patterns of cities which have grown up through history, and will recognize some of these patterns remaining in cities of our own time.

1. *The Defense City* was an urban form designed to protect its inhabitants from outside dangers. Its chief features were a central fortress or strong point (usually a castle), and heavy, high walls. Such cities were built in medieval times throughout Europe. They have narrow streets, crooked and winding, as shown in Example 27-1. The houses are set close onto the streets, without front yards or spaces between them. Material is invariably brick or stone, for wood is too easily set afire. Certain areas of Boston are built in this fashion, but in most American cities dating from pre-revolutionary days these old, old sections have been made into modern patterns. One can still drive into the heart of many European cities and find the original medieval pattern at the very center, surrounded by the broad, straight avenues of later eras.

27-1

2. *The River City* is a more familiar type in the United States. It made its first appearance on the Eastern edge of the country as early settlers used the rivers to provide easy access to the interior. The main streets parallel the river with others leading away

27-2

from it at right angles. Early settlers placed shipping docks and storage sheds close to the river, of course, so that over the years the large-scale transportation industry grew along the waterfront. As ships became less important, rail and truck firms located there to be close to the warehouses, and the riverfront filled up with unsightly structures and areas.

In addition, early industry used the river for its waterpower. Later, the industry converted to coal and remained alongside the river through tradition, and also because transportation and storage facilities were there. The riverfront section of many American cities has long been the ugliest part of town. Only recently have we learned the value of reclaiming and beautifying the river and its banks.

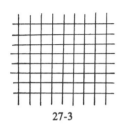

27-3

3. *The Grid City* is by far the most common type seen in our country. It is found in all sections and consists of streets crossing one another at right angles, (Example 27-3) forming "blocks" in which individual lots are sold. Each lot is much like the others, each block and street like all the rest. Various reasons have been given for the popularity of this city type in our earlier days, two of which seem relevant:

a. America was very conscious of its democratic origins, and our people at that time felt all parts of a town or city should be equally good (or bad) to live in. The new cities of the early 1800s were to have no great landed estates, private parks, or rich man's domains as was so common in European cities. Every lot was the equal of every other. The only choice location was "close to the square" around which the business establishments were grouped. Later on, when the railroad came through, these towns and cities suddenly acquired a kind of demarcation line, useful for separating the developing social classes. Even today the phrase "from the other side of the tracks" stands for something of social inferiority, though in actual fact the "tracks" do not separate cities as they once did.

b. These grid cities were created for commercial reasons, rather than for defense. Therefore the equal division of land made possible quick and easy sales of building lots. Furthermore, the straight, right-angled streets made it easy to find any particular address, thus facilitating mail delivery and all sorts of trade and commerce.

4. *The Satellite City* is a more recent type which has sprung up

close to our great centers of population. Clustered about every metropolis are suburbs formed by people who move out some distance from the more congested areas. These suburbs (Example 27-4) often grow to be the size of cities in their own right, but there is one important difference. Their people still earn their livelihood in the city itself, for the most part. They only have their homes in the suburbs. Sometimes the satellites completely ring the city, restricting its further growth, and choking off some of its sources of revenue.

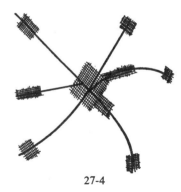

27-4

5. *The Ribbon City* is an even newer phenomenon. Many new expressways, turnpikes, and interstate highways have encouraged builders to extend homes, motels, service stations and small businesses outward from the city in long tentacles whose central core is the high-

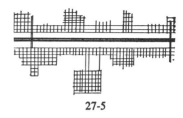

27-5

way. Some of these settlements (Example 27-5) are miles long but only blocks wide. Some are beginning to function more and more as cities do, with a kind of coordination needed for an era of fast-moving transport and rapidly shifting population.

6. *The Planned City,* though not new by any means, has received fresh attention in our day and age. Earlier in this chapter, such a city plan was described, and its features noted. The reasons for such cities are of interest to the student of the arts. First, and perhaps most important, the planner hopes he will be able to avoid those costly mistakes which occur when a city grows without a plan. Almost every one of our major cities has had to spend millions of dollars on redesigning itself, so the planner of the new city builds into it those features which cities are finding most desirable. The plight of the great metropolis today is oftentimes a sorry one, its present condition having come about through a series of fairly well-defined stages.

The Growth Patterns of a City

1. Early growth stages of major American cities were marked by the industrial expansion which our nation experienced in the late 1800s, especially after the Civil War. This period saw the establishment of great factories and industrial districts in the cities. Workers'

homes had to be built within walking distance of these areas, so that factories were usually surrounded by blocks of houses, multiple-dwelling units, tenements and "flats." The area was usually smoky and crowded, with little provision for parks and playgrounds.

2. The second stages of development saw the establishment of various kinds of transportation, such as local railroad and trolley lines. The better-paid classes of workmen would be able to leave the factory districts and purchase land farther away, along the railroad line. At outlying stations a few miles outside the city limits, small communities would begin to grow. The homeowners would usually be in the white collar and junior executive class.

3. As we entered the 20th Century, a third stage of city development occurred, brought about directly by the invention of the mass-produced automobile. In the 1920s, Henry Ford's "Model T" came within the financial reach of many workers, and suddenly our population achieved a new level of mobility. Now the laboring man no longer had to live close to his work. Two, five, even ten miles was not too far to drive to the shop or factory. He need not live on a suburban rail line, either, but could go anywhere that roads would take him. All of a sudden the middle-class worker fled the factory area and swarmed out over the countryside, creating new suburban areas and satellite towns by the thousands.

4. Immigration and further rapid industrial expansion went hand in hand. We needed more and more laborers to fill the great numbers of jobs we were creating. The railroads, mines, factories and farms desperately needed workers. They came from Europe and Asia in great numbers. These people arrived poor, for the most part, and took the lowest-paying jobs. They filled up the cheap-rent housing around the factories, housing that earlier waves of workers had been able to leave for better homes in the suburbs. After some years of working and saving, the immigrant family might be able, in turn, to move out to the suburbs also, making way for still another wave of immigrants. Each move left the tenements and flats in worse shape, and it was not long before true slum conditions prevailed.

5. Traffic problems mark the next stage in the life of the city. The growing number of commuters, many with cars of their own, brought about a frightful congestion in traffic which has persisted to the present day! Earlier streets had to be widened, expressways cut through, bus service extended, and so on. Despite all these measures, the size and number of private cars outstripped the road systems and

parking facilities, and conditions worsened. In the late 1800s, the average speed of horse-drawn traffic in downtown New York City was greater than the pace of modern vehicles today!

6. The flight of businesses from the center of the city marks yet another stage of development. Many of America's large cities had become so uncomfortable and dangerous that people refused to come downtown to shop. The prospect of driving through the surrounding slum areas, on narrow, traffic-choked streets deterred many people from visiting the city. So it was only natural that the large department stores, shops, and services moved out to where their customers were. Beautiful branch stores were set up in the richer suburbs, and great shopping centers arose featuring ample space to park, open air free from dust and dirt, easy highway access, and new, clean buildings. This, of course, further depressed the downtown city center.

7. Cultural difficulties now began to make themselves felt. The great orchestras, theatres, museums and libraries which were the pride of the city began to feel the lack of support which had made them possible in an earlier generation. The people with money now lived elsewhere, and those who had remained were not able to pay taxes on a similar scale. The slum-dweller not only could not support the city institutions; it required a greater share of the tax dollar to take care of *him!* Slum areas need more police surveillance, more fire protection, more health support, and more social workers. As slums spread, city costs rise and city income drops, creating a vicious circle which is most difficult to break.

8. Restorative measures mark the present stage of development in many of our cities. In order to correct the evils which had developed earlier, cities examined their futures, and found them dark. Planners were brought in and money appropriated to help out. Among the principal measures taken were:

a. Traffic control through the construction of new access freeways, improved signal systems, establishment of supplemental subway, bus, and train lines.

b. Slum clearance by massive rebuilding of substandard areas. One move involves tearing down blocks of close-packed two- and three-story buildings and erecting high-rise apartments which will take care of the same number of people, but leave more open space between.

c. Attracting shoppers and visitors to the city center again is being approached in several ways. Some cities have created pedestrian malls by barring streets to vehicles, placing trees and grass plots down the centers of the streets, adding sidewalk cafes and benches along the curbs, and so on. The visitor may stroll about and enjoy shopping without the dust and noise of the usual city traffic.

d. Air pollution control has been enforced by many large cities with a resultant clearing of city air. People no longer leave because of this particular problem in many areas, and visitors need not avoid the city because of its smoke and smog.

e. Waterfront cleanup for those cities fortunate enough to have a river or lake within their boundaries has created areas of surprising beauty. Instead of being an area of rotting warehouses and dirty wharves, many a waterfront is now a lovely park attracting many visitors.

f. Zoning laws, customarily a feature of city government, have been strengthened. A zoning law specifies what type of building may be built in a certain part of a city. In this way, a residential area may not be invaded by a factory or service station. Loose application of zoning laws has permitted the growth of nightmarish areas of hot-dog stands, garages, used-car lots, drive-ins and other features of the entranceways to our great cities. Better zoning can regulate this and make our cities much more attractive.

g. Building codes are closely related to zoning. These regulations control the types and construction of buildings in the city, and are aimed at setting standards for quality and safety. Sometimes the codes do this by specifying exactly what kinds of materials the builder must use. Such codes are not as good as those which specify standards which the materials must meet. Suppose a building code states that all hospitals shall be built of brick and concrete (for fire safety), and later on a kind of plastic or a type of laminated wood is invented which is not only fireproof and as strong as concrete and brick, but lighter and cheaper. It could not be used under that sort of code. Very likely the brick and cement manufacturers would oppose changing the code, as would the unions of bricklayers and cement workers. The losers would be the general public, of course, having to pay for hospital services. When such codes cause industries to locate in other cities where they are allowed to use modern, efficient building materials, the codes are often re-examined and overhauled.

h. The depersonalization of city-life has been the subject of much thought in our time. Ways have been sought whereby people would be drawn together, get to know one another, share a sense of responsibility toward their community, and take an active interest in their immediate neighborhood. Under this arrangement, the city planner or zoning commission marks off an area of some blocks, and cuts off all through traffic. Only those who live there are allowed to drive to their homes. Sometimes alternate streets are completely closed off, making them into long playgrounds on which the children may play without fear of being hit by traffic. As city traffic flows around this island, its inhabitants are drawn together by several means. A central day-nursery and child-care service brings many mothers and children together, establishing the beginning of a community spirit and bonds of friendship. A shopping center offers another meeting place for the people, and, in addition, there is usually a school, church and laundry where people can meet. A movie house and various small shops help create a small-town atmosphere within the large city. The super-block should have its own alderman on the city council, so as to create a political bond among the people. When this is accomplished, the people within the area may begin to feel pride in their community and responsibility for keeping it up. Then they will have the advantages of both the small town and the metropolis.

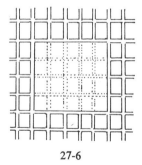

27-6

The Future of the City

Predictions as to the future of cities vary widely among experts. Some think the city has expanded beyond its useful limits, and that the future will see a decrease in city size and population. They base their predictions on such factors as:

1. Communication inventions, which allow us to share much of the excitement and immediacy of the city life via television, radio and telephone while living anywhere we choose. As such communications improve, we may find it possible to "work" in the city but never go there! Certain directorial jobs are handled in large part today by long distance phone calls. Salesmen often do their work without actually meeting the prospect face to face. As this becomes more common, many who must live in a city today may find that no longer necessary in a few years.

2. Transportation improvements make it possible to reach almost any city in a matter of a few hours from anywhere in the nation. Commuters who formerly could live only ten or fifteen miles away

can now live fifty or more. When access to city advantages is easy and rapid, the need to live in the city disappears.

3. Self-contained housing units are also adding to the dispersal of population. As cheap electric power becomes widely available, farm homes will have all of the advantages of city houses. The farmer's house today is air-conditioned, has frozen food storage, television, phone connections with anywhere, and the latest in labor-saving devices. The earlier ideas of country life as primitive have been changed. America is dotted with lovely country homes whose owners may be anything from real farmers to business executives, lawyers, doctors, or small businessmen.

Those who predict added growth of cities have strong points in their favor, too. Among these we find:

1. Cities offer even greater business and job opportunities than ever before. Cities are not only attracting people daily but their own birth rate is adding thousands of newborn babies to the total every year. These, in turn, create an increasing demand for goods, services, education, and recreation. The demand draws still more people, who produce still more population growth.

2. City planning efforts are making metropolitan areas more attractive all the time. As slums are cleared and handsome new apartments rise, people who had moved out into the suburbs are now moving back. It is still preferable to live within walking distance of one's work, and when living conditions are good, people will return to the centers of cities again.

3. New city apartment complexes offer incredibly diverse environment for living, in many cases. The latest apartment houses are really residential skyscraper-cities! One's car is garaged on the lower floors where there are parking facilities for all the dwellers. Service stations and repair shops are right in the building. Above them may be food stores, beauty shops, restaurants, doctors' offices, a moviehouse, and so on. The living quarters, being above these levels quite some distance from the streets, are quieter, cooler places to live than would be available anywhere on the ground level. The added convenience of living close to one's work is a powerful attraction.

SUMMARY

Cities are complex and fascinating phenomena of our national life. Their operation, advantages and disadvantages, their future for America should be of concern to every citizen in this time.

PROBLEMS:

Problem One: Look up statistics for your state, and for the United States, on the population shift from rural to urban areas. Show in chart or graph form what is happening.

Problem Two: Find out what plan is in operation to guide the growth of your town or city, or a nearby population center.

Problem Three: Make a survey of the cultural institutions (orchestras, libraries, museums, galleries) of your state or general area. What relation does their location have to the population density?

Problem Four: Visit with the owner or manager of a local supermarket or department store. Ask him where the many items on his shelves come from, where their distributors are situated, and where their manufacturing plants are. By this survey, show how the large city acts as a "funnel" for commerce.

Problem Five: Make an informal survey of your classmates, or of members of the senior class, to find out how many would like to start their job careers in a large city, and why.

Problem Six: Interview a number of adults as to what they like and dislike about big city living. Tabulate their responses to find out their chief likes and dislikes.

Problem Seven: Study carefully a map of your town or city. If you live in a rural area, use one of the nearby urban centers. See if you can divide the city into its different areas (business, manufacturing, transport, residential, slum, etc.) and describe each. What suggestions do you have for improving the present conditions?

Problem Eight: Find different traces of past stages of growth and development in your town or city. Should these traces be removed, or would it be helpful to preserve them? Why?

Problem Nine: Find different types of cities in your state or region (grid, satellite, ribbon, etc.) and show how their maps differ in appearance. How might life in these cities be affected by their different forms?

Problem Ten: What problems are being encountered by the cities in your area as they grow? Do any of these coincide with the eight mentioned in this chapter?

Part Seven

LOOKING INWARD

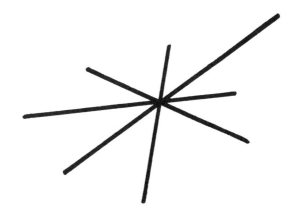

CHAPTER 28

PERCEPTION:
PSYCHOLOGY OF THE ARTS

So far in this book, we have paid a great deal of attention to the work of art, but this is only part of the problem. The work of art still must be seen or heard by someone. This involves the idea of "perception," the study of incoming sense impressions, and how we interpret them.

The average person, if he thinks about the problem at all, considers perception an easily explained process. We see or hear something, and we understand what we have seen or heard. Unfortunately, the process is far from that simple. Perception, in its simplest form, involves at least three aspects; first, the physical functioning of the sense organs; next, the interpretation of the information which they furnish the brain; and third, the effect upon this interpretation of our cultural and social training. In other words, the ideas we form about things in the world may not correspond at all with the "reality" of those things. This will become clearer as we proceed. Let us first focus our attention on the sense receptors, those marvelous organs which act to give us information about the outside world.

The Sense Receptors

In addition to our eyes and ears, which furnish us perhaps the greatest amount of data about what is going on outside ourselves, there are other channels of information available. One of these is the sense of smell, another is the sense of taste, and the third is the sense of touch. We get valuable information from each of these senses. Escaping gas cannot be seen, tasted, felt or heard --- our sense of smell provides the sole warning of this danger. Spoiled food can sometimes be detected by smell, and possible danger averted. Our sense of smell can be highly trained to the point where it can be used for the chemical analysis of products, but in most people it is left undeveloped because other senses provide sufficient information. This sense has been used very little in the world of the arts.

The sense of taste provides us with valuable information also. Food may be rejected if it doesn't "taste right." We often perform a kind of analysis by taste when we attempt to guess the ingredients of a dish by the various tastes we can identify in it. Again, this sense may be much more highly trained than it usually is. Taste, like smell, has had little application in the arts area.

The sense of touch is involved not only with the pressure sensations of touching something, but with sensations of heat, cold, pain, and so on. All of these are related, arising as they do from nerve endings in the skin and flesh. Were it not for this sense, we would not know when we were being physically hurt, when our teeth needed attention, when our bodies needed rest! The whole idea of "pain" is that it acts as a warning signal to the brain that something is wrong somewhere. The sense of touch, unlike taste and smell does have some application in the arts, but not much. Industrial products and appliances which are made to be used and handled do, it is true, require the designer to consider how they will feel to the user when he touches them. Most statues and works of architecture are not touched, and no paintings are, of course.

The other two senses, sight and hearing, form the great bulk of our perception in the world of the arts. Let us briefly examine each one from its purely physical standpoint.

The Eye

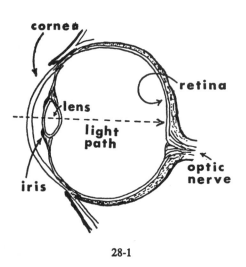

28-1

The eye is a marvellously sensitive organ which functions like a camera but with abilities that no camera ever possessed. It can focus on anything from a few inches to infinity; its "light meter" lets in just as much light as it needs by automatically opening and closing its light aperture (the pupil); it can see stereoscopically and in full color; it will focus on what you are interested in, and ignore something right next to it; it has a self-cleaning device which keeps the lens free from dust at all times; it has highly variable "shutter speeds," and it lasts from 75 to 100 years with few serious maintenance problems. No camera today can meet these specifications.

In operation, the eye sees when light rays are reflected from an object and pass through the cornea, are focused by the lens, and fall on the retina. Here the rays activate the chemicals in the retinal cells, creating nerve impulses which travel through the optic nerve to the brain. The brain then registers the sensation of vision. Two general types of retinal cells are known; the "rods" which allow us to see variations in light and dark, and the "cones" which can detect colors. The rods help us to see in dim light and the cones in bright.

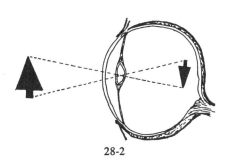

28-2

Like all camera lenses, the eye reverses the images that come through it, so that they fall on the retina upside down, as shown in Example 28-2. Our brain somehow reverses these images so that they look correct to us. A simple experiment has been devised to show that the brain really does this. The subject is asked to wear special goggles that reverse his vision, so that everything looks upside down. If these goggles are worn continuously for several days, the brain will again reverse its interpretation, and things will look normal again to the wearer! If the glasses are then removed, everything will seem to be upside down for awhile, until the brain can again re-interpret the impressions from the eye. Finally, all will return to normal once more. This is just one of the ways in which the incoming sense impressions may be "wrongly" interpreted by the brain. Others will be discussed later.

The Ear

Our hearing mechanism is remarkably sensitive and accurate. It can detect a faint sound requiring almost no energy to produce, and it can tolerate sounds millions of times louder without damage. No man-made sound system possesses the delicacy and adaptability of the ear in so compact a space.

The mechanical functions of the ear are well-known. A brief description will suffice at this point, but if the reader desires more information he should consult an encyclopedia or science text. Sound waves enter the outer ear (A) as seen in Example 28-3, which serves as a focusing device to catch the faint air pressure waves and funnel them into the auditory canal (B). The waves travel down this canal until they reach the eardrum (C) at its end, which separates the outer from the inner ear. On the far side of this eardrum there are three small bones

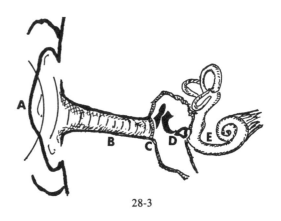

28-3

called the hammer, anvil, and stirrup (D) which act as levers to magnify the tiny air waves, transferring their action to the cochlea (E). The original sound energy is multiplied nearly 200 times by means of all these mechanisms.

Inside the cochlea there is a marvelously sensitive system for changing the mechanical action of the hammer, anvil, and stirrup into fluid pressures, for the cochlea is filled with liquid. As it spirals back into the head, the cochlea, no larger than a bean, is found to contain tiny compartments along which the incoming pressures form wave crests. It is these crests which help us to distinguish low from high pitches.

The walls of the cochlea are lined with nerve endings, and when a pressure crest acts on a given spot in the cochlea, the nerves there signal the brain that a certain sound is being heard. With the original air pressures of sound now transferred into electrical impulses in the brain, we conclude our description of the auditory apparatus, and turn our attention to the vast and virtually unsolved problems of how our brain interprets what the ear hears and the eye sees.

THE PSYCHOLOGY OF PERCEPTION

The connection between the senses and the brain is known to be a vital one. In the past few decades many experiments have been conducted which reveal some of these connections. The following factors have begun to emerge:

1. *Sense stimuli and brain development seem to go together.* Animals raised from birth in healthy but soundless, colorless surroundings have less mental capacity in solving problems than normally-reared animals. There is strong evidence that children have the same needs for rich and varied stimuli in their childhood environment.

2. *Brain functions depend on continued stimuli as a necessary condition for normal thought.* Subjects who have been deprived of incoming sense impressions (by being kept in total darkness and absolute silence) find that after a time their minds would "invent" visions and sounds for them. They "saw" the most amazing but vividly real things while in their isolated states. Prisoners kept in solitary confinement reportedly go "stir crazy" from lack of outside stimuli. Men who have sailed alone for months on the ocean report that even under conditions of comparative richness of sight and sound impressions, the monotony and isolation can lead to hallucinations.

It is for these reasons that the child who lacks a rich environment of sense impressions in the form of good music, interesting colors, forms and lines, will have some difficulty in the learning process. A child who lacks such stimuli altogether, through deafness or blindness, will find it much harder to learn. His only avenues are such comparatively poor ones as touch, taste, and smell. Yet despite terrific handicaps, the brain will develop if fed information with which it can operate and grow. Such people as Helen Keller are proof of what the mind can accomplish even with such handicaps.

3. *Perception is a clue to mental health.* As we have come to realize that the mind and the senses are closely linked, we now use sensory evidence as a measure of mental adjustment. If a football player has been hit hard and appears to be in some temporary mental confusion, the team physician may ask him to answer a few questions such as "Who am I?" and "How many fingers am I holding up?" This quick check on the mental processes gives a rough-and-ready clue as to the functioning of the mind at that moment. If perception is accurate, we know the mind is clear. If the answers are hesitant, trouble is indicated.

Mentally disturbed people may reveal their state of mind to a trained clinician, but not in any plainly visible way. The psychiatrist often learns much from his patient as they work together. Tests involving the senses may include such procedures as viewing ink-blot patterns, and describing what is seen in them. The patient's perception thus may reveal something of the way his mind operates, giving the psychiatrist clues as to his client's difficulties. Unlike many other parts of the body, the brain cannot be easily opened up for examination. And even if it could be opened up, a mental difficulty could not be seen. We must rely on secondary symptoms in our work with such illnesses.

4. *Incoming information is processed.* Something in our brain acts as a kind of censor for the information which is important, and that which is not. Just as a busy executive has secretaries to sort out

his mail and his visitors, the busy brain has some sort of information processing system. If you will stop right now and listen carefully, you will hear a lot of noises you were totally unaware of a moment ago. The "mental receptionist" in your brain was keeping them from reaching your conscious mind until the textbook specifically asked you to become aware of them. Then they become important, and were admitted to the higher levels of the mind. The greater part of the sense impressions you receive are so handled. Apparently these unimportant stimuli are left cooling their heels in some cerebral anteroom but are never completely dismissed. Under the deepest hypnosis, it is said that people can recall trifling details of what happened in former years, meals they ate, the weather, items of clothing and so on from decades earlier.

Existing memories may also be processed by the mind, as in the case of people who "forget" dental appointments, names of disagreeable acquaintances, terrifying events, and so on. Children who lived through war bombings and daily sights of death and destruction in their immediate family environment sometimes lost all memory of such incidents. Oftentimes the mind succeeds in blotting out such memories only to have them crop up in nightmares, so disguised as to be difficult to account for.

5. *Incoming information is organized.* The first impressions a baby's mind receives are vague and almost meaningless because there is no "filing system" set up to put each new impression into a proper slot. As the child grows, the filing system should grow in complexity, and size. Children who have rich and varied experiences, and those who read a lot, are apt to have a more comprehensive system of filing than those who have lacked such experiences. Several factors appear to be present in this classification-and-filing system our mind operates:

a. Basic information is handled in fairly small doses. Suppose a person is shown two red disks, one darker than the other, after which they are hidden. If one of them is then revealed, the subject will be able to tell which one it is without difficulty. If three disks of varying shades are used, the difficulty of identification is no greater, but let four, five or six disks be used, and the accuracy of identification falls off sharply. Seven seems to be the maximum number of items of one kind that can be handled with any degree of accuracy. The same may be proved with regard to varying shapes, tones, tastes, odors, and so on. In fact, in some of the senses, the number of similar items that can be accurately handled is even smaller.

b. Types of information are combined by the mind to make the choice of identifiable items larger. Thus, in the case of disks, we could add differing shapes to the shades of red and get, instead of three disks which could be identified with one hundred per cent accuracy, nine! The dark red disk would now come in star, circle, and square shapes, as would the medium and light red ones. Add a third variable, perhaps texture, and we have twenty-seven disks that may be identified one hundred per cent of the time. We now have three dark-red, star-shaped disks, one rough, one pebbled, and one glossy. We will be able to pick out any one from all the rest. It is in this way that we are able to identify the millions of varying objects about us. Of thousands of faces we see, no two look exactly alike, with the rare exceptions of identical twins. We make rapid reference to our mental filing system of facial shapes, eye-colors, hairline, skin texture, mouth contours, and so on, and we come up with a classification of the face we see. Our mind quickly tells us, "That's a stranger" or "That's my mother."

      c. Information entering through the sense channels is checked against "structures" in the mind. Throughout the learning years, we are constantly engaged in creating larger and larger structures out of the information we possess. The mind tends to see things in large, interrelated fields. If the field is strong enough, the mind will tend to force new information into it, even if it does not properly belong there! A good example would **A** be the three figures at the right, Example 28-4. A, B, and C are seen as three views of transparent containers. However if C were shown by itself, most people would describe **B** it as a figure eight bounded by two straight lines. The fact that it is included in an overall mental structure consisting of other representations of containers makes us see it as a similar object. **C**

There are a number of experiments in which people are asked to solve a problem, using only the materials in 28-4 the room where they are seated. If the solution calls for water to be poured into a pipe in order to raise a ball to the surface, the test subjects will frequently overlook a pitcher of water and ice cubes on the table of the psychologist. Water for drinking belongs in a different category, and the subject finds it difficult to transfer it to a problem-solving category.

A similar problem involves fastening two sticks together in order to make a longer one. With this longer stick, the subject can reach something he needs to get for the experiment, but he is not given anything to fasten the sticks with. A "No Smoking" sign is plainly hung from a string on the wall of the room, but again the subject has great difficulty making the mental transfer of this object from the category of "room furnishing" to "problem-solving equipment" and hence almost always overlooks it. Oddly, people who are watching others try to solve the problem can often see the solution plainly!

Carefully tabulated experiments such as these have shed considerable light on larger human problems of creativity and problem-solving. For one thing, when we wish to be creative, we must learn to break out of those mental categories which are so useful most of the time. We must learn to see all of the aspects of the problem in a fresh light, not taking anything for granted. And it helps if we can "externalize" the problem, see it from the outside, as if we were advising someone else.

A type of structuring process which the mind uses has been termed "coding." We know what the Morse code is, a series of dots and dashes which stand for letters of the alphabet. If we set out to learn it, we find ourselves having to memorize each letter, "Dot-dash is A, dash-dot-dot-dot is B" and so on. The first attempts to use the code are very slow. We have to think of every letter, identify every separate pattern. Presently, however, we will begin to recognize words as larger patterns, then phrases and sentences. We no longer think of a word as having separate letters, but as a total pattern. Our reading patterns undergo the same kind of coding procedure. We learn to read in phrases rather than single words. Incoming sense impressions are taken into the mind as groups of messages rather than as single items.

When a student makes an outline of a lecture or a book, he is attempting to codify and structure the information so that it no longer remains a somewhat bewildering mass of facts. Instead, he tries to group these facts within a smaller number of idea structures so that the mind may more easily deal with them. The experimental evidence that the mind can deal best with five to seven separate items seems to be the basis for the common rule that a good outline should contain not more than five or six main headings.

6. *Incoming information can be altered through conditioning.* Because the mind and the emotions are inextricably linked, incoming impressions become tied in to both. The sound of a word, if it is the right one, can cause a person to blush, perspire, experience increased heart beat and blood pressure. That particular combination of vowel and consonant sounds has somehow acquired the power of triggering a whole set of emotional responses. The same sound heard by another person might occasion none of these responses at all!

Certain works of art become the triggers which set off unexpected emotional explosions. One person viewing a painting of a nude model may be moved to feelings of violent anger, shame, or disgust. Another viewer may have no reaction of this kind whatsoever. In the first case, the incoming sense impressions have been conditioned by the viewer's background and training so that he reacts strongly. In the other case, the viewer accepts the information given him by his eyes without such conditioning. Whether the first viewer's attitude is "good" or "bad" is outside the scope of this discussion.

7. *Sensory information can be interpreted in many ways.* The problem of how we evaluate what our eyes and ears take in is indeed a complex one. We might offer the following ideas as to what sometimes happens:

a. Sense impressions are affected by what happens immediately before or afterward. A simple experiment will illustrate. Place three containers of water on a table, as shown in Example 28-5. Place your left hand in the hot water and your right in the cold. After a minute or so, quickly plunge both hands into the room-temperature water in the middle. The result will be a sensation of heat in the right hand and of cold in the left, yet the water is the same stimulus for both!

28-5

The same sort of interpretation problem is often encountered in music where a certain harmony will sound very dissonant in one place and quite mild in another, depending on what comes just before it. A particular color will look bright amid certain other colors, but dull when placed alongside different ones. After listening to army barracks language, a single swearword has little shock effect. Let that same word come from the mouth of a teacher during a classroom lecture, and the context will give it plenty of emphasis. Good students make use of this factor, and study when there are no "before and after" distractions.

b. Sense impressions are strongly affected by the social-cultural-economic status of the person receiving them. An interesting experiment was performed by Le Shan to find out difference in perception of "time" by children from lower, middle, and upperclass homes. He asked each of the youngsters to tell him a story, and discovered the amount of time covered by the "plot" to increase with the raising of the social level. The stories of lower-class children were largely set within a day's time. The middle-class and upper-class children covered up to a week or more in their stories. Le Shan points out that the lower-class child often comes from a home where life is lived on a day-to-day basis with little permanency. The middle-class student, however, is encouraged to think about future rewards much more.

Families of the upper-class group tend to extend their views of time backward for several generations, as they are more conscious of their ancestry, and also view the future farther ahead. Thus the child's social and economic life trains him to regard time in segments which will vary with his personal background.

Social background also has been shown to affect our interpretation of size! A poor child will overestimate the dimensions of coins and bills, while a rich one will not. Similarly, the hungry person will see a vaguely defined image as something having to do with food, while at another time when not hungry, he will tend to see it as something else.

SUMMARY

The mind depends upon the information fed into it by our five senses. Our actions are based on this information. The incoming data is not sent directly to the conscious mind, nor is it given equal weight when it does arrive there. Instead, a number of grouping, coding, and interpreting processes come into play which apparently serve to make the vast amount of information manageable. Finally, the sensory information we get serves both as a means of keeping us mentally healthy, and as a measurement of that mental health.

The study of perception is a comparatively new field of investigation, and our knowledge of what goes on in the mind with reference to sensory impressions is still extremely limited. As man investigates his own thought processes with more and more insight, he may find presently undreamed-of keys to human behavior.

PROBLEMS:

Problem One: Think of some experience you have had in which your interpretation of the data furnished by your own senses was incorrect. Explain as carefully as you can what happened, and why.

Problem Two: Think of a simple experiment to illustrate the fact that you cannot always believe what you see. Perform the experiment and write an account of it.

Problem Three: Think of and perform a simple experiment designed to prove that the mind may misinterpret what the ears hear. Write up your experiment and its results.

Problem Four: Think of and perform an experiment similar to those in Problems Two and Three, testing one of the other senses.

Problem Five: This textbook gives an elementary account of the mechanism of the eye and ear. Write up a report on the mechanisms of the other senses.

Problem Six: Keep a diary of what you receive in the way of information from all five senses during the length of time it takes to eat a sandwich.

Problem Seven: Report on an experiment other than those in this book, which was made in the field of perception by a psychologist. Discuss the reasoning and method which was used to "prove" what was discovered.

Problem Eight: If you know a doctor or other professional person who meets people with problems, ask him about some of his cases, especially those involving perception and interpretation. Prepare a report on one or more such cases. Names of patients will under no circumstances be mentioned.

Problem Nine: Team up with a classmate to find out how much auditory information your brain censors for you. Let the classmate record every sound that he hears while listening carefully. At the same time, you should be reading an interesting short story, keeping track of any sounds you hear while reading. Compare the lists afterward.

Problem Ten: Look up the subject of "hypnotism" and report on its relationship to perception and memory.

Problem Eleven: Explain as well as you can how you are able to do some simple act involving perception, such as catching a ball, combing your hair before a mirror, putting food in your mouth, and so on. Try to think of and explain every part of the action. You will find that this requires a great deal of thought and writing.

Problem Twelve: If it is true that our minds organize impressions into larger structures, find one of these which your mind has been using, and show how it operates, if you can. You might try to outline what you know within one of these fields or structures.

Problem Thirteen: Give an example from your own experience to illustrate how incoming sense impressions may be "conditioned" so that you interpret them in a different manner from some of your friends. Try to explain where your conditioning came from.

CHAPTER 29

CREATIVITY

Our particular society has placed great emphasis on "progress." Since the middle ages, Western man has sought to improve his lot, to make life on earth better, to seek answers to his most pressing problems, and to make the world a better place for his children. Some societies have not been as enthusiastic for progress as we have been. Ancient Egypt, for instance, remained virtually unchanged for thousands of years, and American Indians had lived much the same life as their ancestors had for generations, until the white man arrived.

Progress, in a sense, is an attitude toward life, and has resulted in some bad things as well as good. Though our life-span has been increased materially, the automobile kills and injures hundreds of thousands in our nation alone each year. While medicine conquers disease on one hand, science has perfected fantastic weapons capable of destroying whole cities in a single explosion. Nevertheless, Western man, and now virtually all mankind, is committed to the idea of progress, to technological and social change. We all fully expect life to be different in twenty-five years, or even in five! Jobs change with great rapidity; new industries are being born daily; half the products on the market today were unknown a decade ago. Life indeed changes rapidly, and man must learn to change along with it.

Wedded to constant change, our society seeks the man who can produce the new ideas such a world demands. On the highest levels of achievement, a half-dozen top thinkers can give one nation superiority over others in the technological race. Needed also are the tens of thousands who have the insight and ability to translate the theorizing of the top men into practical accomplishments. The nation seeks the great philosophic thinkers who can make clear what life is, or should be. The world looks for the great artistic thinkers to interpret man's quest for truth and beauty in works of music, sculpture, painting, poetry, and architecture. In short, the world and the nation need creative thinkers as never before. The future depends upon what these people do to solve the terrifying problems that loom ahead.

A Definition

What is creativity? Earlier generations had the notion that creativity was some unmeasureable, mysterious quality given to a select few. Now, though we do not entirely understand its workings, we have a more logical idea of it. Creativity is the ability to unite previously separate and known factors into new combinations, usually with the purpose of solving a problem or of creating a work of art.

We believe today that this ability is given in some degree to everyone, and that it can be developed and trained greatly. In this sense, creativity training may be compared with athletic training. All of us are born with undeveloped potentials in sports. Many of us may develop skills in football and basketball. Others in bowling and golf. Some of us develop our potentials very little in any athletic way. We are similarly all born with creative potential, but few become skilled in using what they have. A great many more of us build up our athletic skills than we do our creative ones, and this is scarcely surprising. Our schools, after all, pay far greater attention to the former.

Uses of Creativity

Another early belief was that creativity was at work only in the arts. Now we view it as a part of almost any kind of activity. Invention and research certainly require creative thinking, and so do business ventures, advertising, manufacturing, and teaching. A recent experimenter found that creativity was an important factor in the sales records of clerks in a large department store. Those who had high sales also scored high in tests of creative ability. Many of the great creative thinkers began their careers in much the same fashion as the average person, but their creativity carried them up and away from the clerks, secretaries, waiters, and laborers who lacked the imagination to do better.

One field recently given much attention is creativity in students. Good scholarship (not necessarily good grades) requires a creative approach. If people need to develop their creative potential, it follows that school is the logical place for this development to begin.

Creativity in the Schools

A number of studies in recent years have pointed out the fact that schools have done very little to encourage creative thinking on the part of students. One way of finding this out has been to select hundreds of the most creative adults in various fields, and look at the grades they were given in school. If these people are today's leaders, today's top thinkers, it seems reasonable to suppose that their school grades would reflect this in some way. To put it another way, the grading system of the schools should have indicated those leadership qualities in one way or another. Almost invariably, however, the creative adult was found to have made only medium grades in school. This tendency to get middle grades persisted through college and graduate school in many cases. Rarely failures, such students were seldom top grade-getters, either. Apparently the schools had placed a premium on something other than ability to think creatively, at least insofar as grades were concerned. Now why would schools *not* give the highest grades to the most creative thinkers, if this is what we value so highly in our adult population? One answer lies in the characteristics of the highly creative student.

Characteristics of the Creative Student

First, such a student is an individualist in his thinking. He has great enthusiasm for things he regards as important, and little liking for other things. Such a student may ignore assignments he is given, while carrying on elaborate work at home on other phases of the same subject. His ideas of what should be done may vary from those of the teacher, or of the text, and when made to conform to others' wishes, he will sometimes do poor work. His grades on such required work will, of course, be low.

Second, a creative student may see little use for memorizing, drill, rote learning, and similar activities. When required to do these things, he may do them poorly or even avoid them. More than occasionally, the creative student will use his abilities in figuring out ways of *avoiding* work which doesn't interest him.

Third, a student with creative abilities needs and wants recognition for his accomplishments, which he may find difficult to get. Neatness, volume, and accuracy often count for more than originality on many school assignments. Some instructors at all levels of education unfortunately insist that students follow the teacher's way of doing things exactly, thus actually penalizing original approaches.

In this same vein, creative students find strong pressures from their classmates to suppress their creativity. The student who can produce new ideas should be honored by the school as much or more than the student who can throw a ball or jump over a bar. But very often the student with an abundance of ideas is made to feel "different" and is ridiculed. Of course, he *is* different, but so is the basketball star. Both can do something the majority cannot. Both have skills that the rest of us may not possess, and certainly both may have the determination and will-power to excel, which is the mark of a champion. Both may bring honor to the school and the community, and both should be equally honored.

Fourth, the creative student is able to think creatively even under some pressure. This is especially true after the student has learned the rewards of creative thinking, and has some successes with idea production and problem solving. At first, creative thinking may be hesitant and infrequent. Early training can stamp it out rather easily, after which the student learns *not* to think creatively but rather accept the rewards of conformity.

Fifth, the creative student finds emotional satisfaction in this activity. The thrill of turning a problem over in the mind, seeking a clue to its solution, then getting a key idea and working it out --- these are emotional satisfactions which creative thinkers experience. Such pleasures of thinking are often listed by creative people as their chief motivation.

Sixth, the creative student is likely to be a disturbing factor in the classroom. He will ask questions that are difficult to answer, and steer discussions into obscure pathways. He may insist on explanations to questions which bother him, even when it is holding up the orderly class discussion. It is recorded that Albert Einstein as a youngster was asked to leave school because he persisted in asking questions which none of the teachers could answer. When the creative minds of children are inhibited in the schools, or anywhere else for that matter, one of our greatest national resources is being wasted.

The Creative Student, and the Disturbed Student

It should not be assumed from the foregoing statements that any student who gets mediocre grades or who pesters his teacher with questions all the time is possessed of a creative mind. Some students cause trouble in class situations because their level of intelligence does not permit them to keep up with the regular pace of work. Others are troublemakers because the ordinary work is too slow for them! The surface appearance of their actions may be much alike, the causes far different.

Then, too, one must remember that just because *some* creative people were frustrated when they were in school, this does not mean that all frustrated students are potentially creative. Many times the reason for low grades lies in poor background, lack of willingness to work, inadequate preparation, poor health, and other factors unconnected with creativity. The puzzling thing is that all misfits tend to look alike, and sometimes the minds with the high potential get identified with the opposite group.

Tests of Creative Potential

Testing for creativity has been stressed in recent years. Such tests cannot take the usual forms such as True-False, Multiple Choice, and so on, for these do not allow the student to think in a creative way.

If we agree that creativity involves the combining of known factors to produce new results, then our tests must make use of this particular sort of activity. As an example, take this question:

"What would happen if the pull of gravity were to decrease by one-half?" The student with little creative ability might list several consequences on the order of "We would all weigh half as much." The creative thinker would be able to list pages of things which would come about as a result. His mind would range over many known factors, putting them together with the new factor, and come up with such consequences as:

    a.   The shoe manufacturers would suffer because shoes would last twice as long.

    b.   Need for dieting would decrease, and demand for the more fattening foods would rise.

    c.   Trains and cars would spin their wheels a lot more because they depend for traction upon their weight.

    d.   There would be fewer knockouts in boxing, less weight being behind each punch.

    e.   New records would immediately be set in pole vaulting, high jump, etc. Basketball nets would have to be placed a lot higher, football uniforms and padding redesigned, golf courses made longer, and many other changes in sports carried out.

    f.   Waves on the ocean would go higher than ever before.

    g.   A gallon of gasoline would run a car farther.

    h.   The pull of the earth (now less because of weakened gravity) could not hold the moon in its accustomed place, and it would spin off into space.

    i.   Rockets could take off from earth much more easily.

    j.   Trees would grow a lot taller.

    k.   Snow would take longer to fall, and shoveling it would be easier.

    l.   Less deaths might result from auto accidents and falls.

    m.   Hurricanes could blow things away more easily.

    n.   Wrestling would be twice as spectacular, as would circus aerial acts, trampoline stunts, balancing acts, and so on.

    o.   Fire hoses could squirt twice as high, and so would other liquids under pressure such as oil wells and geysers.

    p.   Fences for animals would have to be raised.

    q.   Stairsteps could be made higher.

r.   Buildings could be built with half the strength now needed.

s.   The oxygen in our blood might "bubble" and cause what is known as "the bends", suffered by deep-sea divers.

t.   Statues in stone could be made larger without fear of their weight cracking the lower portions of the sculpture.

u.   Bands could march a lot farther in parades without tiring. Heavier instruments could be carried than are now possible.

Such answers are one kind of measure of a student's ability to get new ideas by combining old ones in new ways. The creative mind will not only come up with more of such ideas, but their quality will be better. A second test of creativity is the ability to see a problem when it exists. Take the following situation:

A high school boy is asked to go to a movie. It is up to him to decide whether to go or not. The following facts may or may not be important in helping him make up his mind:

1.   It is Tuesday, April 9th.   2.   He is a senior.   3.   The weather is warm and pleasant, with a full moon.   4.   It is a double-feature, consisting of a western and a musical.   5.   The student comes from a small town.   6.   His father is a lawyer.   7.   The student ate a hearty supper.   8.   His grade average is a C plus.   9.   The invitation came from a male classmate.   10.   The parents do not object to his friend.   11.   Neither of the movies is objectionable.   12.   The track season is in full swing at the high school.   13.   This small town is 75 miles from New York City.   14.   The student owns a sports car.   15.   He likes jazz music.

What problem or problems does this young man have? The perceptive reader will spot several. Perhaps the most important is that, given a background of some money (sports car) and social standing (lawyer father) this student will be expected to go on to college, perhaps even enter a profession. His present grade average is low, however, and he will need to raise it to at least a B in order to be accepted in many colleges. With this in mind, the young man should certainly not waste a week-night on movies but should be studying for the finals soon to come. The fact that this is happening on the east coast, where college competition is keen makes study and grades all the more important.

A possible sub-problem concerns the sports car. A series of recent studies has shown direct relationship between low grades and ownership of a car. The great majority of car owners in high school and in college get lower grades than do non-car owners.

Creative thinkers will be able, on the whole to look over the various factors in a situation and see where problems exist. The nonthinkers seem never to be able to anticipate their problems, but wait until they are too large to solve.

Yet another test of creativity is the ability to "expand" or "alter" a problem. Some writers have urged us to think of *adding, subtracting, multiplying,* or *dividing* when we face a problem situation. Let us try it with the problem of "solving the traffic situation in New York City." A creative mind will be able to *add* new dimensions to the problem in this fashion:

> *The problem is not just New York City alone but it lies partly in the tremendous influx of people from the outside. Tourist routes, commercial carriers, sightseers, overseas traffic all must be controlled to deal effectively with the total problem.*

Subtraction would throw more light on the problem:

> *Suppose we "take away" some factor in the traffic situation. Most obvious is the private car. Ban all private vehicles from Manhattan Island, and traffic problems will largely vanish. Other alternatives would be to do away with all street parking, thus greatly expanding the road space for traffic. Private cars larger than compacts might be restricted, or one might do away with all two-way streets.*

Multiplication offers these possibilities:

> *Link all eastern cities in a traffic control network with uniform laws. Pool research money for work on common problems. No sense in Philadelphia and Boston duplicating what New York has done. Find out what cities in foreign lands are doing with their traffic problems. Use computers to regulate traffic control devices. Increase the size and number of highways, parking lots, garages, etc.*

Division of the problem will help, too.

> *Instead of tackling the enormously complex problem all at once, we should isolate one segment at a time, or divide it into manageable proportions. For instance, we could concentrate on a much faster, cheaper type of commuter train which would lure people into leaving their own cars at home. Or we could concentrate on building multi-level roadways so as to separate car traffic from trucks and buses. We might try to work on only one section of the city, or use an outlying suburb as a test program for our ideas.*

The creative mind may do other things with a problem such as changing it into another problem entirely. Among such changes might be the following:

1.   Forget about making it easier to get people into and out of the city, and concentrate instead on providing housing close to their work so that they can walk! This would reduce traffic indirectly.

2.   Instead of building ever-wider highways into cities, why not design a city to be built around and over the highway? Such a city would have a central core of high-speed thoroughfares and be essentially long and narrow.

3.   Expand the use of present TV, telephone, radio and other communication devices so that people won't have to come to the city to do business or to meet others.

4.   Set up and collect taxes for entering the city, to be paid by all non-residents. This will provide funds for needed improvements and at the same time reduce the number of those wishing to enter.

The above ideas are a few results of thinking about a problem creatively. Not all of them are usable, but in the process of creative thinking we are only looking for new ideas, not trying them out. If enough novel approaches are suggested, perhaps one or two may contain elements of usefulness.

SUMMARY

The whole idea of identifying and encouraging creativity in schools is still so new as to seem startling to many people. Furthermore, we are not at all sure of how it works, how best to bring it out, or what to do with the student who has it, and the one who seems to lack it. Nevertheless, we are sure that creativity is a precious quality and that everyone possesses the power of creative thought in varying dgrees. This power is of great value to the student and to society. Therefore we must respect and encourage creative thought and work wherever and however we can.

PROBLEMS:

Problem One: Find the origin of five different major inventions, tracing each one back to the inventor's original idea. Does there seem to be a common technique here in finding and defining a problem?

Problem Two: Name five good and five bad things about "progress." Suggest a means of attacking the bad features and solving them.

Problem Three: If possible, find out what kind of childhood school experiences various creative leaders had. What encouragements and discouragements did each have in school?

Problem Four: Show how creative thinking might be useful to the following people: a baseball coach, a fireman, a teacher, a doctor, and a shoe salesman.

Problem Five: List five things your school could do to encourage creative thinking among students. Use your own creative powers to work out these suggestions.

Problem Six: If you were a highly creative student, and your teacher had to carry on the program of instruction at a slower pace than you liked, what things could you do which would allow you to learn at your own pace, yet not disrupt the others?

Problem Seven: Think of subjects and situations in which rote learning is necessary. List at least five subjects, and five situations.

Problem Eight: Student "pressures" can be useful in keeping the trouble-maker in line in a class, but may sometimes be wrongly applied to the highly creative student at the same time. What suggestions have you for telling which is which?

Problem Nine: If your class contained a really expert creative mind, what ways would you recommend to encourage him?

Problem Ten: Name areas in which you like to solve problems. Give any reasons you can think of as to why these areas are rewarding ones for you.

Problem Eleven: Make up a short test to measure the creative potential of a pre-school student, of a sixth grader, of a high school student.

Problem Twelve: Expand, alter, or switch one of the following problems into as many others as you can.

1. How to expand the vending-machine business.
2. How to stimulate foreign travel.
3. How to increase interest in the arts in America.
4. How to become famous.
5. How to learn to like modern painting.

CHAPTER 30

CREATIVE THINKING AND
PROBLEM SOLVING

After learning something in the previous chapter of how and why man creates, we must now study how to harness our own creative powers and put them to work. But first we must distinguish clearly between the several kinds of thinking which man engages in. These kinds of thinking were outlined in the introductory chapter, " Learning to Learn" and are:

1. *Analytic thinking,* in which we gather data by careful observing and testing, then draw inferences from these data, and finally test those inferences under similar conditions to see if they will continue to prove themselves correct.

2. *Assumptive thinking,* in which we attempt to find out what has happened in the past by carefully searching out original sources of information, evaluating these to make sure they are valid, and drawing conclusions from them in the light of what they reveal.

3. *Skills thinking,* in which the main emphasis is upon a physical performance based upon practice, guided by the mind.

4. *Moral thinking,* in which we view actions and their results in the light of a set of personal standards of right and wrong.

5. *Aesthetic thinking,* in which we are as much concerned with the sensory intake as with the mental processes which make use of it. Here we judge experiences as "beautiful," "drab," "exciting," or "ugly" according to our standards, and within the framework of the experience itself.

All of these areas of knowledge, or modes of thought, can be dealt with in two ways; in a critical way, and in a creative way. The two are opposites, yet closely related.

Critical Thinking

This kind of mental approach to a situation or problem begins by pointing out what is wrong. It stresses the negative side of the picture, advises what will not work, dwells on what solutions have been tried and have failed. If an idea is put forth, someone thinking critically is sure to point out that it will never work, or that it is too new to be tried, or that "we've never done it that way."

Critical thinking is, however, of great value. It can and often does stop us from making foolish and costly errors. It teaches us to be cautious, and not act before we have measured the consequences; it teaches us to look for pitfalls, mistrust the unknown, the visionary, and the something-for-nothing scheme. Critical thinking is quick to spot propaganda and straying from the truth. It mistrusts the imagination, the dream-world, the "hunch," and the idea of luck. We all need the ability to think critically, and find ourselves doing it much of the time.

Creative Thinking

This kind of mental approach to a situation or problem capitalizes on the ability of the mind to make new combinations of familiar ideas. It takes into account, however, the fact that in order to make these combinations, the mind must be free and uninhibited. It must not feel that its thoughts will be laughed at, or scorned. It must feel no limitations on what it can think about, nor how wild and wide-ranging those thoughts can be.

The importance of this matter of "new combinations of familiar ideas" cannot be overestimated. Most great inventions came about as the result of the inventor's seeing old things in a new light. The creative scientist may discover important new relationships in facts known to many. Artists take lines or colors used by everyone, and combine them into startling new works. Authors use the same words as the rest of us, but their power to find new combinations of plot, character, setting and idea far surpasses ours. The creative thinker, in short, somehow can gear his mind up to a level which most people cannot match. Is this some innate ability he has? Was he born creative? Recent research and study answer these questions with a strong negative. All of us are able to think creatively, we are told, if we but learn how and practice.

Among the leaders in the field of teaching creative thinking have been Dr. Alex F. Osborn and his associates in the Creative Education Foundation. These men and others have changed our concepts of teaching creativity so greatly that now there are courses in "creative thinking" alongside the more traditional subject-matter courses in what to think *about*.

These creative thinking courses stress one fact above all, critical and creative thinking do not mix! The ability to think up new ideas and discover new relationships is severely limited by our tendency to criticise these ideas as they occur to us. We may come up with a fresh new idea which at first glance may be impractical, but if we use that idea as a steppingstone to others, one of these second-generation ideas may prove the very thing we can use. If, however, we stopped on the first impractical idea, and felt foolish for having even mentioned it, our idea production will have ceased.

Osborn's book, *"Applied Imagination"* (Scribners, 1957) lists seven steps in the creative process:

1. Orientation --- pointing up the problem.
2. Preparation --- gathering pertinent data.
3. Analysis --- breaking down the relevant material.
4. Ideation --- piling up alternatives by way of ideas.
5. Incubation --- letting up, to invite illumination.
6. Synthesis --- putting the pieces together.
7. Evaluation --- judging the resultant ideas.

Osborn stresses that these steps are not to be considered as necessarily coming in the order stated. Frequently our ideas come in random fashion while we are still trying to pin down the problem, and we find ourselves carrying on several steps at the same time. Generally speaking, however, the steps are all parts of the process of creative thinking. Here's how they work:

Step One: *Orientation.* Before creative thinking can be applied to any problem, we must know what that problem is. Most of us have a number of worries or gripes, things which bother us in our daily lives. Psychologists tell us that we should sit down and write out on paper what these worries are. In doing so, we begin to state them as specific problems, and when we see our worries as problems we can begin to deal with them. As long as they are only vague worries, they will remain unsolved.

The world is full of problems waiting to be recognized. The creative mind looks for such problems. Many an invention began with a dissatisfied man who did something about the source of his uneasiness. Many successful people have applied the creative thinking process to the problems in their own lives, and have solved them to reach new heights of achievement.

Perhaps you are worrying about what the future holds. You think about the prospects of getting a job, earning money, marrying, buying a home, raising a family, and so on. This is a vast problem area, one which is present in almost every young person's mind to some extent. What might be done to orient or define the basic problem more clearly? First, you can ask yourself such questions as:

a. What type of job would I really like to have?
b. What sort of education is necessary to get that job?
c. How long will this preparation take?

d. What will it cost? Can I afford it?

e. What sort of person do my future employers want?

f. How can I prepare to be that sort of person?

As a result of these and other questions, you will find yourself getting a clearer picture of the one problem area of your future vocation. Once you have decided on the sort of job you would like (realizing that this may change as you work on the problem) you are ready to take the next step.

Step Two: *Preparation.* At this point, you could really investigate that job, and you might also want to investigate the educational setup necessary to prepare for it. More questions come up:

a. What sort of future does this work hold?

b. Is there chance for advancement for a hard-working employee?

c. What will I learn by taking this job?

d. Would it be a good experience which would later on help to get a better job?

e. What kind of college should I attend, if any?

f. How can I be sure of being admitted? Of staying in?

Step Three: *Analysis.* You now have a fairly clear idea of the kind of work you would like to do. Further analysis of the situation might yield some surprises. Suppose you wanted to be a bookkeeper. You might learn about salaries, openings, training necessary and so on, but as you analyzed the work you might also find that bookkeepers are gradually being replaced by electronic office machines, data storage systems, calculators and so on, so that in another ten years there will be few openings in the field!

You might decide that your own abilities could profit by some analysis, too. There are extensive tests of aptitude and achievement now available which offer help in self-analysis. Young people go into various lines of work for the wrong reasons. It looks glamorous, or easy, or financially rewarding, or fun. Perhaps their parents push them into something they, the parents, think will be suitable. Some analysis of the situation may save a great deal of unhappiness and frustration later on.

Step Four: *Ideation.* Now we are ready to turn the brain loose on the problem. The problem in this case will be a more limited one because of the need to conserve space in this textbook. A large problem such as deciding on a career would take too long to fully discuss.

You have decided to get a job working on a Western Ranch this summer. You have thought through the first three three steps, so that you know that this is what you want to do, that it will pay well, that you're suited for it, and that such a job is going to be good for you. Now you are faced with the need to think up ideas on how to land such a job, especially if you live somewhere other than near ranches of this type. In this step you will remember that *any* idea is as good as any other in this stage of the game. You will sort out the good from the bad later on. Taking a note pad, you try to think up as many ideas as you can for 30 minutes. Here are some you might come up with:

a. Write letters to a lot of ranches asking for work.

b. Look around town for somebody who knows a ranch owner.

c. Hitchhike out west to where the ranches are; something may turn up if you are on the spot.

d. Subscribe to a few western newspapers, and read the want-ads.

e. Advertise your services in western local papers.

f. Advertise on a western radio or TV station.

g. Hide out near a ranch and ambush a regular ranch hand. When he doesn't show for work the next morning, apply for his job.

h. Offer a rancher a small sum of money to let you work free, just for the experience.

i. Offer to work on a "money-back guarantee." If the rancher isn't satisfied, you will return the salary.

j. Borrow money to go west --- repay it as you get work.

k. Get a buddy to threaten a rancher with a gun, and then you come along and run him off. Rancher will be grateful and give you a job.

l. Pose as an author writing a book on the life of a rancher. Ranch owner will let you work so he can be in your book.

m. Offer to write a feature article each week about life on a ranch, and sell the idea to your hometown paper. Money from the articles will go to repay job-hunting expenses.

n. Find some other way of getting to stay on a ranch; as a tutor for the rancher's children, perhaps.

o. Become a salesman for some product used on a farm. This might enable you to earn more money, and allow you to visit many ranches.

p. Offer daytime baby-sitting service to ranchers with small children.

q. Practice marksmanship and trapping, then advertise your services as exterminator of coyotes and mountain lions.

r. Take up gambling and win ranch of your own.

s. Investigate sales of government surplus land. Acquire some remote land and camp there for a summer.

t. Buy a grubstake and pan gold for a summer. A strike would repay you for your trouble.

Step Five: *Incubation.* Now is the time to put the problem away for a day or a week, and let the subconscious mind take over. The ideas you get when you return to the problem are often better than the earlier ones. The phenomenon known as "inspiration" often occurs at this point. The complete solution to a problem pops into the conscious mind quite suddenly, but only after that mind has been working on the problem for some time. And, of course, many times inspiration doesn't happen at all. Part of the technique of solving a problem creatively is getting started on it soon enough to allow this to happen. Many people simply give their minds too little time to come up with good ideas.

Step Six: *Synthesis.* We now can look back over the ideas we had and see how they might be combined or broken down, enlarged or extended. The very first idea of writing letters to ranchers suggests several secondary ideas:

a. Get ranchers' names from magazines devoted to ranching, horse and cattle raising, and so forth.

b. Get your local mayor, school officials, minister, or other professional person to write a letter of recommendation to go along with your application.

c. Ask your local veterinarian to let you help him, and in this way you could learn many practical things about animal care which would make your services more valuable. Get the veterinarian to endorse your application after you have worked for him.

d. Get help from your English teacher in writing the best possible letter of application.

e. Write the letters in plenty of time to get a job --- don't wait until it is too late. All of this takes planning.

f. Send self-addressed envelope with stamp for rancher's reply.

g. Call rancher long-distance after he has your letter. This will allow him to ask a few questions, and impress him with the fact that you are serious.

These seven secondary ideas which have grown out of the original one make it more valuable. This is the way in which an idea can grow until it eventually turns into a working solution for your problem.

Step Seven: *Evaluation.* Judging the resultant ideas is sometimes easy and sometimes difficult. In the case of idea "b", it might be useful, and could certainly be combined with the first idea. Idea "c" doesn't seem to be so good. A hitchhiker is rarely taken into a job, especially if he doesn't know where he is to look for one. However, being close to the source of work would be of help. Idea "e" is good, but its cost might be prohibitive. The local library might carry a few papers from those areas. Idea "f" is too expensive. Besides, ranch hands who advertise in these mediums would likely be regarded with suspicion. Idea "g" can easily be dismissed as involving crime. However, that idea might give rise to a better one. Try job hunting in an area where there is an outbreak of flu or some other mild epidemic. Jobs will be opening up more readily. Perhaps areas near larger cities would have more jobs available, since ranch hands might tend to take higher-paying work in the urban areas. The other ideas can be evaluated in this same fashion, some being immediately discarded, others revised and added to for new approaches.

Applying Creative Thinking to Art Problems

The range of artistic problems which concern us is often surprisingly large. Even people who think they have no problems concerning the arts may be mistaken, for an unrecognized problem is just as much a problem as when it is noticed. Education should train us to be sensitive to problems; to be able to spot them before they grow too large, and solve them. Some likely places to check are the following:

1.   *Personal appearance* --- if you feel awkward and wish you had more poise, you may have a problem in moving gracefully, in which case the art of dance has many answers for you. Or it may be in the cut and style of your clothes, or the colors you wear. An understanding of the visual elements of line, color, texture and value would offer insight into such a problem.

2.   *Communication ability* --- many of us feel inadequate in talking to others. Understanding and practice in the use of the elements of speech may be called for. Literature holds many examples of the way in which great men conveyed ideas through speech. A careful study will give one a sense of sureness when talking. Writing may likewise be a problem area. Literature alone among the arts can help solve this problem.

3.   *Boredom* --- the curse of modern man is the possession of too much free time and not enough training in how to use it wisely. The endless round of TV watching and club activities may fill up the vacant hours but these do little for enrichment of life. Man needs a mental challenge now and then, not just busywork.

The arts have been engaged in asking the deepest and most penetrating questions for thousands of years. The pursuit of such questions is the perfect antidote to boredom, for who can become bored with the problem of his own reason for being on this earth, with defining what is good and evil, with the problem of understanding history and man's works. A study of Michelangelo's Sistine Chapel frescos, the plays of Shakespeare, Goethe's *Faust*, and Wagner's *Parsifal* show that artists in all fields have wrestled with these problems and have come up with striking answers. The arts are full of such examples.

4. *Local conditions* --- many local problems have an artistic basis in part. Unsightly slums come about as a result of property owners' and renters' disregard for their surroundings. Even a city-wide cleanup might not help for long, because people who were content to live in ugliness once will do so again. Look for a solution in long-term education, in enrichment of the child's artistic life, in making slum dwellers aware of what beauty is and what it can do.

Local conditions in business may reflect the presence of aesthetic problems, too. The loss of trade experienced by downtown sections may be due to the unpleasantness of the shopping experience. When artistic considerations are given thought, and the arts are used to make the shopping areas more pleasing to the customer, business will usually improve.

The arts, then, may offer solutions to one's problems. By applying creative thinking to these and other areas, we may be able to deal with such problems more effectively.

PROBLEMS:

Problem One: Keep a record of one day's activities, noting how frequently you made a critical judgment about something, and how frequently you used creative thinking. Is there any change from school-hours to non-school time? Did you have your most creative thoughts in the morning or evening. Was there any pattern noticeable?

Problem Two: Try to apply Osborn's seven steps in the creative process to a problem of your own. Write out your thinking for each step.

Problem Three: Hold a creative thinking session with several of your friends. Write down every idea you get, and do not attempt to judge which ones might or might not work. The following problems might prove interesting, although you should try your own also:

    a.   How can I make people like me?

    b.   How can my club earn money?

    c.   How could our school become famous as an educational institution?

    d.   How can the number of auto accidents be reduced sharply?

    e.   How can mankind keep from destroying itself with modern weapons?

Problem Four: Using one of the five problems above, go through the steps of preparation and analysis, writing down what you think of, or learn about the topic.

Problem Five: Make a tour of your home town or neighborhood, keeping your eyes open for signs of problems which have not yet been officially recognized. Make a list of these and ask your parents which of the problems they feel is most pressing.

Problem Six: Look about you carefully in your school. Make a list of problems the school has. Choose the one you think most important and write a paper on its possible solution.

Problem Seven: Define and attack an artistic problem which you have found in your home, school, church, or community.

Problem Eight: Show evidences that your understanding of the principles of creative thinking is helping you in your schoolwork.

Part Eight

LEARNING TO JUDGE

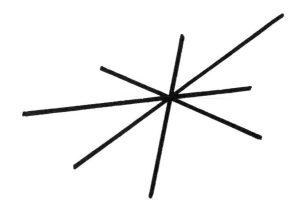

CHAPTER 31

JUDGING THE SPACE ARTS

When a work of art and a human observer meet, a two-way process is set in motion. The work "speaks" its message to the observer, a message which is sometimes coded, concealed, and complex. At other times it is plain and understandable. This is one side of the picture; the other is contained in the observer's interpretation of that message.

We learn something about the work of art from the comments and criticisms which the observer makes about it but more than that, we learn a great deal about the observer himself. If we watch and listen to a number of people in an art gallery as they view a painting, we can easily tell which ones have some understanding and artistic sensitivity and which ones do not. Their comments and judgments will be accurate indications of their tastes and intellects. Judgment, therefore, is not a thing to be undertaken lightly, yet without judgment we cannot form our own taste standards or raise our level of appreciation. It is not so much a question of "to judge or not to judge" --- we all make judgments of works of art all the time by our looks, gestures, attendance at art shows or refusal to attend, by the things we read or don't read, the magazines we subscribe to, and so on. We simply cannot help making some sort of judgment in the world of the arts. The question is, then, "How shall we judge, and on what basis?"

For the great mass of people, judgment or choice is based simply on like or dislike. "I know what I like" is the only criterion most people have. Unfortunately this can be reversed to "I like what I know" just as easily, which means that the person is condemned to a single level of enjoyment and understanding. He chooses only what he likes, and likes only what he chooses. Only some forcible experience such as having to study about the arts in a course, can jog such a person into the learning experiences which may give him the capacity to like something different and extend his range of understanding.

Having come this far in this book, the reader is in a much different position from the average person. He has been led into many new understandings and insights, and has been encouraged to make many new approaches to the arts. For him, the problem of judgment is one of collecting all of this information into some sort of outline which can be remembered easily. Armed with this, he will be able to approach a new work of art with the confidence of a person who knows what to look for and how to interpret the impressions he receives.

One final word before presenting these outlines. Despite all the sets of standards, outlines, check sheets, or rules for making critical judgments, the process remains a subjective, personal one. Nobody can make a meaningful judgment for you --- you must work that out for yourself. You will learn from others *about* works of art, but you must always make the final choice alone, based upon what you understand. The present practice of following newspaper and magazine critical reviews without question is absurd, and it shows how little our people are trained to think for themselves in matters of art. The following guides are presented solely with the idea of summing up what you have studied about the various areas of the arts. Your judgment will depend on the depth of your knowledge and the level of your understanding at the time the judgment is made. As you continue to meet and judge art works, your powers will grow, and your tastes will change. Things you now like may later seem simple, and works which seem remote now may become familiar and deeply enjoyed as you mature.

JUDGMENT OUTLINE FOR PAINTING AND SCULPTURE

I   Representational Aspects

Does the artist try to imitate nature, distort it, abstract from it? Why has he done this --- to call attention, emphasize, shock? Are there objects, colors, lines, etc., in the work which stand for something other than themselves (symbols)?

II   Functional Aspects

Was the work made as a record, remembrance, likeness? Did it compete with the camera in this function? How successfully? Were there educational uses for the work of art? Religious uses? How well did it function in these areas, if at all?

III   Aspects of Medium

What is the material used? In painting, what coloring matter, mixing agent, and surface are featured? What techniques of applying paint to surface are in evidence? Do these suit the subject and function (if any) of the work? What are the limitations and possibilities of this medium (oil, watercolor, fresco, tempera, etc.)? How well has the artist worked within these possibilities?

In sculpture, what material is used? What are its strengths and weaknesses? Has the sculptor taken these into account? What techniques has he used for producing this work?

IV   Elemental Aspects

Line --- straight; horizontals, diagonals, verticals. Curved; fast, slow. Skeletal, outline, contour, edge lines, etc. What kinds of lines are used in the work, and why? What effect has the artist achieved through use of line?

Color --- hue; primaries, secondaries, complementaries, warm and cool hues, advancing and receding hues, analogous and other schemes. Tints, tones, shades. Does the artist use color as a predominant feature of the work of art? Would the work lose interest greatly in a black-and-white version?

Texture --- is the texture of the work (painting) real or imitative? Does the texture serve an important purpose in the work? Was the artist using texture to show off his technique?

Value -- is the work "high in value" (bright) or "low in value" (dark)? Are there strong contrasts in values? Are these used to bring out important features of the work? How is the work of art placed with regard to illumination? If a sculpture, does it make use of light-and-shadow values effectively?

Perspective --- (painting). Does the work make use of perspective? If so, is it one, two, or three point perspective? Is it geometrically accurate? If not, why not? Is the perspective linear, aerial, or both? How is it achieved (converging lines, overlapping, position in the picture, etc.)?

Volume --- does the work show a three-dimensional quality, or is it flat design? How is a feeling of depth or roundness attained?

V   Structural Aspects

Does the work show an easily recognized form? Is it a simple form or a complex one? Are separate forms combined into the overall picture or sculpture? Does form seem more important than content?

VI   Aspects of Meaning

What was the artist trying to say in his work? Do we now read additional meaning into it? Has any of its meaning been lost? Is there a literal and a symbolic meaning to be found in it? Is the meaning consistent with the artist's own time? What does the work tell us about the age in which it was made? Do you like or dislike the work, after having considered all of its aspects? What are your reasons?

JUDGMENT OUTLINE FOR ARCHITECTURE

I   Functional Aspects

   A   Choice of the Site

   Is the structure suitable for the part of the world where it is found?

Does it suit the climate? Have soil type and topography of the building lot been taken into account? Do zoning laws permit the type of construction needed, and have building codes restricted the work? Will this site increase in value? What patterns of growth are detectable in the area? What will be the traffic problems?

B   Choice of Floor Plan

Are the room functions suitably worked out? Can inhabitants move freely without disturbing one another? Is privacy of both sight and sound assured where needed? Can temperature and humidity be controlled when needed? Can lighting levels be regulated if desired? Will the plan assure easy and inexpensive maintenance? Will the structure bring to its owner the prestige he wants from it?

II   Structural Aspects

A   Enclosure of Space

Does the interior seem cramped? Does it seem smaller inside than it looks from the outside? Why? Is the total space cut up into boxlike rooms? Do rooms flow into each other, where desired? Is the outdoors "brought in" by means of patio, screen porch, breezeway, glass wall, and so on? Do the ceiling heights reflect the proper interior atmosphere?

B   Style

Is the style of the house or building copied wholly, or in part from the past? Does the style seem to fit the locale? Does the style help the function, or hinder it? Does the style fit the owner's preference or personality?

C   Materials

Are local materials used where suitable? Does the choice of materials carry out the functions of the building most effectively? Do the various materials fit with one another? Are tensile, compressive, and shearing strengths present as needed? Are any of the materials used for symbolic or prestige reasons only?

D   Construction

Are the walls "load-bearing"? Is there a metal skeleton about which the structure is built? If the arch is used, what forms of this technique are found? If concrete is used, has it been reinforced, prestressed? Is the foundation adequate? Is there evidence of good or poor workmanship? Does the construction stress simplicity or complexity? Are there constructional techniques in evidence which have been "lost" over the centuries?

III   Symbolic Aspects

A   Location

Is there a practical reason for the placement of the structure, or a symbolic one? Which direction does the building face, and why? Is it on a hill, cliff, a certain street, or in a particular section of town which might have symbolic value?

B   Structural Shape

Is the building's shape in any way significant? Is there something symbolic in its height, width, size? Does the front of the structure show special treatment? Are there towers, porches, portals, arches, domes, chimneys, picture-windows, and so on which might have more symbolic than practical value?

C   Meaning

Does the structure seem to be an architectural embodiment of some ideal or spirit? Could it serve as an architectural trademark, or perhaps as a landmark? Does it combine beauty with efficiency? Does it tell us something about the era which produced it? About its architect, and owner? Having studied it, do you like it? Do you think it deserves being preserved, or should it make way for other works of architecture?

PROBLEMS:

The central problem in judging a visual work of art, at least for the beginner, is to understand it well enough to make a judgment which can be defended. The problem would be exactly the same in any other field, from judging livestock to judging military operations. A good judgment is always based upon knowledge and experience. Therefore, the problem must be met by study and practice, and more study and practice. This can be done in a number of interesting ways, and will afford much pleasure in years to come:

1.   Purchase visual artworks for your room or home. Live with them, learning about their qualities through long association. Try to acquire original works if possible (lithographs and etchings by well-known artists may be ordered through catalogs for the price of a pair of good shoes)!

2. Go to art shows, galleries and museums any time you can. The experience gained from seeing masterworks at close range is unforgettable. The knowledge gained from this book will find many applications.

3. Visit all buildings and houses with an eye for their constructional details, their use of space, proportion and style. Pay especially close attention to buildings by famous architects, studying these structures as you would any masterwork of painting or sculpture.

4. Subscribe to art magazines. These will provide you with not only news of the art world, but instructional articles, color plates to study, offers of works for sale, notices of new books, and so on. Through such reading, you will continue to learn at your leisure, and build up a surprising background in the arts. There are many excellent periodicals on painting, sculpture, architecture, the home, photography, and movie-making, to say nothing of other visual art areas such as antique collecting, jewelry design, flower arranging, and so on.

5. Become more sensitive to the elements of visual art in everyday surroundings. Line, texture, and value are as interesting in a littered alley as in a Romanesque basilica. Colors may be found in the oily ramp of a gas station as well as in a Titian painting. Perspective can be noted while driving down a highway, not only in a Dutch landscape of the 17th Century. Look for design in appliances, sculptural detail in furniture and mass-produced goods, and look for proportion in magazine advertisements. The visual arts are everywhere, from the church to the market, as well as in masterpieces. Your life can be one exciting search for art elements and principles, and your judgment of these will grow more and more sure.

6. Take any opportunity to participate in the area of the visual arts that you can. Classes in sculpture and painting are found in many places, and anything learned there will make your understanding of these areas more profound.

CHAPTER 32

JUDGING THE TIME ARTS

Judgment in the time arts is like judgment in the space arts; it must be based on experience and understanding. Whenever we make a judgment, we expose our own artistic background, or the lack of it. Your principal task will be to continue learning about music and literature so that you may improve your judgment. This will be, of course, a lifetime task, but one that will become increasingly enjoyable as you pursue it. The following outlines are only summaries of what you have studied thus far. Many more points and refinements will be added as you grow in experience and wisdom.

JUDGMENT OUTLINE FOR MUSIC

I   Representational Aspects *(Program music)*

Does the music have a descriptive title *(Don Juan)* or a non-descriptive one *(Symphony No. 40)?* If the former, does the music really seem to be describing its title? Are imitative sounds used (church-bells, thunder, etc.)? Do instruments take the roles of characters in a story? Are episodes marked by dynamic and tempo changes? Did the composer leave program notes describing the story or picture he tried to set musically? Would the music be equally interesting without the accompanying program? Are musical "symbols" used?

II   Functional Aspects

Does the music serve some purpose --- dance, work, masking, ceremony, commercial, therapeutic? Is it suitable in length, instrumentation, tempo, dynamics, and form for the function it serves?

III   Aspects of Medium

Does the music employ voices, strings, brass, woodwinds, percussion, electronic instruments? In what combinations and numbers are these used?

IV   Elemental Aspects

Pitch --- is the work "monophonic" (single melody line), "polyphonic" (several melody lines at once) or "harmonic" (melody with chords) in nature? Does it combine these in its structure? Are the melodies scalewise or leaping? Are harmonies common ones (I-IV-V etc.)? Do motives play a large part in the work?

Duration

Meter --- is the piece in duple or triple meter? Is the beat or pulsation regular throughout? If not, why is it changed? Is the meter a strong factor in the piece?

Tempo --- is the music fast, slow, or varied? What purpose does tempo play in the work?

Rhythm --- do rhythm and meter coincide often? Are the rhythms fairly simple, or intricate? Is there much rhythmic repetition? Is there syncopation?

Volume --- is the work loud, soft, varied? Do dynamic levels coincide with sections in the composition? Are strong accents present? How are crescendos and decrescendos used?

Timbre --- how are the various "tone colors" used in the work? Would it sound better or worse if played by some other combination of instruments? How much does it depend on timbre for its effectiveness?

V   Structural Aspects

Is the work written in one of the familiar forms (sectional, contrapuntal, sonata-allegro, variation, suite, etc.)? Does the form fit the content and/or the function of the music? Is the structure fairly easy to follow, or does the music stray from the common formal pattern? Does the form seem more important than the content?

VI   Aspects of Meaning

What does the work tell us about its composer? About the era in which it was written, the society which produced it? Has its meaning changed since it was written --- do we interpret the music differently now than formerly? How much of the total effect of the music is due to the performer, and how much to the music itself?

JUDGMENT OUTLINE FOR LITERATURE

I   Aspects of Subject

Is the work wide-ranging in subject, or limited, and why? What is the author's purpose in treating such a subject? Is it realistically handled? What has been left out for purposes of compactness and storytelling effect? Where does the subject fit in the God-Man-Nature triangle? Is it a subject of fantasy, the dream world?

II Functional Aspects

Is the work of suitable length for its purpose? If it is written for the stage, is it "good theatre," that is, effective as a play? If an essay, does it explain or instruct while retaining literary interest as well? Does it have a moral or religious function? Does it fulfill its function at the expense of its quality as a work of literature?

III Aspects of Medium

Is the language handled well, with grammatical structures and word meanings contributing to the effect of the work? Is this work a translation from another language? Has it been translated from another medium (novel into play, for instance)? If so, what has been added or deleted, and how effective has the change been?

IV Elemental Aspects

Sound Elements

Are the sounds of words used to intensify their meaning? Are there assonance, consonance, rhyme, onomatopoeia, and so on? Are the words arranged in repetitive phrases for effect? In meters, line lengths, etc.? If so, which ones are used (iambic pentameter, trochaic tetrameter, etc.) and why? If there is rhyme, is it regular, off-rhyme, internal rhyme? Does the rhythm of the words always match the meter, and if not, why not?

Elements of Sense

Are there visual or auditory images painted by the author? If so, how well does he use the basic elements of sight and sound in his words? Are there, perhaps, images properly belonging to the other senses?

Are the words precise or deliberately confusing in their total effect? How well are the traditional factors of characterization, setting, plot and action handled? What is the basic story, and how is the plot (actual sequence of events in the work) arranged to present that story?

What "point of view" is maintained by the author, or who is it that is telling the story, and from what vantage point? What is the essential conflict about which the story revolves? Why is this of importance to the reader?

V Structural Aspects

What is the overall form of the work (novel, play, poem, etc.)? Within each large category, what special form is evidenced (sonnet, couplet, quatrain, etc.)? How does this structure contribute to the effectiveness and meaning of the work? In the case of a poem does the form actually restrict the poet's message?

VI   Aspects of Meaning

What does the work tell us about the time in which it was written? What were the large issues of this era, and how well does the work cope with these? Is the "message" of the work worth the effort taken to produce it? What meaning does it have for our own time and life? Is there something of the "eternal" about the work that will give it meaning in centuries to come? Will it speak to men of other times and places?

The outlines presented in this and the previous chapter have dealt only with the separate time- and space-arts. There are also, of course, a number of arts which combine these. Rather than present complete and separate outlines for each, let the reader apply those points from each of the outlines which apply, and add to them the questions listed below:

QUESTIONS FOR JUDGING THE MOVIES

1.   What types of camera shots are used to open the action? To set the atmosphere? To delineate character?

2.   How do the camera angles further the telling of the story?

3.   How are the various cuts, fades, wipes, dissolves, etc. used in the film?

4.   If color is used, does it particularly enhance the mood or effect of the story? Would it be just as effective in black and white?

5.   Is the music used to good effect? Is it imitative, accurate in a historical sense, kept in the background suitably? Are musical numbers introduced tastefully?

6.   Is the camera allowed to tell the story, or is the movie more like a filmed stage play? How important are spoken words to the total effect? Are there important sections where no words are used?

ADDITIONAL QUESTIONS FOR TELEVISION

1.   Does the program have a "live," immediate quality, or is it a filmed version?

2.   Are the more intimate setting and size of the television screen taken into account in the presentation?

3.   Is the program worthy of the time and money spent to produce it? Does it challenge the viewer in any way? What is its function?

4.   Are the commercial messages introduced at appropriate times, and are they tastefully done?

5.   How does this particular program differ from the usual run

of television fare? Does it show imagination, or is it a "formula" plot and story?

QUESTIONS FOR JUDGING THE DANCE (Serious, modern dance)

1. Are the physical elements used well in the creation of the work (force, direction, level, etc.)?

2. Is there a plot or story? If so, are the movements appropriate to this "program"?

3. In what ways does the dance present contemporary ideas, questions, thoughts, philosophy?

4. How do the musical and the physical movements, rhythms, tempos, accents, and so on compare and contrast?

5. Are the techniques of the dancers appropriate to the work being presented?

6. Are costumes, settings, and general appearance suitable to the subject of the work, if any?

QUESTIONS FOR JUDGING CITIES

1. Does the city, or part of it, show a recognizable form or pattern? Is this pattern a relic of another era? Does it fit today's needs? Is it worthy of retaining?

2. Is the city a comfortable place to live? Is it clean, safe, not too crowded? It is exciting, with many alternative forms of entertainment and activity?

3. Does adequate living demand more-than-average expenditure? Are prices and services within range of the average dweller?

4. Are traffic patterns suitable for both motorist and pedestrian? Are there adequate forms of transportation other than the private car? Can one enter and leave the city quickly and easily? Are there sufficient parking facilities available in forms which do not restrict the building space of the downtown area?

5. Does the city possess good cultural attractions, such as museums, symphony orchestra, colleges, art galleries, and so on?

6. Are there well-defined zoning laws which will regulate the future growth of the city in patterns that are pleasing and yet economically attractive?

7. Are the local building codes just, and will they permit the ready use of the latest materials?

8. Are there slum areas, and if so, what steps are being taken

to clean them up? Are steps also planned for retraining the slum-dwellers so that they may become responsible citizens?

    9.   Does the city possess a master plan for its future growth? If so, what care went into its designing?

    10.   Are the approaches to the city unsightly, or do they present a good front to the traveller and visitor?

PROBLEMS:

    The basic problem in judging the time arts and the combined arts is the same as that for the space arts --- attainment of understanding and experience. There are certain things that the student may do to continue his growth in the arts. These will be much the same kinds of things suggested at the close of the previous chapter; attending concerts, plays, dance programs, and so on. Additional suggestions are:

    1.   Build a collection of good music on records and tapes. Hearing a favorite sonata or symphony every so often will soon bring about its own form of "education" which can be gained in no other manner. Such music need not, at least not always, be listened to attentively with score in hand. It may be used for quiet evening background music, for masking other sounds while the children are getting to sleep, and so on.

    2.   Learn to watch television and the movies with a more critical eye. Most of us accept these for entertainment only, but they can and should be much more than that. Both at their best are much greater arts than those examples of them we usually see. Subscribe to a serious magazine in the field of the movies, and you will soon learn there is more to the films than most of us realize.

    3.   Become more familiar with the resources of your town or city. A metropolis has untold wealth in the great variety of things that one may find there. These range from the smaller delights of window-shopping and sampling different restaurants to the greater ones of the theatre, ballet, and opera house. Think of the city as a great and complex work of art, partly made up of buildings and partly of people, moving and changing all the time. Get to know its good points and try to change its bad ones.

    4.   Make an occasional attempt to participate in the time arts. This might involve taking music lessons, trying out for a theatre group,

or studying creative writing. Each venture into the arts from the production angle will make you a keener judge, and give you more pleasure as a consumer.

A FINAL WORD

Through the course of this book, we have tried to open doors to the arts. These doors are now just barely open, but through them you are able to glimpse those long "avenues to the arts" that are so much fun to travel. The journey will take you all the rest of your life, and you may never go as far as you would like, but the fun is in the travelling. The best wishes of the author go with you on your journey.

*****

INDEX

332

DATE DUE